Writing in the Sand

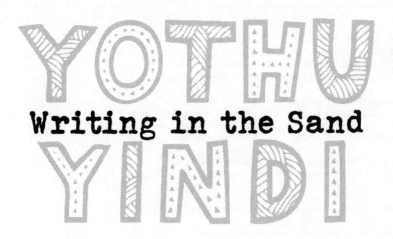

YOTHU YINDI
Writing in the Sand

MATT GARRICK

ABC BOOKS

Aboriginal and Torres Strait Islander readers are respectfully advised this book contains names, images and descriptions of people who have died.

This book was written in consultation with senior members of the Gumatj and Rirratjiŋu clans. Permissions for the use of names and images of the deceased have been granted. The author has not used the first names of people who had died recently at the time of publication.

 The ABC 'Wave' device is a trademark of the Australian Broadcasting Corporation and is used under licence by HarperCollins*Publishers* Australia.

HarperCollins*Publishers*
Australia • Brazil • Canada • France • Germany • Holland • India
Italy • Japan • Mexico • New Zealand • Poland • Spain • Sweden
Switzerland • United Kingdom • United States of America

HarperCollins acknowledges the Traditional Custodians
of the land upon which we live and work, and pays respect
to Elders past and present.

First published on Gadigal Country in Australia in 2021
This edition published in 2024
by HarperCollins*Publishers* Australia Pty Limited
ABN 36 009 913 517
harpercollins.com.au

Copyright © Matt Garrick 2021

The right of Matt Garrick to be identified as the author of this work has been asserted by him in accordance with the *Copyright Amendment (Moral Rights) Act 2000*.

This work is copyright. Apart from any use as permitted under the *Copyright Act 1968*, no part may be reproduced, copied, scanned, stored in a retrieval system, recorded, or transmitted, in any form or by any means, without the prior written permission of the publisher. Without limiting the author's and publisher's exclusive rights, any unauthorised use of this publication to train generative artificial intelligence (AI) technologies is expressly prohibited.

A catalogue record for this book is available from the National Library of Australia

ISBN 978 0 7333 4181 6 (paperback)
ISBN 978 1 4607 1378 5 (ebook)

Cover design by Lisa Reidy
Front cover photo by Bob King/Getty Images
Back cover photo © David Hancock
Author photograph by Michael Franchi
Map by Map Illustrations, mapillustrations.com.au
Typeset in Baskerville by Kirby Jones
Printed and bound in Australia by McPherson's Printing Group

This book was written on Yolŋu and Larrakia lands.

It's dedicated to all Yothu Yindi members,
past and present, for rocking Australia
(in more ways than one).

And to the memory of Dr B Marika,
for your wisdom, humour,
compassion and bottomless cups of tea.

And to Gus:
follow the river; follow your dreams.

Contents

Introduction: A Message of Hope ix
  by Yalmay Yunupiŋu
Introduction: Following the Dream xi
  by Witiyana Marika
Author's Note xv

Prologue 1
1 Diamond Dogs 7
2 Child and Mother 21
3 The Educator 38
4 Swamp Stomp 51
5 Back in 1988 67
6 The Good Oils 79
7 The Highway Beckons 92
8 The Brother 109
9 Well I Heard It on the Radio 121
10 Into the Mainstream 139
11 Hollywood Calling 155
12 Australia Tunes In 168
13 Freedom 181

14	Raypirri	193
15	A Global Nation	206
16	One Blood	220
17	Garma	234
18	The New Millennium	246
19	Fire on the Hill	259
20	Yolŋu Medicine	269
21	The Drummer	279
22	The New Guard	291
23	Goodbye, Crocodile Man	304
24	A Flame Reignited	319
Epilogue		331

Glossary of Yolŋu Words	335
Some Key Concepts	339
Acknowledgements	343
Notes	347
Yothu Yindi Discography	357
Lyrics Permissions	361

Yalmay Yunupiŋu, teacher, linguist, human rights advocate.

Introduction

A Message of Hope

Yalmay Yunupiŋu

This is a very, very unique story. It's about my husband, Mandawuy Bakamana Yunupiŋu. He was born on 17 September 1956, and as the world knows, he was the lead singer of the Yothu Yindi band. He started the Yothu Yindi band in 1986 together with Witiyana Marika, because they were already in a *yothu yindi* relationship; as we would often say, they were mother and child. He was the very lucky son, a gifted and naturally talented son, of Makurrŋu, his mother, and Mungurrawuy Yunupiŋu, his father. They would've been very proud to see him sing onstage if they had still been alive.

Through his music, Mandawuy carried the true colours of green and gold, Australia, and red, yellow and black, his Yolŋu (Aboriginal) heart. He was a builder of bridges between all races.

As an educator and school principal, he planted seeds of a Both Ways curriculum with exceptional talent and courage. He was a human rights advocate who fought tirelessly right up to the time of his illness, trying to help make a better place for his people.

His songs echoed across Australia, through mountains, land, sea and through the skies. These are songs about the rich culture of the Yolŋu people, of the land, the sea, everything that is in our universe and that is interwoven. It is a dynamic culture; ancient but still very much alive today. Mandawuy shared his culture and stories with the world through songs. Through his songs he would always talk about balance: it was his theme word for every tour the band ever made. Balance was his universal weapon, his message of hope, truth and peace. Many people were shocked and devastated when he died on 2 June 2013. He left a powerful legacy behind. The legacy of a Yolŋu rockstar educator. But his sweet memory will not disappear. Through this book we salute the Yothu Yindi band for the enormous contribution they've made nationally and internationally. Their story is shared to remind us all how they've helped make a better place for the many nationalities and cultures who now call Australia home.

Yirrkala, Northern Territory, May 2021

Introduction
Following the Dream
Witiyana Marika

When I was a kid growing up back in the sixties and seventies, there was a song by Elvis Presley called 'Follow That Dream'. That song, that Elvis song, inspired me. I said to myself, 'I'm gonna make it in the world.' Through my Yolŋu culture, I got there.

My father taught me how to be a survivor, to be a leader, to learn the country. He taught me everything. So, by the time Mandawuy was ready to form the band Yothu Yindi, he saw that I was a strong man coming up. Ready to give our Yolŋu culture to the world.

After we started the band in the eighties, non-Indigenous and other Indigenous people down south, they saw us, and they thought, 'This is the power.' We were powerful, and they loved us. And in Yothu Yindi we were a family, a family of balanda and Yolŋu. Yothu Yindi is a story about Australia coming together. It's a unique story for Australia, especially how Mandawuy showed the way and did so much to inspire

Witiyana Marika, co-founder of Yothu Yindi.

this country. This story won't forget him, or myself, or the other band members, who all contributed to creating a better future and building a bridge over troubled waters in this nation of ours. On this journey we give thanks to people like Alan James, the manager who made everything possible; friends in the industry like Michael Gudinski and Michael Chugg, who helped us reach the national stage; and many others who walked with us on the way, including Paul Kelly, Peter Garrett, Jimmy Barnes, Jack Thompson, John Trudell and Quiltman, Bart Willoughby, Neil Finn, Slim Dusty and Joy McKean. And our families, who always stuck in there for us, through all of it.

Looking back, there's pride and also sadness. This is our story, our footprint, in this book here; I think readers will appreciate it. They'll love it. They'll cry. They'll think about a time they saw and heard us onstage, when Yothu Yindi presented that power, from this soil in Arnhem Land, to the rest of the world. From the bush to the big smoke. Now we want the political people in government to see that power too, to finally see the need for a treaty; we want our voice to be recognised.

We celebrate Mother Earth and Father Sky; and we are the cycle of life.

Yow manymak.

Yirrkala, Northern Territory, July 2021

Author's Note

Under the shade of a school awning in the remote Gumatj homeland of Biranybirany, the plan for this book was hatched. It was June 2018, and a memorial was being held to commemorate the life of Yothu Yindi's lead singer at the place where he wrote the first lines of 'Treaty' with Paul Kelly. I was working for the band as their media coordinator for the event, covering the story for Darwin's *NT News* and shuttling other journos out to the site in my beat-up Holden Frontera. Sitting with Yothu Yindi mainstays Witiyana Marika and Stu Kellaway, I held out the dictaphone as they shared memories of times long gone; from the band's early meeting at a sound check in the Arnhem Club, to being signed by Mushroom, to writing their biggest hit. On that day we began a collaborative journey to record the story of this incredible band and the many exceptional humans who have played in it. In more than one hundred interviews, from backyards and homes in Yirrkala and Gunyaŋara, to coffee shops and parks in Darwin, and Zoom conversations reaching to Ireland, the US, New Zealand and all around Australia, those connected to the band have shared their tales, from the funny and awe-inspiring to the desperately sad.

For the best part of the last decade I've worked as a reporter in the Northern Territory, in East Arnhem Land, Darwin and Alice Springs, including as the editor at Arnhem Land's *Arafura Times* newspaper in Nhulunbuy. I've been privileged to cover Yothu Yindi at some pivotal later moments: from their ARIA Hall of Fame induction to the tragic death and funeral of lead singer Mandawuy (whose wife, Yalmay, has permitted his name and image to be used in this book). Taking highlights from more than thirty years of the band's history, and thousands more of Yolŋu history, this book can only hope to shine light on fragments of the Yothu Yindi story – a story of breaking down barriers and giving voice to the movement for Indigenous recognition, a story that continues today. While Yothu Yindi's founding singer was not here to add his voice to the interviews, the reflections of his bandmates, teaching colleagues, family and friends illuminate his vision for a brighter future for Yolŋu in Australia.

As with the band's name itself, Yolŋu languages are a critical part of telling this story – as Mandawuy once said, 'Language is power' – so you'll find Yolŋu Matha words scattered throughout the book, with a glossary at the end.

This book starts and finishes where its first sparks were lit – the same place the first lines were written for 'Treaty' – in Biranybirany. In the Ancestors' days, Biranybirany was a place of peace-making, of *Makarrata*, a starlit courtroom where clans

Author's Note

in dispute would gather to reconcile under ancestral law. More recently it was a place of education and of music, where a song calling for justice awoke the spirit of the land once more. This is that story: the story of Yothu Yindi.

Matt Garrick, 2021

Freedom

(Mandawuy Yunupiŋu)

We've been working on a course for change
Trying to work out a balance
Sometimes I feel I'm so alone
And I wish you were here

Making money can be one thing
Building bridges can be the other one
All it takes is understanding now
To make that dream come true

You and me bayma
We can make it happen — freedom
You and me liya-wayma
We can see it through — freedom

Many thousand years of history
Of a culture that is still to be told
This is only just the beginning now
I guess we'll have to work it out

You and me bayma
We can make it happen — freedom
You and me liya-wayma
We can see it through — freedom
You and me bayma
We can make it happen — freedom
You and me liya-wayma
We can see it through — freedom

You and me — we can make it happen

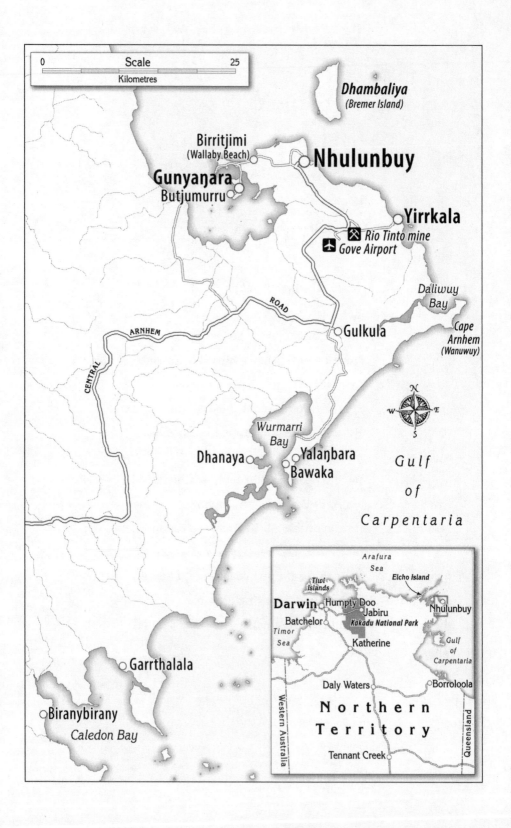

Prologue

On a lonely patch of the northern Australian coastline, a sweet, sad ceremony is getting underway. It's 7 June 2018. The smell of burnt eucalyptus and the smoke of a slow-roasting barbecue carry on the dry season breeze. A makeshift stage has been trucked into the remote Gumatj homeland, 130 kilometres down a potholed dirt highway from the nearest township of Nhulunbuy, on which a sweaty crew tune guitars and test amps beneath the brutal glow of the East Arnhem Land sun. A posse of scrappy camp dogs watch curiously as guests climb out of their packed 4WDs and filter into the site. A soundie sorts the speakers and a distinctive guitar groove blasts out. The vocals carry over the grounds:

> Well I heard it on the radio,
> And I saw it on the television …

It was out here at Biranybirany, between beers and by the flames of an open campfire, that the first snatches of the Yothu Yindi song 'Treaty' were hashed out in 1990. A spark lit that would eventually spread into a wildfire. The early embers of a game-changing political anthem, with a chorus that was never meant to make it out of the rehearsal room. An ARIA Song of the Year and its video clip – remember those kids backflipping on the beach? – that opened the eyes of a generation. The Biranybirany speakers blare:

>   Treaty yeah! Treaty now!

A couple of the (eight!) credited songwriters on 'Treaty' are reunited here for this sombre occasion. Its lead author is physically absent, gone from this world, but his spirit blazes strong in the hearts of those congregated. On this morning, they're here for him: it's a memorial, out at the birthplace of his biggest hit, to mark five years since he passed away. Mats are splayed on the dust under a hodgepodge of marquees set up in a ring around the central ceremonial arena. The guests shuffle in, sitting to await the day's proceedings. Among these visitors is a famous musician, keeping low-key among the crowd. He stands with his hands behind his back like a polite schoolboy.

Suddenly, the dull murmur of the crowd is broken by the reverberating clack of two pieces of wood being knocked together in a driving beat – *tock tock tock* – and the purposeful holler of a sort-of marching band leader revving up a procession. This leader is Witiyana Marika, the charismatic co-founder of Yothu Yindi. Between a frizzy mane of black

Prologue

hair and a blooming grey beard, his coffee-dark face resembles a lion as it concentratedly prepares for a hunt. He's at the head of a pack of around thirty painted warriors, both Yolŋu and balanda, black and white, all men. *Bilma* (clapsticks) clasped in his hands, Witiyana cracks them together in time, an ancient metronome ringing out. He begins the *manikay* (song). He's singing out 'Maralitja' ('Crocodile Man'), a Yothu Yindi track about the late frontman's Gumatj clan identity. Witiyana steers the troupe towards the large sandpit that's been deposited in front of the stage, at the heart of this open bush auditorium. The famous musician in the audience is suddenly summoned from across the pit by Witiyana.

'Paul Kelly!' shouts the Yothu Yindi songman. '*Yow*, Paul Kelly!'

Out in the wilds of East Arnhem Land, in this tiny blip on the map, the renowned Australian singer is called into action. Paul Kelly takes a few steps forward as Witiyana guides him into the procession. In a flash, this otherwise inconspicuous figure, a stark contrast in his blue polo to the painted men surrounding him, is at the centre of the march as it moves across the sand. It's headed towards a large boulder draped in yellow fabric by the stage.

Witiyana instructs Kelly with earnest glances and hand signals. The southern musician offers a gracious smile, which is quickly abandoned as he absorbs the seriousness of the impending moment. The warriors stop just steps before the boulder.

Witiyana's chants have hit an urgent climax and now sing out alone and acapella across the ceremonial grounds. Still bellowing, he takes Kelly's arm and guides it onto the boulder, to the sheet of yellow fabric. Kelly has evidently grasped his role and stretches out his hand to remove the sheet. For a second, his otherwise passive face is marked by sorrow. The boulder has been bared for all to see. The warriors stand still; a sea of furrowed brows staring at this rock. On the stone lies a plaque bearing the words:

```
My tongue is the flame, gathered, prepared and alight.
    It burns with truth carrying me across the land
                   of my backbone.
            Dr Mandawuy Bakamana Djambayaŋ
             Djarrtuṉdjuṉ Yunupiŋu AC,
            September 17 1956 — June 2 2013.
```

A photograph sits at the plaque's centre – a wide smiling face rounded by crow-black curls, a face once recognised across the nation. It's Mandawuy Yunupiŋu. Gumatj songman, school principal. The charming Yothu Yindi band leader who burst from the NT wilderness to become one of the most famous Aboriginal men in the country.

He was a man of many names. His surname, Yunupiŋu, means 'a rock that stands against time'. He was a man of fire; in his own words: 'fire is my clan symbol. Fire is my life force.' With Yothu Yindi he once took that fire – that rock-and-roll torch – around the entire world, spreading a message of equality, of working together, of the power of the Yolŋu voice.

The *bäru* was his totem animal, the spirit of his ancestors, dancing deep within his soul. He was a crocodile man of the Gumatj clan and this hamlet of Biranybirany was his homeland.

On this day in 2018, the sun beams down, but an undercurrent of grief runs cool in the crowd. Paul Kelly wipes a speck from his eye and Witiyana grasps him around the shoulder in solidarity as the warriors stand gazing at the plaque, heads bowed. Then, in a sudden flurry, like a tide returning out to sea after the crash of a towering wave, the procession is over. The warriors dissipate and grab a seat in the sand, awaiting the next part of proceedings.

The musicians make their way up to the stage.

1
Diamond Dogs

Yirrkala, 1976: an almighty din was clanging out from the old school hall. Although rough, it was still recognisable as the gravelly howl of John Fogerty and distorted strains of his rock outfit Creedence Clearwater Revival. Grinding guitar lines rolled heavy and fast like a road train clanking up the neck of the Stuart Highway. Minimal chords, three or four, max. Songs about the rain, the ceaseless rain. As the singer's voice climbed to the climax of 'Who'll Stop the Rain', the monsoon was keeping rhythm against the hall's roof. But the deluge couldn't dissuade a stream of kids from poking their noses in through the door to see what was going on, to have a giggle and yell with glee.

It would turn out to be the first gig of a local cover band. Modelled by a group of brothers on their faraway heroes of the stage and spotlight, and an early precursor to Yothu Yindi, the band was called the Diamond Dogs. Jangly guitars, crackly amps, raw as a plate of buffalo tartare.

'We started belting out songs; people came saying, "Ay, what's that noise? Must be something!"' says Djawa Yunupiŋu, once the Diamond Dogs' lead singer, between belly laughs. 'Kids comin' up, and we were busy singin' out our songs from Creedence Clearwater, Rolling Stones, Beatles, and Elvis of course – the king of rock and roll.'

The band's name was a nod to the David Bowie album, whose title also had a local resonance: the diamond was a shining symbol of the Yunupiŋu brothers' Gumatj clan. 'The idea 'round that, around David Bowie's album, struck me,' says Djawa. 'My totem is the dog. It's my Dreaming. And the diamond is me, my clan. I twisted David Bowie's name round, to me, to my clan. And my brother said, "That's good! Let's stick to that."'

Djawa's in his sixties now, lean and affable, with his top foliage turning silver. He's the younger brother of two former Australians of the Year – Galarrwuy and Mandawuy (previously Bakamana) Yunupiŋu. One is nowadays an elderly land rights legend; the other was the original lead singer of Yothu Yindi.

But when the Dogs formed, they were just young men, teenagers, sniffing out new songs. 'I'd just come back from Kormilda College, before that big wind came, Cyclone Tracy,' says Djawa. 'I'd come back for a Christmas break, and with me I'd brought some songbooks. Brought some records with me too … my brother already had a guitar with him, he bought one in Darwin. We had one amp, we shared the amp, and a rhythm guitar. We were on the lookout for a bass guitar – they were pretty hard to find in those days. But there was a spare bass in the church, so we decided to ask the parish there if we could use it. And they said, "Look, go, you can take it. We don't need it." That was very generous of them. So, we started practising, practising.'

There the Dogs were born. Their main line-up consisted of three teen brothers born from different mothers – Djawa, Bakamana and Balupalu Yunupiŋu, with their mates Harry Gumana on bass and Mawalan 2 Marika on guitar, and a revolving door of drummers slapping the skins.

Their base was the Yolŋu community of Yirrkala, a former missionary settlement that lies against the stingray-laced shores of the Arafura Sea. It was the birthplace in 1963 of the fight for Aboriginal land rights, after the Australian Government gave an international mining consortium the green light to dig up Yolŋu traditional lands for bauxite, without consultation. It was the trigger for a drawn-out legal and political battle, in which the brothers' father, the powerful Gumatj chieftain and artist Mungurrawuy Yunupiŋu, was a pivotal player, and eldest brother Galarrwuy also had an important role.

In Yirrkala, millennia-old sacred song cycles and ceremonies run parallel to a rock-and-roll beat; the traditional ways of the elders are in an endless tug-of-war with the gleaming lures of the white man's world. It's a place of balance, precarious as that may be at times.

Here, the Dogs would gather their cheap equipment of chapped guitars and frayed drumsticks and bash away long into the night. It was modern rock thrashed out in an ancient corner of north-east Arnhem Land where Yolŋu society – complete with its own traditional law, education, politics, maths, music, art, astronomy, dance, real estate and supermarket – has operated cohesively for thousands of years.

In a Yirrkala backyard, a tarp is spread out on the grass, sun beating down. A toddler just learning to stand hops, shaky but fearless, around the yard in a nappy. Yalmay Yunupiŋu leans back on the plastic, stretching as if trying to reach deep for a memory, always keeping one eye locked on the baby as he toddles off to try to wreak havoc. Her late husband was Mandawuy Yunupiŋu, known prior to the late 1980s as Bakamana Yunupiŋu (among other names, including Tom). Now, the steadfast mother of their six daughters (and a growing number of grandchildren and great grandchildren) is taking time to preserve and record old memories.

'The first band that he started before we got married was Diamond Dogs,' says Yalmay. The memory sparks a burst of laughter. 'It didn't go anywhere. It wasn't that big. They played down at the oval, where the basketball court is. I still have fond memories of that, where they played some of their first Diamond Dogs gigs.' She talks of how music was in her husband's blood. It had been swirling around the Yunupiŋu brothers since their earliest days of childhood. 'Music lived in him because of traditional music that he had already.'

The brothers' father, Mungurrawuy, was a traditional Gumatj composer. He'd also owned the first ever wind-up gramophone in Yirrkala and had an enviable collection of vinyl, particularly of old tribal recordings. His sons would study intently this strange musical object, its tuba-like protuberance blurting out sounds as crackly records spun round and round. Over his lifetime, the bearded Mungurrawuy also fathered a mighty brood; according to his son Djawa, the clan leader had about eight wives who collectively contributed more than fifteen children to the proud Yunupiŋu lineage.

Now also a clan elder himself, Balupalu Yunupiŋu – another original Diamond Dog – sits at the Gove Boat Club overlooking the waters of Melville Bay, just a few kilometres from his community at Gunyaŋara (Ski Beach). With a stubble of beard showing on his usually clean-shaven cheeks, he's reminiscing about the roughshod outfit he and his brothers pulled together all those years ago, inspired in part by the sounds of their father's old gramophone. 'He was the first one to get one of those. And we used to listen to that. We used to carry it everywhere, my brothers, and listen to that,' says Balupalu, sipping on a beer and chuckling. 'It was mainly the old songs – Yolŋu songs – like on the land and all that. We would've been teenage, thirteen or fourteen.'

As a natural progression, the boys started to hunt around for instruments, so they could play the sounds themselves. 'We decided to ask our older brother [Galarrwuy] to get us some band equipment and we started singing,' says Balupalu. 'Started off with Creedence; we loved the Creedence. I got really excited. My brother [Bakamana] went into Darwin, went everywhere, and collected all the old tapes, like Status Quo, Joe Cocker and some other music as well. He'd bring it back and he'd play it for us, and we liked it.'

The siblings had paid attention when a 21-year-old Galarrwuy had had a shot at the music business years earlier, recording a land-rights-inspired single with bush balladeer Ted Egan in 1969, called the 'Gurindji Blues'. They were still in school when the single was released on vinyl, but it showed them what was possible, and so, with Galarrwuy's help gathering some gear, they fired up.

The band's focus at that stage was only on covers. Bakamana 'hadn't ever thought about writing his own songs yet,' says Balupalu, about the man whose lyrics and tunes would one day alter the global perception of Australian music. 'We started up a different kind of music back then, all *ŋapaki* [non-Indigenous] music.'

Despite their amateur stylings and dodgy equipment, the Diamond Dogs had a good run. They were booked for gigs at the nearby Walkabout tavern, and travelled out for shows in other East Arnhem communities such as Galiwin'ku and Milingimbi. When talking about her husband's first foray into the universe of rock and roll, Yalmay Yunupiŋu peals with laughter, an infectious high-pitched chortle. 'They were pretty rough at the time,' she offers. 'Very rough boys at the time.'

Like a shooting star, the group burned out just as it was heating up. 'We lost our gear,' shrugs Balupalu. It was over, but not without some positive – albeit discordant – notes having been hit along the way. The imported songs of the Diamond Dogs had started Bakamana's rock-and-roll heart beating.

At this stage, however, playing in a band was very much a side hustle for Bakamana; his main calling was education, and he worked as a teacher's assistant at the Yirrkala School.

Bakamana had grown up in a row of houses so close to the sea that the front doorsteps were almost lapped by the incoming tide. It's a place named Raŋi, in Rirratjiŋu

Land rights legend and Gumatj clan leader Galarrwuy Yunupiŋu, pictured here in his youth, was a big influence on his younger brothers, including Yothu Yindi's lead singer. *(Fairfax Media Archives)*

language, and goes by Beach Camp in English. From here you can watch the wet season storms cross the horizon, a wall of rain marching towards Yirrkala. Of an evening, an old man named Bälun would position himself by the campfire, serenading the kids with Slim Dusty songs on an old acoustic. Bakamana would perch beside the old man, soaking in the country ballads before Bälun's crooning was sucked away by the westerly winds.

Another of those kids raised up in Raŋi was Dr B Marika – an elder, artist and the NT's Senior Australian of the Year in 2020. (Dr Marika sadly passed away, aged sixty-six, in July 2021, just as this book was going to press.) 'Bälun had taught himself how to play string guitars, and Bakamana would sit with him,' says Dr Marika. 'He was the first teacher that he had for playing musical instruments.' Steaming cuppa in hand, she peers out to sea from her home at Raŋi, and thinks back to a largely untroubled childhood. 'We all grew up in Raŋi, our old people living here, his parents, my parents, cousins, yothu yindi: family. Gumatj and Rirratjiŋu. We lived in corrugated iron houses, nothing like you see today.' Dr Marika motions to the surrounding scene. 'A sand bed and a couple of blankets. Our showers were the creek. We'd shower in there and then go off to the mission school, bare feet, hardly anything on our backs. We literally grew up together, along with his wife, my sister Yalmay. I didn't see any hardships when we were growing up as children – well, obviously there were health issues. But our parents were still nomads.'

Their families were trying to buck the encroachment of western culture and carry on with their traditional lifestyle –

hunting, gathering, walking the country or travelling the coastline in their *lipalipa* (canoes). Across Yirrkala, music was a pervading presence, woven in with the sea, the wind and the nightly beach bonfires. The elders would sing ceremonial manikay – songlines dating back thousands of years to mark animals, rocks, trees and ancestors – to the earthy drone of the *yidaki* (didgeridoo) and the clacking of the bilma. Thrown into the pot with the traditional sounds were the hymns of the Christian church, which Bakamana and his peers learned at mission school during the day, and the more contemporary strains of country music, which came crackling through a couple of portable wirelesses.

At school, the students learned 'typical European manikay' like 'Edelweiss' from *The Sound of Music*, a song named after a white flower found high in the Swiss Alps. Dr Marika recalls the children loading into a bus for a school excursion to visit the nearby early mining developments, where on the way they sang in harmony to American troubadour Woody Guthrie's 'This Land Is Your Land'. A song that speaks of the freedom of all folk sharing the different corners of a wide country, it seems an ironic choice by the mission school educators, considering the land rights battle being waged between the Yolŋu and the mining company at that time.

In the hall of the mission school, the students would refine their harmonies in choir practice. The boys and girls were being readied for an annual competition that saw hundreds of Aboriginal kids from remote communities gather in the Territory capital each year. It was called the North Australia Eisteddfod: a festival of music and dance, which tallied among its early winners a talented teenage Yolŋu dancer named David Gulpilil, who would become a renowned Australian actor and star of films such as *Storm Boy* and *The Tracker*. Dr Marika recalls: 'We learned at home and practised our singing and all of that, then we used to get carted over to Darwin for the big Eisteddfod festivals and competed with other Yolŋu communities. I'm sure we won one or two recognitions.'

Another girl from those mission school days was Merrkiyawuy Ganambarr-Stubbs, now the principal of Yirrkala School. She recalls Bakamana as a class showman with a show-stopping smile, who would have his fellow pupils in stitches. At the school, the missionaries called him by his English name, Tom, and his best friend was Jerry – a real cat-and-mouse team. '"There goes Tom and Jerry!" we would all say.' Merrkiyawuy cracks up at the memory. 'And they were funny. Really funny. And they would make us all laugh. We were all growing up together in a big family.'

She recalls pattering into a teacher's house years later and witnessing the Diamond Dogs in full churn. It was the first time she'd ever heard her schoolmate sing. 'I remember going there just once and listening to them singing and practising, and saying, "Ay manikay, ay *latju* [beautiful]!" Just encouraging them. It was all my uncles at the beginning.'

Yalmay and Bakamana had been schoolmates too, and in 1979 they were married in the 'tribal way'. Yalmay says, 'It wasn't like a marriage in the white way, in a church. It was just small, with immediate family. His family came to where I lived and we had a meeting. There it was agreed we would be married. And I packed up my things and went to his home.'

There's one story from her husband's Diamond Dogs days that brings tears to Yalmay's eyes, an incident that could've altered her own trajectory, and that of Australia's pop music scene, for the worse. 'I would watch my kids and also my grandkids, and I would think back to this story, and I would think to myself, "These kids wouldn't be here, and I wouldn't have married him, and I wouldn't have had grandkids,"' she says, eyeing her tiny grandson as she speaks.

Bakamana's niece, Banbapuy Ganambarr, remembers the night well, as Bakamana spent it with her late husband, Billy Gaywṉdji Maymuru. She tells the tale as Yalmay listens on. 'They were really great mates. Always drinking together, always driving to town, always hitchhiking together,' says Banbapuy. 'And in those days we only had a handful of cars in Yirrkala, and sometimes people used to go by boats. They'd launch from where Raṉi is, around the point, and then park their boats on the seashore at Nhulunbuy, at Town Beach. Then they'd go and drink, and come back on the boat.'

Bakamana had turned up at his niece's family home. He strummed the JJ Cale song 'Magnolia' to her toddler son on guitar, then soon enough, he and Billy were on their way. They made tracks down towards the shoreline. 'I saw them walking around down to the beach, and I said, "Aren't you hitchhiking?" And they said, "No, we've got a boat parked down at the beach."'

Their tinnie puttered off, until it was just a silhouette on the horizon. It's about a fifteen-kilometre trip by sea, skirting rocky coastline, from Yirrkala to the nearby mining town of Nhulunbuy.

The hours ticked onwards. The pair didn't return. 'I was worried because I knew something was wrong. And I kept getting up, waking up and waiting for them outside,' Banbapuy recounts.

She later learned her instincts had been correct: something had gone awry when they were halfway back to Yirrkala. 'They were having a party, they were drinking in the boat, singing and singing and singing, and then my husband turned around and saw that my uncle was gone. And the moon was not up, there was no moon, it was a dark night. And [Billy] straight away knew that [Bakamana had] fallen off the boat. So, he took off his shirt and dived in, and started going like this' – she gesticulates to show his arms moving wildly, here and there – 'He was sinking.' Billy miraculously landed a hand upon Bakamana's shirt and hoisted him back up onto the boat.

'When they came home they were all wet,' Banbapuy says. 'And I said, "What happened?" And they said, "Uncle here, he fell asleep."'

That event sometimes flickers through her mind, she says, and she quietly offers thanks to her deceased first husband for saving Bakamana's life. 'I thank him and say, "Thank you for saving my uncle's life, otherwise he wouldn't have been famous, and no Yothu Yindi would've existed."'

By 1984, with the Diamond Dogs exiled to history, the Yunupiŋu brothers had a new group on the go, the Wäwa Mala ('Group of Brothers') band. For this band, Bakamana had joined forces with a balanda janitor from Yirrkala School, a musician named Graeme Kelly, who'd spent years travelling through Asia and the Pacific. 'We met each other and caught up and just hit it off, and started jamming and playing music, mostly just guitars and stuff, but talkin' about this mix of traditional and modern music and putting it both together,' says Kelly, now seventy and living in Tasmania. 'We both had very similar ideas. And so, we just spent a lot of time together, talkin' about it and jamming and writing a song here and there, and going to play it, and then sort of coming up with ideas about that. It was a good, positive start.'

On his journeys through the Solomon Islands and New Guinea, Kelly says, he'd seen groups merge their traditional sounds with electric instruments. It was a new idea for Arnhem Land. The Wäwa Mala band started to incorporate some of the elements that would eventually become the backbone of Yothu Yindi – the yidaki and *buŋgul* (traditional dance).

'I think it was an important time to get it happening,' says Kelly. 'Mixing the two ways together, the mainstream, the Yolŋu and the balanda, and getting it out there.' The brotherhood was now reaching well outside of the Yunupiŋu family circle to form a group without borders, black and white together, creating enough of a cacophony to carry across the Gulf and into Queensland. It was drawing a map for Yothu Yindi to follow.

The cacophony would also be the bane of Yalmay's existence, keeping her and her baby daughters awake into the wee hours. 'It was very hard at the time. They would have lots of parties, parties I didn't like. It was just noise everywhere, all around. Sometimes it would go from early hours of the night till late.' Despite the hardship caused to her young family by her husband's early attempts as a rock-and-roller, Yalmay acknowledges the importance of the racket. 'It was something that his vision was leading into. He didn't think he was going to be a big famous man later,' she says. 'It just happened.'

The brothers were a crew of rough diamonds – but soon enough another young leader would emerge from Yirrkala's musical talent pool to help them shine.

2
Child and Mother

Bakamana Yunupiŋu had his eye on a young fella in Yirrkala community: a disciplined student of traditional knowledge, with a powerful lineage and a neat tuft of jet-black hair. He was barely out of boyhood but he could already hold a crowd; his dances at ceremony were a blaze of movement, his yidaki playing a rumble of thunder across the landscape. He was bold, strong and proud. Slightly cheeky, but good-hearted. His name was Witiyana Marika, of the Rirratjiŋu clan. The son of Dadayŋa 'Roy' Marika, the clan's leader. He was Bakamana's sister's son, the musician's nephew. In *gurrutu* (Yolŋu kinship) terms, he was the yothu to his uncle's yindi.

And, as Witiyana reflects now, 'He saw me, saw that I was something.' Bakamana's judgement was on the money. Plenty of primped-up rock-and-rollers spend years carefully cultivating their image. But for Witiyana, the charismatic co-founder of Yothu Yindi, now sixty, rockstar swagger flows as naturally out of his being as fish swim along East Arnhem's Cato River.

With slack jeans, reflector sunnies and a ready, beaming smile, wherever he goes in the NT or across the world, he gets noticed. And so it was with his uncle, who Witiyana says 'chose' him for what would become a lifelong collaboration – at least for one of them – to take Yolŋu knowledge from their isolated home community in Arnhem Land out to the world.

'He saw me as I was growing up and learning all that powerful knowledge,' Witiyana says, motioning with his hands as if to physically summon up the recollection. 'One day he would choose me, because I'm *ralpa*; I do as I'm told what to do from my father in a disciplined way, because I had been disciplined in my mind, my spirit, to do ritual, culture. I was still a young boy when [Bakamana] was in Diamond Dogs. He was older than me. He saw that I had lots of talent, and like, "This boy has got something," you know? Powerful. Power there.'

In the years to come, Witiyana would translate that cultural power onto the stage – striped in *gapan̲* (ceremonial clay) and bellowing out thousands-of-years-old songs to wide-eyed white suburban kids. He would become the captivating traditional showman of Yothu Yindi, the foil to Bakamana's guitar-carrying troubadour.

'He would just stand there, beautiful, bold in his gapan̲ and holding his bil̲ma, just singing,' says Darwin musician Todd Williams, who was side of stage for some of Witiyana's earliest performances to southern audiences. 'Going into these Sydney pubs, and having these manikay sung in these places, you could just see people's jaws dropping.'

Yothu Yindi's former drummer Bart Willoughby, a stalwart of South Australia's music scene, says watching Witiyana's early performances was akin to watching a star soprano belt it out in an opera house. 'When Witiyana would sing, he knew how to fill up the whole area with his voice, like an opera person,' Willoughby says. 'But that technique came from out in the bush. He'd be sitting out in the bush, and he'd have to train himself on how to fill up the whole area, from a young age. By the time he got to America and started singing, he had the same power as an opera singer. A technique of how to fill up the whole air.'

As well as a performer, songwriter, ceremonial leader and ARIA Hall of Fame entrant, in 2020 Witiyana added to his startlingly impressive CV the title of big-screen actor, pulling off a key role in a confronting film about the NT's frontier wars, *High Ground*. On this particular day, he's sitting out the back of the Rirratjiŋu Aboriginal Corporation office in Yirrkala, elbows propped against a scratched wooden tabletop and looking out over the view of the Arafura Sea. He reaches for a half-opened tobacco pouch to roll a cigarette. He shouldn't really be smoking; a tapering scar across his chest from an aortic valve replacement suggests this with severity. But drag away he does.

He's thinking back to the start of things, decades in the rear-view mirror, to times before Hollywood record deals, TV interviews, endless bus tours and backstage parties. He's recalling a time when it was just him, his uncle and their families, trying to keep living the traditional way. Hunting magpie geese and spearing stingray. Cutting yiḏaki from stringybark trees. Trading stories, songs and secrets. Knowledge.

'My father stood for the land and sang for the land and managed the land at that time,' he says. 'So, as I was growing up, I became a part of that life. And growing up I got to a certain age, six, seven years old, I was learning manikay. I was singin' manikay along with Dad. Eight, I was getting stronger, nine, ten years old, learning dance.'

Witiyana's father, Roy, remains imprinted in NT folklore for taking on the mining industry when his people hardly had a voice. He was a serious ceremonial leader and a showman, with a chiselled face like a skull, as Witiyana describes it, and a central figure in the fight to attain Aboriginal land rights in Australia.

The bulldozers had come to East Arnhem Land with little warning in the 1960s. As had the dynamite. Some Yolŋu thought they were being bombed, and while this wasn't the case, it was the beginning of a kind of war. In 1962 the Australian Government granted mining exploration rights to a multinational consortium, Pechiney, for more than 300 square kilometres of traditional Yolŋu land. It planned to extract bauxite, a type of rock, red as Uluṟu, that contains the raw material needed to produce aluminium, a lucrative commodity used to construct most of the world's trains, cars and cans.

The consortium was preparing to dig up dirt that for tens of thousands of years had been home and hunting grounds of the area's Aboriginal custodians. The elders were livid. Rirratjiŋu and Gumatj leaders, Roy and Mungurrawuy among them, rallied the elders from all thirteen clans of the Gove Peninsula to rail against the mining. They soon took their fight to the nation's capital.

A mural in Yirrkala honouring the work of land rights pioneer and artist Roy Marika, father of Yothu Yindi co-founder Witiyana Marika. *(Blue Douglas/mural by Mike Makatron and Cam Scale)*

A teenage Galarrwuy helped his father and the clan leaders draft the Yirrkala bark petitions – signed, typewritten letters plastered on bark and bordered by traditional designs, which spelled out their inherited rights to the land 'from time immemorial'. They sent two petitions to the federal parliament and the House of Representatives tabled them in August 1963. '[The petitions were created] to try to help explain to the government and the mining company the spiritual relationship we have with our land,' says Bakamana in the 1994 Yothu Yindi documentary, *Tribal Voice*. 'This was Australia's first land rights claim.'

Politicians noted the grievances of the Yolŋu, and created a committee to travel to Arnhem Land to hear their concerns firsthand. The committee sat down in the scrub and gave the impression they'd listened. But, by and large, the clan leaders' voices were ignored by Canberra.

By 1968, the consortium Nabalco had been granted a special mineral lease to expand its operations, including the creation of a nearby town to house its workers. On one occasion, in 1969, senior clansmen gathered at the top of a sacred hill site named Nhulun, which had been partly bulldozed by the mining firm. Up there, *gara* (spears) in hand to demand an end to the desecration, they performed a special ceremony known as the 'Land Rights Galtha Buŋgul', calling for respect. A photograph of the Yolŋu clutching their gara on the hillside hit newspapers as far south as Sydney's *Daily Telegraph*. In one concession to the elders, the company agreed to keep the traditional name of Nhulunbuy for the township, in preference to its chosen name of Gove, after a World War II pilot.

But the mining operations still went forward at full tilt and, aghast, Roy and the traditional owners took their fight a step further. With prompting from supporters, they entered the balanda legal arena and waged a high-profile Supreme Court battle *(Milirrpum v Nabalco and the Commonwealth of Australia)* which, heartbreakingly, they lost in 1971. Justice Blackburn ruled that under Australian law, the Yolŋu had no claim to ownership of the land.

Witiyana was then just ten years old, but remembers clearly his father's and the elders' sorrow. 'They were devastated. We felt like we were nobody, like terra nullius, like they say. But we didn't let it beat us. We are survivors. It doesn't matter about that white man's case not recognising us, it doesn't matter. They only lived by their law and their society – but they can't sing the land. [The clan leaders] didn't forget that ruling. But they always knew who they were.'

In the court case's aftermath, the elders finally had some success – albeit a far cry from their original goal. Although the mine forged ahead, their legal tussle had laid the groundwork for the *Aboriginal Land Rights (NT) Act* to be written into law in 1976. It was a watershed moment, an opening for other Aboriginal clan nations around Australia to follow suit and demand recognition – and royalties – of and for use of their traditional lands. The younger generation, including the future members of Yothu Yindi, took notice.

When Witiyana reached his early teens in the mid-1970s, he felt the pull of the south. Under his father's instruction, he travelled to Melbourne, where he would spend a few years as part of a trailblazing dance troupe, Bwung-Gul Aboriginal

Culture Group, run by Ralph Nicholls, son of Indigenous AFL legend Sir Doug Nicholls. 'We were teaching buŋgul to Koori mob all over the suburbs, as well to balanda schools, going around and introducing our culture,' Witiyana says.

Here, the singer's eyes were opened to Australia's 'material world'. He learned English and how to tread in the ways of the whitefellas. He also popped up on primetime TV, cutting dance moves alongside Ossie Ostrich for an episode of *Hey Hey It's Saturday*. 'I would've been fourteen, fifteen. Almost an adult. My mind and life was changing.' Witiyana's fingers slice the air, plucking at the memories. 'I wanted to check it out, the new way, white man's society. How they live. From the bush to the contemporary world. On the television you would see Indigenous people talking English, and I'd say, "I want to learn to talk like that."'

Witiyana's father summoned him homewards around 1980, when he was nineteen; the young man was needed in Yirrkala. After decades of fighting for land rights, the Rirratjiŋu's leaders of the 1960s and '70s were rapidly ageing. The old warriors were dying out, and they needed to ensure the next generation could carry on their knowledge. How to stand strong in the modern age. How to sing the land to life in an age of television, fast cars, beer and cannabis. These kids weren't perfect, far from it (the story of a teenage Witiyana and his mate crashing a night-patrol paddy wagon in Nhulunbuy comes to mind as an example). But at least they were willing to give it a crack. 'I was leading the way, you know?' Witiyana says. 'I was listening, ralpa, to my father.'

Child and Mother

But shaping the community's future wasn't his first priority. His uncle had put an idea into his mind.

By the mid-1980s, in Yirrkala, the Wäwa Mala band had downed tools, and Bakamana was looking to embark on his next musical incarnation. He called on his nephew.

'He'd come round and say, "Hey, Witiyana! Let's make some songs,"' Witiyana recalls. 'We would jam together, jamming, jamming, and then getting chords right, our melodies right. He was quite into his teaching, but he was stepping into music at the same time. He was breaking through.' As well as clan manikay, Witiyana says, 'there was blues, a little bit gospel, sometimes we'd play gospel, and rock and roll. And country and western as well.'

With Bakamana's guitar and Witiyana's growing mastery of yidaki, bilma, manikay and buŋgul, they twigged they could pull something together, something fresh yet ancient, a mix of the contemporary and the traditional. Pop music grounded in the planet's history.

And with Bakamana's Rirratjiŋu nephew now involved, they were no longer the wäwa band – they had moved beyond brothers. It was the start of a yothu yindi band. 'One night we were sitting around saying, "Ah, we'll have to change the name,"' recalls their early bandmate Graeme Kelly. 'And somebody come up with Yothu Yindi, and they just all got so excited about it – everybody goes, "That's just perfect!" That was a new era then.'

The two relatives of different clans: the Rirratjiŋu and the Gumatj. Men of opposite moieties: the *Dhuwa* and the *Yirritja*. Or as Witiyana explains it: 'I'm his yothu and he's my yindi.'

Yothu yindi is part of the strict Yolŋu kinship system, gurrutu. It allows opposites to co-exist respectfully – those of different clans, land, ceremonies, songs, totems. It's a system of balance. Yothu yindi dictates marriage, ceremonial obligations and land ownership between individuals and between entire clans. It is a cycle with no beginning and no end, carrying on infinitely over hundreds of generations.

It's a 'child and mother' relationship; the mother, the yindi, must always be there to care for her young one, yothu, and vice versa.

'Yothu yindi is child and mother, so it's opposites,' as Bakamana explained years later, in the *Yothu Yindi: One Blood* documentary. 'And that's basically the principles that govern our lives … within those two elements of philosophy, yothu and yindi.' And as Galarrwuy put it so eloquently in *The Monthly* in 2008: 'My inner life is that of the Yolŋu song cycles, the ceremonies, the knowledge, the law and the land. This is *yothu yindi*. Balance. Wholeness. Completeness. A world designed in perfection, founded on the beautiful simplicity of a mother and her newborn child.'

In the Yirrkala School janitor's one-room shack that night, a new Yothu Yindi relationship was conceived. As Kelly recalls it, the name 'sorta just popped out'.

In the months ahead, Yothu Yindi would have their first ever onstage performances, low-key affairs at the Gove Surf Club, the Yirrkala School, and a town square event for Australia Day. 'At the Yirrkala School they were very popular and everyone was excited,' says Kelly. 'Everybody could see what we were doing and were quite positive and supportive of us to keep at it.' Importantly for the Yolŋu men, they'd always consult with the clan leaders before performing any traditional songs in public, to make sure they weren't breaking any cultural protocols. The elders had their backs, and usually sent them off with a tick of approval: go for it.

Since his rough early days in the Diamond Dogs, Bakamana's musical repertoire had been refined – he'd even penned his first handful of songs. Graeme Kelly tells of how he and Bakamana wrote a track called 'Crying in the Rain' after a community funeral. 'We went to a funeral one night and it was just bucketing rain,' he recounts. 'And all the women were out dancing in this rain, and crying, as happens in those ceremonies, and it was quite emotional. We walked back to my place after that, and he just goes, "We gotta write about that." So we just sat down and wrote this song … it was a fantastic song.' The track would eventually be named 'Yolngu Woman' and land on Yothu Yindi's debut album.

Bakamana's first ever tune had been born a few years earlier during a stint working as assistant principal at Shepherdson College in Galiwin'ku, on Elcho Island. Staring out to the sunset, he'd been inspired to turn his hand to writing, spurred on by relatives from a pioneering Yolŋu band called Soft Sands. Now largely consigned to obscurity, Soft Sands' influence on the NT's most celebrated artists, from Geoffrey Gurrumul Yunupiŋu to the Warumpi Band, was unsurpassed in the day. Dressed flash in matching cowboy shirts and stetsons, Soft Sands made inroads into the competitive country music scene, touring hard and playing at flagship gatherings like the

Tamworth Country Music Festival. They were the first Yolŋu band to ever tour the US and Canada.

The tales of this intrepid act were captured in a doco called *Chasing the Music*, about the arrival of rock and roll into Arnhem Land, shot by brothers Rob and Stu Courtenay. 'Soft Sands came out of the church and went a country and western style, culminating in them winning in Tamworth – I mean, to win in Tamworth you've got to be pretty bloody good,' says Rob from his home in Adelaide. 'They were really good musos ... and they were happy to break away from the church, from the sort of mission music, into exploring their own, and using the music as a vehicle for the songlines.'

The filmmaker says when Bakamana saw Soft Sands in action – roping a band together, rehearsing, recording, 'it was like a light globe went off in his head': 'It was like, "Wow, that's how you go about making a band!" He would've just been jamming probably daily with the cats from Soft Sands during his time on Elcho. He would've learned everything from that year. Not everything, but a lot, about music.'

Soft Sands also helped convince Bakamana to jot down on paper the opening lines of his first Yothu Yindi song, 'Djäpana (Sunset Dreaming)':

> Look at the sun,
> Sinkin' like a ship,
> And the sunset,
> Takes my mind,
> Back to my homeland,
> Far away.

Child and Mother

> It's a story,
> Planted in my mind,
> It's so clear, I remember,
> Oh my, oh my sunset dreaming
> Wo djäpana, wo warwu,
> Wo rramani, Wo galaŋgarri …

'Djäpana' would become one of Yothu Yindi's most enduring hits, climbing the ARIA singles chart, with its remix still a dancefloor staple in the Top End. Djäpana translates to sunset – the exploding Arnhem Land evening sky splashed with an easel of pinks, oranges and the occasional streak of green. The lyrics spliced English and Gumatj languages, and rang with a helpless homesickness; the author missing his home in Yirrkala, separated by hundreds of kilometres of land and sea.

'It was one afternoon when the sun was setting down,' explains Bakamana's wife, Yalmay. 'He was always outside and looking out at the sea. And he was homesick. Sometimes looking at that djäpana, sometimes people feel homesick, missing family at home. Sometimes djäpana also means someone has passed away.'

Sunsets on Galiwin'ku, Elcho Island's most populous community, seem to engulf the island every evening – and so too, as Bakamana discovered, did music. He spent his nights there in the early 1980s jamming away, on one of Australia's northernmost islands, and one of its most fertile grounds for fostering Indigenous sounds, as the glowing djäpana dipped into the sea.

'We sorta had our DNA reconfigured': Midnight Oil frontman Peter Garrett (centre) says his band's tour across the remote Northern Territory in 1986 with the Warumpi Band was a formative experience. *(Ray Kennedy, The Age/Fairfax Media)*

Child and Mother

Once Bakamana had moved back to Yirrkala, one day in 1986 a wiry, tightly wound rockstar would shoot through the community and leave a profound impact on him and Witiyana. A Yolŋu man from Elcho Island with a gravity-defying afro and Mick Jagger swagger, George Rrurrambu Burarrwaŋa was the frontman of an exciting Central Australian outfit called the Warumpi Band. During Warumpi gigs, George would stalk the stage like a panther on the loose, swivelling his hips, pitching his hands in the air, sitting down, leaping up and screeching lyrics with an accented urgency. Bursting from the Red Centre community of Papunya, the Warumpis – a four-piece made up of George, a Victorian named Neil Murray and two brothers, Sammy and the late G Butcher – were on the rise thanks to a handful of hook-laden local hits and glimmers of interest from the south. (If Yothu Yindi would one day become Australia's Beatles from the bush, the Warumpis would counter as their slightly grittier, wilder Rolling Stones.) The Warumpis had set off into the nation's dusty heart on tour alongside Sydney pub rockers Midnight Oil, who were in the clutch of an outback awakening. As Oils singer Peter Garrett says of that tour's impact on his band, 'We sorta had our DNA reconfigured and our understanding of Australia reconfigured in pretty substantial ways.'

The two bands played in rarely visited corrugated-iron communities like Warburton, Kintore and Yuendumu along the Tanami Track. The Oils were pegged as the headliners, but the crowds of Aboriginal onlookers at each stop were there mainly to catch sight of George in full flight, as the Warumpis belted out 'Blackfella/Whitefella', 'Waru (Fire)' and a string of rock-and-roll songs in Luritja and Yolŋu Matha languages.

When this unprecedented tour wound its way north into Arnhem Land, the double bill readied to perform on the back of a truck trailer on the lawns of Yirrkala church. Hundreds of hardhat-wearing bauxite miners from Nhulunbuy couldn't believe their luck – the Oils! They jumped in their utes and zipped down to see the towering singer, Garrett, sweat it out in the tropical heat. An author was there to document the moment – a wordsmith whose story would in time intertwine with that of Yothu Yindi's own. Dubbed a 'thinking man's drinking man', *Rolling Stone* writer Andrew McMillan dispatched a book from the tour, *Strict Rules*, reporting: 'there are a couple thousand people at the show, the whites from Nhulunbuy reclining by their eskies in deckchairs at the front or on their feet by the stage. The local Aborigines sit in the shadows on the hill behind.'

Yothu Yindi's earliest incarnation – Bakamana and Witiyana – were among those in the audience. And according to Witiyana, as they watched George and the Warumpis light up the stage that night, his bandmate was taking some serious mental notes. 'That's when we were inspired by Warumpi Band,' he says. ''Cause he was doing that mix of contemporary and tradition, on his own, George Rrurrambu. So [Bakamana] thought, after we formed the band in '85, he said, "See that? We gonna twist that round, you and I." He told me, "We can make it different." Big rockstar that came in, because he had to start everything else. Took off. Warumpi. So he's the one who we were inspired by. Yeah!'

Warumpi had laid down a gauntlet to the whole community, says Yirrkala educator Leon White, who was in the audience and remembers an electric feeling in the air. 'I think the challenge for Yirrkala was, "Can we do the same?" Because here they were hearing a Yolŋu guy sing and ... boom! George was absolutely amazing.'

Neil Murray and the Butcher Brothers pounded along to wildman George, a tight backbone to the bouncing brain out front. Then came the Oils, who delivered what McMillan described as a set of 'dynamism and passion, a strong and humorous performance': 'It's a beautiful night. People are responding – they're calling out for songs! Clapping! Cheering! Slapping palm fronds against the stage! Hurling the fronds, wrenching them off the side of the semi and spearing them onto the stage.'

Peter Garrett himself still remembers it well. 'It was a great night, one of those beautiful, mellow sort of soft nights, not much wind,' he says. 'And just everybody, every single person scattered in different parts around, some up the front, some sitting under trees at the back. Just the whole thing was very, very special.' The sun slipped into the horizon and spilt a tin of dark purple paint over the scene. It was over and the Midnight Oil juggernaut jetted onwards, across the bay to Groote Eylandt, and deeper into the bush.

But in its wake, Yothu Yindi would apply the valuable lesson given by Warumpi. The puzzle pieces were falling into place: a blending of the ancient and the new. A hot new sound to be born in a brutally hot part of the nation.

3
The Educator

It was an afternoon in late 1985, and the barehanded beats of African drums were echoing down the hallways of Yirrkala School. A touring group of master drummers had been brought to the East Arnhem Land classrooms by the Australian arts council, which was being managed in the NT by a long-haired former barramundi exporter by the name of Alan 'AJ' James. After the showcase ended, James received a whispered request from one of the schoolteachers: 'Bakamana Yunupiŋu wants to meet you.'

'I didn't know who that was,' James says from his regular table at the Roma Bar – a long-standing institution of Darwin's cultural landscape. 'But I said, "I'm staying at the Walkabout hotel in town. Tell him I'll be finished after four o'clock." So, he came and met me there.'

Bakamana rocked up to the Walkabout with a black beard on his cheeks and a rousing handshake. A few friendly words were exchanged, and the arts council official and the school principal-in-training strode into the bottleshop, stacked up with a six-pack of VB, then took off at pace to Bakamana's house in the beachside settlement of Gunyaŋara. Out by the water's edge, they sat on the sand as the former Diamond Dog strummed from his early songbook.

'We sat down on the beach and he played me, I think, three songs on his acoustic guitar. He said he wanted to get into the music industry. He knew that I was the manager of the then famous Northern Territory band,' James says with a wry smile, 'the Swamp Jockeys, which somehow gave me the credibility of being the person that might be able to get him into the music industry. And at the end of that meeting, I remember as we walked away from the beach, I said, "Well, if we're gonna work together mate, you're gonna need a passport. Because we'll go places." And in my mind, that was the beginning of the journey.'

Alan James would one day become pivotal in Bakamana's life, as the manager of Yothu Yindi. But that era was yet to come. At this point, Bakamana had a different kind of revolution to pull off.

The Yirrkala School sits on a hill in the community, just a stone's throw from an overgrown banana farm and the red bush track leading down to Ganarrimirri (Shady Beach), where children swim and play under the watchful eyes of hawks winging overhead. It was here from the late 1970s that Bakamana, a gifted bilingual communicator with a disarming smile, had begun to find tangible ways to help realise a vision of his elders: a Yolŋu-controlled school, with Yolŋu teachers planted in every classroom and Yolŋu languages spoken proudly. It was part of a broader agenda for Yirrkala's self-determination, and was a radical shift from the English colonial school model of the day.

'The end result is to get people to think like Yolŋu and get away from the balanda approach which automatically tries to define what's best for us,' Bakamana told the *Land Rights News* in 1988. 'We will end up with an autonomous Yolŋu institution offering Yolŋu courses … we're definitely not saying that balanda knowledge is no good. It's there all the time and we come up against it, so we need to know some of it. But we'll decide what we need of it.'

To this day, many in the sector still view the trailblazing teacher and principal as an educator first and foremost, with his years as a globetrotting musician simply a continuation of this role.

Bakamana's wife, Yalmay, was also a teacher at the school. She's still there all these decades later, fighting for a fairer system for her people. Yalmay and Bakamana began to raise up their family while both on the books there.

As a teacher, Bakamana was often seen glued to his acoustic guitar. He lugged it wherever he walked around the community, and in class he'd sometimes strum his lessons. 'The guitar was always on his back,' says his former colleague and close friend Kathy McMahon. 'He had a way of teaching that was very Yolŋu. It's like at ceremonies, where kids can do what they like more or less, unless it's something really serious. So, he taught like that. And usually he used music.'

One of McMahon's favourite memories of the man she calls her *ŋapipi* (uncle, in the Yolŋu kinship system) was an impromptu trip to Darwin to watch Dire Straits in 1986. The British superstars' *Brothers in Arms* concert was one of the biggest rock shows ever to light up the Top End capital; it remains one of its most legendary.

It was pelting with rain, the Darwin Showgrounds soggy as a four-year-old's bedsheets. The band members of Dire Straits were throwing wary glances at each other, visibly nervous about being fried onstage by a short-circuiting amplifier. But the revellers remained undeterred.

'[Bakamana] was right in the front. It was pissing monsoonal rain, and he was just there in front of [Dire Straits frontman] Mark Knopfler, just air guitaring,' McMahon laughs. 'The look on his face was just like, "My hero is right here in front of me!" I'm sure Mark Knopfler would've noticed. It was so good. And I knew that night, look, this guy, he just loves music. It's in his soul, this rock stuff. Soaking wet, we didn't care less.'

The story didn't end there. Kathy McMahon and a couple of other balanda teachers were hauled in for disciplinary proceedings for leaving Yirrkala to attend the concert without having been formally granted time off for the night, but Bakamana had their backs. In the regional education manager's office, the Gumatj man spoke on behalf of the non-Indigenous teachers. And according to McMahon, he laid it on thick. 'He says, "I'm here to speak for them. We have a strong belief in culture and cultural activities, and for these three balanda, Dire Straits is a cultural activity, and they have a right to go to Darwin so they don't miss out on things." And the manager just looked at us, and looked at him, and went, "Oh, spare me. Out you go." And he tore up the notice.'

One of Bakamana's early mates and educational mentors was a man named Leon White, a diehard Carlton AFL supporter with an equally lifelong passion for improving remote NT education. In both Carlton and bush schooling, he continues to struggle to see big wins. White, a surname that suits his long, snowy beard, was tight with Bakamana as the Yolŋu teacher rose through the ranks. They would hunker down at Nhulunbuy's Walkabout hotel and the Arnhem Club, their 'regular spots', where for hours they'd debate ways to fix Australia's woes over a few cold schooners.

'He was quite prepared to push challenging ideas, but at the same time ... the outcome of the discussion is what he was looking at, not necessarily agreement,' White says. 'He wanted to get a conversation going.'

This ability to argue a point without prejudice was part of the teacher's nature, says White, and one of his great attributes, which in years to come would see him recognised as a cultural bridge-builder on the national stage. But in those days, as an Aboriginal man from the bush, he may as well have been shouting his ideas to the wind. Decision-makers entrenched in the Territory's education department seemed to care very little about the wishes of the Yolŋu, and were more intent on retaining the status quo. 'He was treated abysmally by people in bureaucracy, really,' says White.

Bakamana was also confronted by some of the nastiest elements of institutional racism: hurtful comments tossed off flippantly by those fearful of a coming change. Former Yirrkala School principal Greg Wearne was present when one of Bakamana's peers branded him a 'coon' at an Arnhem

Land principals conference. The Gumatj man had just been promoted to the role of co-principal alongside Wearne. 'It was late at night, principals sitting around having a drink, chatting. Bakamana was there, I was there ... and the conversation was quite pleasant, sort of patting him on the back a bit,' says Wearne.

Bakamana went to bed and the grog-fuelled conversation swung around. Criticisms were thrown, accusing him of having been granted the promotion because of his race. 'One of the principals tried to sort of dampen things down and said, "Come on, you guys, he's a colleague,"' says Wearne. 'The comment came from one of the other principals: "He's not a colleague. He's a coon." And that, of course, is embedded in my mind to this very day.'

Bakamana didn't hear the insult himself, but as Wearne says, 'he was incredibly astute, and he knew that this kind of negativity towards his elevation' was rife among other principals.

Kathy McMahon recalls that Bakamana returned from that conference to Yirrkala in a dejected slump. 'We couldn't fight the systemic racism,' she reflects wearily. 'It was massive ... that awful incident where he was belittled in public; he was expecting collegiality and support, not adulation, or anything like that. But that's what he got: "just a coon". You can't imagine it.'

While this breed of racist bureaucrat ('All white and all men,' says McMahon) wasn't listening, or worse, was actively undermining him, Bakamana's elders and Yirrkala workmates stuck by his side. With a determination to change the system in line with the wishes of the old people, he pressed on. 'I had accepted the reality that Yolŋu had suffered for too long from the system,' he told *Land Rights News* in 1988. 'It was time to take hold.'

By the mid-1980s, the Yolŋu quest to transform Yirrkala School was gaining steam, and Bakamana's role was emerging as key: he was on track to becoming the solo school principal. With the support of the elders, he'd enrolled in a course at Darwin's Institute of Technology (an early precursor to Charles Darwin University) and relocated with Yalmay and their daughters to the Territory capital. But the lessons at the institute didn't deliver what he'd hoped for, and his community's goals remained unfulfilled.

In stepped a professor from Deakin University, the softly spoken John Henry, who would become instrumental in helping to change that. Henry visited Bakamana in Darwin at the end of the student's first semester in 1985. 'We discussed his disappointment with the Darwin Institute course and its lack of relevance to his community's aspiration for self-management of their school,' Henry said in 2018. 'During this discussion [he] raised the possibility of Deakin University being an option for [the Indigenous teacher-training institution] Batchelor College's graduates seeking a full teacher-training qualification. This was the start of a project that was to have far reaching benefits for Aboriginal communities across Australia: a project that was to revolutionise Aboriginal higher education in Australia.'

Bakamana's internal cocktail of ambition, disappointment and sense of duty helped create this new course: a partnership between Batchelor College and Deakin, through which he would eventually attain his Bachelor of Arts degree in education. The program was revolutionary in allowing Indigenous students to combine traditional knowledge and practices with the mainstream university curriculum, and to study and file assignments while still based in their home communities out bush.

As he embarked on this new course, Bakamana was plucking at a tune, 'Mainstream', that would eventually land as the opener on Yothu Yindi's debut album. He submitted the original lyrics of 'Mainstream' for a uni assignment, some of which painted a portrait of a unified Australia:

```
            Reflections in the water I see,
              Yolngu and balanda living,
               We're living together now,
       Sharing dreams of the red, black and gold,
                  Dreamtime living now,
                    In the Yolngu way.
         Go, go, go, go, living in the mainstream,
           Go, go, go, go, but under one dream.
         We're living together, we're living together,
        We're learning together, we're living together,
               Yolngu, balanda, balanda, Yolngu,
                       This is Australia.
```

By the author's account, 'Mainstream' is 'a song about Yolŋu having our own mainstream, our own *Rom* (law) which is equal to yours'. Bakamana explains the track in the 2009 book *Reflections and Voices*: 'On a political level, Indigenous and non-Indigenous Australians can complement each other just like the Yolŋu and balanda parts to our two-way school curriculum.'

His main lecturer during the Deakin course, philosopher Helen Verran, is listed in the liner notes of one Yothu Yindi album as their 'consultant philosopher'. 'This must be the only rock band in history to have had a consultant philosopher on their books, so I'm rather proud of that,' laughs Verran.

She says Bakamana submitted the 'Mainstream' lyrics for an assignment about literature and creative writing. 'I think he was probably the only person who submitted song lyrics,' she says. 'Most people would write an essay or a short story or something like that … it was an idea that came out of the ether. And they were good song lyrics, very good, so I think he got a good mark for the assignment … he would've got a high distinction.'

Bakamana eventually made it through to graduation. His name was read out at a ceremony at Batchelor in 1988 and he held his *bathi* (sacred ceremonial dillybag) high above his head. Bakamana beamed a wide smile for the cameras. He had become the first Yolŋu from Arnhem Land to gain a university qualification, no small feat.

It was a breakthrough for his people. But even then, he still had to fight for his recognition. 'On his graduation night down in Batchelor they only had one flagpole – there was a policy about what flags could be shown at departmental sites,' Leon White remembers, still annoyed. 'An Aboriginal flag turned up and got put up, but it was never recognised by the [education] department as an important thing.'

If departmental officials had failed to properly comprehend the milestone moment, many others got it – back home, Bakamana was a hero. His family, colleagues and musician mates gathered for a traditional ceremony at the sandy tip of the Gove Peninsula, a place called Butjumurru (Drimmie Head). It was an elaborate occasion marked in style, with some of the Territory's top brass among the 'hundreds' in attendance, including the NT's chief justice and chancellor of Deakin University, Austin Asche. 'It was a big deal; Deakin people, the administrator, lots of Yolŋu. Everybody was there,' says Kathy McMahon. 'There was buŋgul and manikay and everything, and then there was the skydiving and show-off stuff,' she laughs. In spite of the colourful celebrations on the ground, many of those in the crowd had their eyes on a light aircraft up in the sky. 'I think it might've been Alan James's brother [John James]. One of those boys jumped out with a parachute, and he had the degree, and he came down with it.' According to attendees like McMahon and Leon White, the skydiver landed with Bakamana's graduation certificate in his belt, which a Yolŋu family member then fished out with a spear, before it was eventually passed over to its recipient.

Armed with his degree, Bakamana continued to push ahead. He led the discussions for Yirrkala School's future curriculum, with Yolŋu knowledge at its heart – ceremony, art, music and language – alongside elements of western education. Two knowledge systems side by side, with an eye on quality outcomes for Yolŋu students, just like any other young Australian.

It was a Both Ways education revolution. As Greg Wearne explains, this philosophy spearheaded by Yirrkala School and its principal has now become 'a key word and a key philosophy across lots of fields … Both Ways is sort of the guiding rubric in land management conservation, in health, and so especially when you're in north-east Arnhem Land, you're reminded almost on a daily basis of his contributions.'

With each new step the school took towards the community's vision, people in the lofty echelons of government began to take notice. Perhaps surprisingly, the conservative NT Country Liberal Party Government set the train rolling: in Bakamana's words, they had 'listened to the Yolŋu voice'. By the late 1980s, they'd allowed the Yolŋu to set up a powerful community school council and take charge of their own decision-making. All the work, all the bargaining, all the battles were beginning to come to fruition.

The Yolŋu strength of purpose and cultural identity had prevailed; but it hadn't been by fluke. The Methodist missionaries had only arrived in Yirrkala in 1935, meaning that until then, and unlike many of Australia's southern Aboriginal nations, the region's clans had long been able to continue living in the traditional way, dining off the fruits of their land and sea country, following Yolŋu Rom and speaking up to forty Yolŋu languages – more than fifteen in Yirrkala alone – without interference. The elders had known exactly how they'd wanted to shape their school culturally, because for some of them, even by the 1980s, it had been central to their being since childhood.

But by the time Bakamana had finally achieved his goal of becoming the solo principal of Yirrkala School, in 1991, fate had other ideas. Yothu Yindi was exploding in popularity and its singer was called out onto the road. He took leave from which he would never return.

The Yirrkala School community still celebrates their progeny's achievements as their own. In class, the kids are taught to sing Yothu Yindi songs – both the Yolŋu Matha sections and the English. Recently they learned one of the band's earliest tunes by heart to perform in public, the title track from their 1988 debut, *Homeland Movement*. The lyrics cry out:

> See the campfire burnin',
> And the children are yearnin',
> Talkin' about peace and harmony.
> Yolngu education,
> Is the key for redemption,
> And the homelands centre movement is here to stay.
>
> Power to the people,
> Power to their land,
> Power for culture revival,
> Power for survival.

The legacy of that Yolŋu rockstar at Yirrkala School, three decades after he left to chase his musical dream, still looms large in the current principal's mind. Merrkiyawuy Ganambarr-Stubbs – a proud Yolŋu woman following in Bakamana's footsteps – says the school is closer than ever to attaining the crux of his vision for bush education. 'That curricula that he saw in his mind is almost complete now,' she says.

Sitting out on her back porch, Merrkiyawuy reflects on her predecessor's decision to eventually leave the school he had fought so long and hard for. 'I think [Bakamana] turned to music so he could educate more and a wider audience than being stuck in a school trying to speak up for the bilingual school in Both Ways education,' she says. 'He put that onto himself and became – I won't say a singer – but like a preacher, because to me that's what he was. A preacher, preaching through songs … so that through those songs, he can preach and tell the others: that's what Yirrkala School teaches.'

His classrooms would soon become stages across the globe, his school an entire nation.

4
Swamp Stomp

It's sometime back in 1986. Humpty Doo's liveliest sons, the Swamp Jockeys, are tuning up in the Arnhem Club. In its heyday the Arno, as it was known in Nhulunbuy pub parlance, was the place to be. The mining town's watering hole is nowadays boarded up and slapped with a sign declaring in black capital letters: 'THE ARNHEM CLUB IS CLOSED PERMANENTLY'. But in its finest moments between the 1970s and 2019 (when it was shuttered over financial issues), the Arno was a melting pot of Yolŋu and balanda music, all blaring slightly distorted through ageing speakers to a half-cut crowd.

And so it was in 1986 when Yothu Yindi two-piece Bakamana Yunupiŋu and Witiyana Marika took to the stage and played with a touring bunch of self-proclaimed Territory 'outcasts'. The Arno air was thick with moisture and opportunity. The Yolŋu men were sitting in the beer garden, watching this ragtag crew at sound check. They'd been tipped off to come along by the Swamp Jockeys' band manager, Alan James.

'Me and [Bakamana] saw them at the Arnhem Club, and we had a jam there.' Witiyana pieces together this part of pop music history. 'We were a two-piece band … I was doin' yiḏaki, biḻma, and I was singin'.' The pair hopped up onstage with the Swamps for the sound check, wound up, ready to roll, and showcasing their own songs. A guitar, two voices and Witiyana's rumbling didge.

'We just went, "Wow, you guys are hot!"' Swamp Jockeys bassist Stuart Kellaway recounts of the scene. 'Like, "They're great songs – just come back later on." And we did the gig with them. They warmed up the crowd, 'cause the Yolŋu were just loving it.'

Drummer Andrew Belletty says he was 'knocked out' by the strength of Bakamana's pipes. 'I went, "This guy's got a great voice! He's really confident and he really knows what he wants to do." So I suppose that first sound check led to us doing some workshops with them, to try and get those songs happening,' he says.

Humpty Doo is better known for its plentiful growth of mango plantations and illegal cannabis crops than for nurturing 'raggedy bush bands', but this small town off the highway to Kakadu National Park did produce the Swamp Jockeys – a five-piece guitar band that took their moniker from a slab of strange graffiti scrawled on a corrugated-iron bus stop.

'Someone had sprayed on the side of a bus shelter down there the words "grunt swamp jocky",' explains the band's singer

Swamp Stomp

Todd Williams from his NT Music School office, flanked by band posters and psychedelic art, the gathered ephemera of decades spent in the Top End's creative scene. 'So, my brother Cal and I were doing radio at the time, we were volunteers on the station TOP FM, and we came up with this imaginary band that we called Swamp Jockeys. I would pretend to be the guitarist or something, and Cal would interview me, and we'd try to make it funny and absurd. We did gammon interviews with each other. And then when we actually formed the band, there was really nothing else to be called but that.'

Cal Williams had a rural property at Humpty Doo's Solar Village, about forty minutes from the Darwin CBD, where the Swamp Jockeys would clatter away into the evenings. As Todd tells it, 'We used to gather down there and jam out.'

It was here they spawned their unique breed of 'irreverent country', says Stu Kellaway, an English-born, Papua New Guinea–raised former horticulturalist. 'We loved bands like The Johnnys, Johnny Cash; we loved a lot of country. A bit of Roy Orbison and lots of things like that,' he says from a backyard in Yirrkala.

Along with their twangy outlaw heroes, the Williams brothers' graveyard radio shifts had introduced them to some dangerous foreign sounds such as The Gun Club, Violent Femmes and Joy Division – captivating discoveries in the musically isolated NT capital.

Stu Kellaway and Calcutta-born Andy Belletty had been stewing up songs together since their teenage years. The Williams brothers came to the Top End from Perth in 1970, less than five years before Cyclone Tracy rolled in and obliterated Darwin. Todd Williams says the first mate he made after arriving in the NT at eight years old would turn out to be his comrade at the microphone, the second Swamp Jockeys singer Michael Wyatt.

By 1984 the five Jockeys had all met and properly assembled. 'It was a really interesting, exciting time, because we were all in our early twenties and just inspired by music generally, and just wanting to do music,' reflects Todd Williams now.

The Swamp Jockeys went by two identities: the names on their birth certificates – Kellaway, Wyatt, Belletty and the Williams boys; and their onstage haystack pseudonyms – Stan Stockton (Todd, vocals), Captain Coop (Michael, vocals), Clem Combine (Stu, bass), Dirk Cattlegrid (Cal, guitar), Dan Haybale (Andy, drums) – and their business manager Chuck Mango (Alan James). These blokes were doing more than just imbibing magic mushrooms and warm beer at a bush block down the road from a forty-foot statue of a boxing crocodile. They were, perhaps inadvertently, pushing forward a scene of original NT music, which for years had been mired in blues standards and cover bands imported from Brisbane and the Gold Coast to hit the pub circuit. Darwin's music-thirsty crowd was lapping them up.

'Every pub had a blues band, just the same old shit,' says Kellaway. 'And we sort of tried to steer clear of the blues the whole time, go the opposite to whatever was going on with that. Don't get caught up in that blues riff, because you just never get out. It's like a big bog. We did originals – we were one of the first sort of original bands in Darwin, I guess, because everyone was all about covers. We just weren't real

The Swamp Jockeys putting on a high-energy show in the carpark of the Roma Bar, in downtown Darwin, 1987. From left: Cal Williams, Michael Wyatt, Todd Williams, Andrew Belletty and Stu Kellaway. *(courtesy of Todd Williams)*

good at learning them properly. Even when we tried to, they were always a bit our own versions. But we had lots of fun.'

The Swamp Jockeys made it their mission to bring energy to the Top End's stagnant stages. 'We were always wanting to put on a show,' says Todd. 'Me and Michael would just never stop moving. It's a criticism I have of bands generally, who stare at their feet ... we always wanted to show people how to interpret our music and how to dance to our music by jumping around and by putting out the energy. Because when you put it out, people either look at you and say, "You mob are a bunch of dickheads," or they go, "You guys are great!" So, either way, it didn't really matter to us, because that's the way we loved it.'

One of Todd Williams's specials in this department was a mongrel hop called the 'Swamp Stomp'. He would start the dance onstage – if the term 'dance' is not an offence to those trained in the field – and the audience would follow suit. 'You sort of look halfway between a cassowary and a rhino, I guess,' says Kellaway of the move.

At one stage in the band's lifespan, another drummer was recruited by the name of Colin Holt – a Top End artist known to some for his offbeat portraits of every Northern Territory chief minister since self-government. He recalls the Swamp Stomp with glee. 'It was always great fun. It was always crazy and just have a good time. The audience is on trial, not the band. And you know, make 'em dance crazy, that was our aim. Make 'em do crazy wild swamp dance. Haven't you seen one yet?' Holt offers a guttural cackle. 'It's a Northern Territory specialty, sort of half mixed with Yolŋu and Tiwi and Central Australia, and mad outback jack rockin' – just crazy swamp stomp.'

There were other moves too. The Galiwin'ku Goanna, a trademark of Wyatt's, saw the singer turn in frenzied circles, wheeling and spinning, one hand waving free, clockwise, then anti, round and round, then hopping dizzily back to the mic for a chorus. 'Because we live amongst goannas, and you see their head move in that particular way – their whole body jumps to the left and jumps to the right,' Wyatt says, in stitches. 'And if you see some traditional dancers, they have similar movements to that sort of thing. So it sort of just came naturally. One day I just did it.'

For all the mad larks they were having, the Swamp Jockeys' influences were steeped in something more sober. Growing up in the north they'd come a cropper on some serious bigotry: 'We grew up in a pretty tough Darwin,' says Andy Belletty. 'It was quite different in those days – it was very redneck, very kind of hostile to different people. You know, you'd wear a Hawaiian shirt at a pub there, and guys would just come up to you openly and call you a poofter and tell you to fuck off.'

But amid the NT's unique population balance, where more than 30 per cent of residents are Aboriginal, they'd also been raised with a firmer understanding of Indigenous life and culture than in many other corners of Australia. 'We were very supportive of land rights,' explains Todd Williams. 'It was very close to us in the Northern Territory. It was news all the time. We brushed up against some really hardcore bigots and racists that we went to school with, but at the same time, we grew up with Aboriginal people as well.'

It seemed natural for the band to be active advocates of Indigenous rights, appearing on compilations like the 1989 *Building Bridges: Australia Has a Black History*, and gigging with Aboriginal bands of the era such as pioneering South Australian acts No Fixed Address and Coloured Stone, who'd each already been touring hard for years and raising their voice for Aboriginal pride through songs like Coloured Stone's 1984 classic, 'Black Boy'. 'We used to hang out with those dudes in Sydney,' says Stu Kellaway. 'We knew all the blackfella bands and how hard it was to get gigs.' But their musical allegiances were by no means strictly political. It was more about having like-minded mates who knew how tough the scene could get and shared a love of cutting outback stages to shreds.

Sometimes the Swamp Jockeys would show up in remote communities where balanda bands were a rarer sight than a full set of teeth in Humpty Doo. 'We'd do gigs on communities and blackfellas liked us 'cause we were a little bit mad, you know, and it didn't matter if we were a little bit rough and ready,' recalls the band's bassist.

The Tiwi Islands to the Red Centre and Arnhem Land – the Jockeys found their way to these isolated parts of the Australian wilderness thanks to having two qualified pilots at their disposal in Michael Wyatt and Alan James. They were taking the high way, shooting charter aircrafts through the Top End skies. 'Between those guys we would charter the cheapest, shittiest single-engine planes,' recounts Kellaway. 'We used to rip the seats out, chuck all the band gear in there and just fly across to Arnhem Land, smoking weed and drinking beer all the way. That's business class, mate.' The bassist has memories of jump-starting planes on bush tarmacs 'with a flat battery, having to get a troopie out, just run some jumper leads and kick it over'. Business class.

When Bakamana Yunupiŋu was studying in Darwin in the mid-1980s, he became a fixture of the sweaty capital's nightlife, where fate would often land him near the Swamp Jockeys. 'We'd be at a party somewhere, you know the classic Darwin party under someone's house, wet season, hot as anything,' recalls Kellaway. 'And he was already at the party; we walked in and he was there. We were playin' a Swamp Jockeys set, we were settin' up the gig, and he goes, "Ah, may as well jump up and have a sing."'

Todd Williams says their friendship with Bakamana 'developed pretty organically'. 'We formed a good, strong relationship,' he says. 'And he had lots of great songs.'

The Swamp Jockeys began including Bakamana in their neighbourhood gigs at regular haunts such as the Nightcliff Hotel and Lims, where the bar was caged off by iron mesh. During those exuberant sets, the Swamp Jockeys singers would head offstage for a breather, and the Gumatj man would come out. A headband wrapped around his mop of curly black locks, Bakamana would hit the audience with his own freshly scribed tracks, 'Djäpana', 'Mainstream', 'Journey On' and 'Yolngu Boy'. This last song had recently garnered airplay after Warumpi Band recorded a version for their 1987 album, *Go Bush!*

Bakamana would close his eyes and get right into it, bashing the song out to a room full of whitefellas:

> Hey Yolngu boy
> Under the neon light
> Hey Yolngu boy,
> Under the neon light,
> Come with me see a brand new day.
>
> You see that cycad palm,
> That's the pure eye.
> You see that cycad palm,
> That's the living bread.
> Come with me see a brand new day.

Some of his earliest gigs with the Swamp Jockeys in Darwin, at Lims and the Marrara Sports Stadium, were among Bakamana's first to fully white audiences. 'I think the crowd probably reacted with bemusement, rather than euphoria,' says Alan James. 'Like, "Who is this guy? We're here to dance to the Swamp Jockeys." So, it wasn't anything like, "Wow, Bruce Springsteen's just arrived!"' But Bakamana maintained his cool and kept on smiling through.

'I do remember the first time he played with us, all unrehearsed, he just turned up to the show,' says guitarist Cal Williams at Darwin's Lucky Bat Café. 'It was at the Marrara indoor stadium. And just before he came onstage, we said to him, "What style do you want to do your song in, [Bakamana]? Reggae? Country? Rock?" and he goes, "I wanna rock it like The Angels!" and we go, "Yeah, righty-o! Let's rock 'Mainstream' out!" So we rocked the shit out of "Mainstream".' It may have been a throwaway line but, inadvertently, it cranked the volume for Yothu Yindi's sound. '[It] sort of set up a default rock thing, just purely because he made that comment at the time,' says Cal. 'So we rocked it out. And we rocked it out really hard for the first couple of years.'

Before too long, the 31-year-old teacher was a regular at Swamp Jockeys shows – and he'd often call his nephew in Arnhem Land and reel him into the melee as well. 'Wherever Swamp Jockeys gigs were in Darwin, they would invite him,' says Witiyana. 'And that's where I came along because my uncle invited me: "We should go and put a yidaki sound into Swamp Jockeys, and guitar, acoustic, playing straight in." It was magic. And that's when we got known in the Territory, outside of Arnhem Land, just this isolated area here.'

The band's homemade posters, screen prints featuring a skeletal kangaroo, billed them as: 'The Swamp Jockeys with special guests Bakamana and Witiyana from Yirrkala'.

The Swamp Jockeys soon packed up their swags and rolled south for a handful of shows in the harbour city of Sydney. They were well attuned to the workings of the Big Seedy, having already spent long months there snaffling opening slots for rockers like Spy v Spy and Cold Chisel's former singer turned solo screamer, Jimmy Barnes.

'We did lots of early supports, like Jimmy Barnes at Blacktown RSL roller-skate rink or some show,' Kellaway says. 'It might've been Bankstown. It was out west of Sydney, and we just got hammered by paper cups, because they were all kids and they all wanted Barnesy. And they were just chanting, "Barnesy, Barnesy, Barnesy!" So we jumped in on it as well, making fun of it, and started a bit of a chant game for

Barnesy, and going, "This next song's a Jimmy Barnes song!" and then leap into an original of ours. Next minute, paper cups'd be flying onstage again.'

Witiyana and Bakamana flew down and joined the Swamp Jockeys on the circuit in 1987. The Sydney pub punters nearly spat out their Tooheys in shock. 'I just remember standing side of stage just watching them, and they were in peak form – and it was fucking spellbinding,' Belletty recalls. 'To see these guys in this beer barn with a massive capacity, thousands of people, and there's Witiyana, singing the brolga, 'Gudurrku', and stuff, and it's like, "Fucking hell, this guy's singing manikay on a stage in Sydney" ... I don't think anybody had heard anything like it.'

The outfits scored some attention with a spot on Andrew Denton's early variety show *Blah Blah Blah*, where Bakamana introduced 'Mainstream' as a 'song about white people and Aboriginal people living together'. They were nervous but shone vibrantly on national TV.

At most gigs, Bakamana and Witiyana would come out to warm up the crowd, performing traditional manikay with a yidaki and bilma. Then Bakamana would strum a couple of his own acoustic numbers, before the Swamp Jockeys would step out and join the duo to offer up the full band roar.

Drummer Andy Belletty recalls a bit of magic in that early onstage formula. 'Incorporating those guys into our gigs as we did, we would do these fifty-fifty shows where we would play and then Yothu would play,' says Belletty. 'Cal, Stu and myself would be the engine of Yothu. For me, when I look back, it was a groundbreaking thing.'

The Swamp Jockeys would then stay onstage for their own set, where they'd be accompanied by the Fabulous Flienetts: two professional dancers, Julie-Anne Long and Narelle Benjamin, from Sydney dance-theatre company One Extra. Getting into the swampy spirit of things, the Flienetts presented as outback characters, wearing flynet headgear and allegedly harking from the Stuart Highway stopover town of Tennant Creek. The Swamp Jockeys billed them as 'a pair of delightful young dancers who ... first succumbed to the joys of dancing the Galiwin'ku Goanna during the Great Tennant Creek Fly Plague of 1986'. The Flienetts' contributions to the Swamp Jockeys shenanigans were cut rudely short one evening, when police officers raided an inner city warehouse party and shut off the building's power. Guitars down. The night's noise was damned to a fate worse than those stricken by Tennant Creek's mythical fly plague.

Although the shows were capped with joyous raucousness and a supportive scene, the Swamp Jockeys couldn't sustain a cohesive unit forever. Their dole money was always dwindling, and their musical careers didn't seem to be elevating to a skyward level anytime soon. In reality, the Swamp Jockeys were on the bones of their arses, sleeping on grubby mattresses on the floors of Sydney warehouses and mates' places.

They'd been gigging relentlessly for years but hadn't managed to actually release an album. At one point they did have a crack, recording some tunes in a studio next to the Arnott's biscuit factory in Camperdown, where they'd be greeted by wafts of shortbread on their ciggie breaks. But it wasn't meant to be: the tapes got lost or tied up in contractual

A homemade Swamp Jockeys poster from when they were 'living on the bones of their arses' in Sydney in 1987. This gig was performed in an inner-city warehouse, alongside dancers the Fabulous Flienetts. (Library and Archives NT, Andrew McMillan Collection, MS68)

limbo and the record was never released. 'That was probably the biggest sort of failure in our concept as a band,' says singer Michael Wyatt. 'In five years, with all that publicity … we didn't have a record. Even though it was a lot of fun, I think we didn't take it seriously enough. We didn't understand … it never really occurred to me that the album was a thing that we should've focused on.'

Eventually, the two singers – Wyatt and Todd Williams – decided they'd had enough. 'Sometimes it felt like I was pissing away my twenties, other times it was like the best thing you could do in the world,' says Todd, who nowadays supports up-and-coming bands in the Territory as part of the NT education department's Music School. 'We'd been having a hack at it since '84 and it was mid-'88, and we'd thrown ourselves at the industry. I had to pretty much look in the mirror and say, "Do you feel that you're dedicated and ultimately talented enough to make it in this industry?" And I'd also just met this beautiful woman who became my wife, so I had to say I couldn't do it anymore. And then the other lead singer left about three months after that, and you know, the band morphed into something else.'

In the absence of the two singers a void had appeared, but the rest of the ensemble – Stu Kellaway, Cal Williams and Andy Belletty – weren't quite ready to call it quits. Instead, they stuck with their support act who were gathering steam, the traditional men from Yirrkala: Bakamana and Witiyana.

Kellaway puts it simply: 'The two singers in the Swamp Jockeys got sick of being on the dole and never having any money, so we just sorta ran with these two.'

Witiyana remembers the moment: 'They decided we should make one band. They knew that we should give a chance for a Yolŋu balanda band, a mix, and that's called Yothu Yindi. Doesn't matter, black or white, you still Yothu Yindi. The meaning kinda changed.'

The balanda boys were adopted into the Yolŋu members' families, which kept the notion of a yothu yindi system intact. Yothu Yindi: Indigenous and non-Indigenous. Black and white. An electric guitar and a yidaki. One big family. Australia, get ready for a wake-up call.

5
Back in 1988

For Yothu Yindi, 1988 marked the beginning of things. 'In '88 we took off,' says Witiyana Marika. 'That sound was different, you know? A new sound. I knew. And [Bakamana] told me, "This is going to be something big, ay, 'cause of this sound. Because of our Yolŋu lyrics and balanda – it's going to hit Australia."'

By 1988 they'd recruited a new yidaki player to the lineup, a young maestro of the instrument and a kinship nephew of Bakamana's named Milkayŋu 'Milkay' Mununggurr. 'He was my little brother, but on yidaki he was a master,' says Witiyana. 'He was learning from other clan nations like Dhalwaŋu, rock-and-roll yidaki players, a different way to blow the yidaki. But he jumped in and he changed everything. He was the master, a super boy who could play that yidaki. Black magic. I would have goosebumps every time when we used to sing together, and I would feel that power. He would just give me goosebumps.'

With Milkay onboard, they were ready for a year marked by twists of fate leaping out from around every corner. And like all catalysts for some swell of social change, it had started with a shitfight. An epic one: the bicentenary.

Australia's bicentenary had arrived on 26 January 1988 bearing cringeworthy government ads and catchcries – 'Let's make it great in '88!' – all over the television, buses and everywhere else. The celebrations marked the 200th anniversary of Captain Arthur Phillip sailing the first British ships into what is now Sydney Harbour – the beginning of foreign invasion and settlement, and the start of a long and harrowing road for Australia's Aboriginal people. There were fireworks, a re-enactment of the First Fleet's arrival and parties across the nation's cities, while simultaneously, the same corners of the country were gripped by fiery rallies to rebel against celebrating a date that had seen rights and land stripped from the First Australians.

Ironically, this year proved to be a breakthrough for the newly formed Yothu Yindi band. 'Because it was the bicentennial, everyone got behind Indigenous Australia,' says Stuart Kellaway. 'There were protests in the streets, and it sort of gave us some momentum.'

The black and white members of Yothu Yindi were among the tens of thousands of people who marched through the heart of Sydney's CBD, protesting the bicentenary. 'We were in Sydney during the very first Invasion Day march, and somehow we ended up right at the front,' says founding drummer Andy Belletty. 'Milkay and Witiyana, they had all the instruments, the yidaki and stuff, and they were right

Yiḏaki player Milkayŋu 'Milkay' Munuŋgurr joined Yothu Yindi in 1988. He was known as a master of the instrument across Arnhem Land. *(courtesy of Yothu Yindi)*

down [the front] holding the banner for quite a while, and then we were holding our Yothu Yindi banner in the front row. The march ended up down at the Bondi Pavilion for quite a big gig, and that was probably the first time that I saw Yothu really empowered, because we were in a very Indigenous space. They were super confident, super comfortable, as we were playing to close to a thousand people, I would imagine, that were there because it was an Aboriginal Invasion Day protest gig ... it was a really powerful gig because the people were there to see Aboriginal music.'

So unknown were Yothu Yindi that they were incorrectly billed at this Building Bridges show as the 'Koori Dancers'. But the anonymity wouldn't last. From behind the drumkit, Belletty says he saw a new power rising in the Yolŋu men. 'I could see the energy, and I just remember [Bakamana] turning to me during the first song, and he just had this incredible smile,' he says. 'He was just fucking loving it. He was having the time of his life. It was the first time that I saw those guys really hitting their strides. I think from then on, the band kind of changed gears and really started taking off after that.'

The politically charged mood of the moment wasn't lost on the band, either. One of Yothu Yindi's first studio recordings was a biting take on Australia's British invasion called 'Luku-Wangawuy Manikay (1788)' – which Witiyana translates as 'Foundation Song' – the lyrics of which were scribed by folk singer Ted Egan and first sung by Bakamana's older brother Galarrwuy:

Back in 1988

> There was no fight when the white man came,
> we welcomed him as a friend.
> But we never said that he could have our land,
> because that would be the end.
> If Captain Phillip had landed here and tried
> to take Yirrkala,
> It wouldn't have taken us very long to fix that
> English fella.

Years earlier, when he was still a teenager, Bakamana had ventured from Yirrkala to Sydney with a balanda mate named Kevin Kluken. It'd been one of Bakamana's first trips out of Arnhem Land, and looking for something to do, the pair had decided to trek out to Botany Bay to see the site where Captain Cook first rowed ashore. 'We were talking about places we could go and visit, and I said, "Well, there's Kurnell, the Captain Cook landing site, but you probably don't want to go there,"' says the former teacher-trainer Kluken, now in his seventies. 'And he said, quote unquote, "I want to go there, because I want to see where it all started." Meaning the [British] contact. So we did. And we probably were at least an hour and a half, two hours, just sitting there, imagining what it was like at that moment. He was very considered [about it]. He wasn't one to become emotional or aggressive or whatever. He had a gentler nature.'

Yothu Yindi's manager, Alan James, who'd taken them on when they'd merged with the Swamp Jockeys, believes the energy around the bicentenary helped the group take the next step in their musical journey. 'It was because [that year] there was an immense amount of goodwill in Australia towards Aboriginal causes,' James reflects now.

The band stumped up some cash, around $10,000 from the Gumatj and Rirratjiŋu clans on the Gove Peninsula, so they could head into the studio in Sydney and record the few tunes they had in their kitbag. They figured it would be a demo. They booked some session time at the famous Alberts music studios, the production house which had given birth to some of the biggest songs of Australia's top-billed acts, from AC/DC to John Paul Young.

To save money, Yothu Yindi crashed at the self-described inner city 'squat' of Andrew McMillan, the music writer, who had first connected with the band after a Swamp Jockeys gig at the grungy Hopetoun Hotel in Surry Hills. 'We went back to Andrew's place and that forged a friendship and a semi-working relationship that lasted many years,' says James, who hunkered down there as he toiled to establish the group's profile. 'I ended up camped at Andrew's house for many months.'

McMillan, a prolific journo turned author with an acerbic wit and an astute eye for detail, shifted north to live in Darwin not long after meeting Yothu Yindi. Over the years, the Collingwood diehard who existed on – according to those who knew him – a steady diet of moselle, stubbies and newspaper print, would devote reams of A4 sheets to the adventures of the Territory band, and spend countless hours out on their home soil.

In his 2001 book, *An Intruder's Guide to East Arnhem Land*, McMillan remembers Yothu Yindi's early trek south: 'They stayed in Sydney for a few weeks, camping at my Camperdown squat, drawing the cops at five in the morning with the garrulous chatter of green cans and the haunting howl of *yidaki*.'

In Alberts studios in 1988, Yothu Yindi recorded five of Bakamana's songs: 'Djäpana', 'Mainstream', 'Homeland Movement', 'Yolngu Boy' and 'Yolngu Woman'. These would eventually become the guts of the band's debut album, *Homeland Movement*, produced by Leszek Karski, a musician of bar-hopping Sydney bands Bondi Cigars and The Hippos. Karski was in Yothu Yindi's orbit as he had previously produced albums for Midnight Oil and Spy v Spy.

'After we got those five songs down, Lez said, "You can't put an album out with just five songs on it,"' says Alan James. 'And this was back in the day of vinyl. So, we then recorded twenty-two minutes of Yolŋu manikay – traditional songs. Which I believe was the first digital recording of manikay. And sometime later, when the album finally came out as *Homeland Movement*, one side were the contemporary songs, and the other side, if you flip the album over, you got the traditional music.'

Karski says the recording came with its own special challenges. 'I remember one of the hardest things to record live was to do the clapsticks,' he says from where he now lives in Fremantle. 'Clapsticks have an incredibly piercing high-pitched sound; they get into everything. So we had to position them in such a way that the clapsticks wouldn't bleed into every other microphone. But it was a good time doing it.'

To Karski's recollection, Bakamana's leadership of the band shone through in those sessions. 'He was just a gentle spirit, and he was very powerful in his own way,' says Karski. 'But he was just a very engaging, very charismatic, very gentle man. That was my first impression. And the other guys were kind of looking up to him all the time.'

Between recordings, the youthful Yolŋu men Witiyana and Milkayŋu would run out onto the streets of Sydney's North Shore, clutching their yidaki to try and earn a couple of bucks. 'They were like mischievous kids.' Andy Belletty chuckles. 'They'd run out in their shorts, and they're super black, their skin tone, and there we were in Neutral Bay, which in those days was the most white, middle-class suburb you can imagine. And they would just nick out, and you'd see them down on the corner and they'd be busking.' He bursts out laughing. 'Milkay would be playing this massive studio yidaki, this really long one that he had, and Witiyana would be singing and playing the bilma. And I'd be going, "You guys are fucking awesome." And because they were so different, they'd come back with like fifty bucks within half an hour! I just remember the spirit that those guys had.'

Cal Williams says some days in the city were spent quite literally singing for their supper. 'We did a few shows around Sydney, and we were really broke, all of us were super broke. So we'd go up to Kings Cross, busking for food money. And I tell you what, I've busked for food money without Yolŋu guys, but when you go up there and the Yolŋu guys start doing traditional manikay, holy fuck! "We're gonna eat Chinese tonight, boys! There's a hundred and twenty bucks in the kitty!"'

And so Yothu Yindi in its original format – Bakamana Yunupiŋu (guitar, vocals), Witiyana Marika (bilma, vocals),

Milkaŋu Munuŋgurr (yidaki), together with the former Swamp Jockeys backline of Cal Williams (lead guitar), Stu Kellaway (bass) and Andrew Belletty (drums) – had achieved something personally new. Something the Swamp Jockeys had never managed to complete in their years on the road. Yothu Yindi had recorded an album, although how, if and when it would be released to the world remained an unknown.

With the recording session done and dusted, the Yolŋu men jetted back north, and Bakamana returned to his day job at Yirrkala School. He also went about the business of recruiting more family members into the band.

One of those he approached was a moustachioed Yolŋu dancer named Malati Yunupiŋu – another Gumatj relative. Like Witiyana, Malati had cut his teeth as a teenager touring as part of Ralph Nicholls's dance troupe in Victoria, but says it was 'too cold' for him in the southern states, so he found his way back home to Yirrkala. Here he ran into Bakamana, who asked him to get involved with the burgeoning Yothu Yindi outfit. His trademark mo nowadays peppered with greys, Malati rocks back on a plastic seat at his house in Gunyaŋara. He's casting his mind back to some of Yothu Yindi's first ever international gigs, during that bicentenary year, concerts in which he played a colourful key role. Malati would wow the crowds with his traditional dances, his mimicry of animals scampering through the bush: 'The kangaroo dance is a part of me. I live with it. I grew up with it.'

The first shows abroad were for the Seoul Olympics, in September 1988. 'We were welcomed there with rice wine,' Malati says. 'It was bloody hotter than vodka.'

Alan James had managed to scoop the traditional performers of Yothu Yindi a slot representing Australia at the Summer Olympics, where they'd follow the torch from town to town across Korea, singing and dancing the ancient manikay of their homelands. 'I got whiff that the Northern Land Council had the job of sending an Aboriginal group to Korea for the '88 Olympics, so I went doorknocking,' James says. 'I sat down in front of [Northern Land Council's] Peter Cooke and said, "Mate, I want to do this tour." And he said, "Who the fuck are you?" And after ten or fifteen minutes of toing or froing, he pulled open a drawer and he pulled out a bundle of passports and he said, "Alright, it's yours."'

The events were to be a showcase of Yolŋu culture – no Swamp Jockeys onboard, and, to the immense frustration of Yothu Yindi's chief architect, no Bakamana Yunupiŋu. 'Disgruntled, he sat at home, being a school principal,' says James. 'In those first three or four years, we only worked on school holidays.'

Even as Yothu Yindi began to burst through, somehow the Yolŋu band leader and school principal managed to keep both flames burning, at least for a while. 'He'd work full-time and committed to the educational endeavour, and then in the holidays, off Yothu Yindi would go,' says his former Yirrkala School colleague Greg Wearne. 'He managed that rather remarkably, I reckon, to be able to burn the candles at both ends. And he did, both professionally and socially, he did bloody well!'

The Olympics tour that went ahead without Bakamana had its gold-medal moments. 'When we finished that tour at

Seoul Olympics, we were invited to the palace to a farewell party. And we were all pissed drunk, and eating,' says Malati, nearly falling off his plastic stool in his Gunyaŋara backyard. 'And Milkay pulled out his yiḏaki to play it, and the mayor thought it was a bazooka. He hid behind a table. We said, "No, no! It's wood! It's not a bazooka."'

Another memorable early set was at the inaugural Festival of Aboriginal Rock Music in Darwin, which saw the Yothu Yindi band in full flight, footage of which ended up on a doco, *Sing Loud Play Strong*, alongside acts such as Warumpi Band and Pitjantjatjara singer Frank Yamma. 'What we're trying to do is bringing both worlds together: balanda world of music, and Yolŋu world of music,' Bakamana says in that documentary. 'We draw on the Yolŋu way of music because it's part of our life; it's our foundation. It's what we are. It's how we identify ourselves as Yolŋu. Because the definition for Yolŋu is a person who knows how to sing and dance.'

That film also captures Malati, striped in ochre and bounding across the stage, eucalyptus leaves clenched in his teeth, shaking and leaping as the kangaroo. He still remembers it well: as Stu Kellaway says, 'Malati is amazing – his memory, even though he was one of the biggest drinkers, he's got a photographic memory. He can remember every show, who was there, and what they were drinkin'.'

But six weeks in October and November 1988 are particularly implanted in Malati's heart and soul, six weeks that will remain with him until the day he dies: thirty cities in thirty-six days. Sixteen thousand kilometres. The Diesel and Dust to Big Mountain tour of the US and Canada, in the slipstream of Aussie headliners Midnight Oil. 'From Florida to Canada, the bus was our home. With bunks and all that. We were on the move with Midnight Oil – a convoy. Life on the road, seeing different cities, countryside, beautiful country. It was a dream. My dream came true,' Malati reminisces.

It was a coup for Yothu Yindi, who at that stage had hardly even gigged within the borders of their home country. It was a chance to head out onto the highway with one of Australia's biggest bands at the peak of their powers as they tried to crack the lucrative US market. It was a chance for the Yolŋu voice to be heard across oceans; a chance to leave the bicentennial behind. 'I think the Oils tour was the start of an adventure that I don't think can be replicated, in terms of cross-cultural engagement on a global basis,' says Alan James.

And, according to James, the fledgling NT band landed the support slot on this tour of a lifetime by accident.

6
The Good Oils

The amplifiers boom Witiyana's ancient manikay out across the venue – 10,000 Americans watching, jaws agape, eyes wide. The cracking of his clapsticks fills the room.

Barely a switch flick since Yothu Yindi's formation, they're already travelling the highways of the US for a gruelling 36-day tour schedule, crossing east and west, supporting one of Australia's hottest musical exports: the thumping pulse of Midnight Oil.

More than three decades since his band's breakthrough tour across the heart of America, with Yothu Yindi and Native American act Grafitti Man in tow, Peter Garrett's still talking about its impact. Well, he's attempting to. His voice is coming through in staccato bursts: 'It's telling me … my connection … is unstable …'

It'd be a studio technician's nightmare. Thankfully it's not the vocal track for a Midnight Oil album, but rather a dodgy link-up on Zoom. After a couple minutes of fiddling to fix the connection (from the New South Wales scrub to Darwin – what could go wrong?) Garrett launches into his memories of Yothu Yindi under the blazing lights of America.

'I think the key thing is the impact that it had on the American audiences, who probably had never seen an Aboriginal or Torres Strait Islander person at all, let alone a whole bunch of people in a band, some dressed with ceremonial markings, with dance, with clapsticks, but also with the full paraphernalia of a big rock show.' The famously loquacious singer mulls over his words. 'It was actually really quite different, sometimes challenging, particularly when they sang in [their] language ... and extraordinarily exciting.'

He thinks back to Yothu Yindi's nightly shows: thirty minutes to blow the senses of a roomful of middle-class American kids fed a steady diet of MTV. Witiyana appears, streaked like a warrior ghost spirit, and hollers to the night. Dancers prowl proudly nearby. The backline soon materialises, Cal and Stu, axes on shoulders, alongside the lead singer.

'[Bakamana] was sort of the anchor weight in the middle of the stage, propelled along by a pretty nifty rhythm section,' says Garrett. 'But the intensity, the cultural resonance and the pointy edges of it came from all the Yolŋu, who really just let fly, essentially, whenever they got onstage. They weren't up for that long, they were playing as the support, they were our special guests ... they probably only played for half an hour. So it was one of those maximum-impact shows. Essentially, the lights go down and the band comes onto the stage, and then the lights come up again, and then the audience sort of stands there, many of them either with their jaws heading towards the floor or in disbelief.'

The tour was the product of happenstance that came to a head in an office in Sydney's inner west, in an encounter with a burnt-out band manager with a busted limb. 'I was in the Oils' office on Glebe Point Road, and the manager of Warumpi Band came in with his arm in a cast,' Alan James says. 'He described how the lead singer of Warumpi had broken his arm on the last tour. And that was it – he said he'd had enough and he was quitting, and he pulled the pin. And unbeknown to me, that led to a string of events where the Oils – who were planning their big breakthrough tour in the US – had originally planned on that being Midnight Oil, Warumpi Band and a Native American group called Grafitti Man. Which subsequently became Midnight Oil, Yothu Yindi and Grafitti Man. So, by November, we were touring the US and Canada with Midnight Oil.'

It may well have been a mixture of dumb luck and shrewd opportunism that got Yothu Yindi the US tour. But the opportunity hadn't come from nowhere: a bond between the bands had been cemented a few years earlier, before Yothu Yindi had even properly existed. It was a friendship forged in the skies above Arnhem Land. The Swamp Jockeys' piloting pair, Alan James and Michael Wyatt, had offered to shuttle gear in two light aircrafts to various Top End Indigenous communities for the Oils' *Blackfella/Whitefella* tour with Warumpi Band in 1986. They'd called themselves 'Swamp Air'.

'Midnight Oil had eight aircraft and twenty-two tonnes of gear, and the Indigenous people had never seen so much

PA or heard such a loud noise in their life,' says Michael Wyatt.

He recalls a show on Elcho Island, where the Oils were cranking up for their concert, sound checking as the local mob amassed. He and Alan James were sitting on a beach with a mate when James suggested they head up in the air for a skydive. (James and Cal Williams, among others in the Swamp Jockeys universe, were experienced plane jumpers, and often took impromptu leaps from light aircraft.)

'I said, "Okay, fair enough,"' says Wyatt. 'So, we went and did this parachute jump over Elcho Island. And of course, the people had never seen a skydiver before, so when they see this person jump out of an airplane and see this parachute coming down, they all left Midnight Oil and the stage and came running to the oval to watch AJ land. That evening, Peter Garrett came up to us, licks his finger and puts it in the air and goes, "Swamp Jockeys – one. Midnight Oil – zero." We stole their crowd.'

On Garrett's end, he's still laughing about the absurdity of it: 'It's not a bad entry, really. Well, it was funny, when you think about it, especially for the little kids. All these balanda are suddenly flying in the air without wings!'

All was eventually forgiven. In the following year, 1987, Midnight Oil repaid the favour to the Swamp Jockeys for helping them tour the Territory. They hauled the Swamps along for a five-week, 25-date tour of the Australian east coast, hitting the big cities as well as regional centres like Broken Hill in NSW and the steel city of Whyalla in South Australia.

For the Swamp Jockeys, the tour was a tough hump – they made $500 per half-hour support slot, most of which went on day-to-day food, accommodation and transport costs. 'We drove around cramped in a little Tarago,' says singer Todd Williams. 'Part of the tour we slept outside. In South Australia, Whyalla, we actually had to sleep on the beach, while the managers and the roadies slept in a hotel. We just didn't have any money.'

Despite the rigours of the road, the band from a Humpty Doo bush block learned some priceless lessons from their politically charged counterparts, who had just released what would become their most successful single, 'Beds Are Burning'.

Williams describes the Oils' engine firing up when they headed onstage every night – a well-oiled combo acting completely in gear with a roar like a low-flying Hercules. 'It was like, one, two, three, four … POW! And compared to what we'd just done, it was like, "Oh, shit, this is the stage that we need to get to, to have that solid, big sound." It was a real kind of wake-up call.'

By late 1988, the Oils' machine was firing down the gun-barrel freeways of North America, with the band from northeast Arnhem Land along for the ride. The inclusion of Yothu Yindi and Grafitti Man – comprising activist John Trudell, guitarist Mark Shark, singer Charlene Howard and drummer Milton 'Quiltman' Sahme – was most certainly, as Garrett still attests, 'quite a political statement'. As the former law student and future Labor MP told the *Rocky Mountain News* during the tour: 'The rights of Indigenous people are hardly high on the hip topics of concern these days … Indigenous cultures are survival cultures that haven't destroyed the land.

South Australian music pioneer Bart Willoughby, who played for a stint in Yothu Yindi, with singer Mandawuy (Bakamana) Yunupiŋu and band manager Alan James, on tour in the US in 1988. *(courtesy of Yothu Yindi)*

It's not only an issue that focuses on people's rights, it's a very deep and timely issue.'

The inclusion of Trudell on the tour was a particularly incendiary move for a foreign band. The outspoken activist poet's pregnant wife, three children and mother-in-law had been killed in a house fire ten years before the Oils tour, the day after Trudell had torched an American flag on the steps of US Congress over a lack of rights for Native Americans. There's long been suspicion Trudell's home was set ablaze by political nemeses; the FBI refused to investigate the incident, labelling the fire an 'accident'.

Yothu Yindi's Stuart Kellaway says Grafitti Man opened doors – and eyes – for the Australian act into Native American ways of life on the land across the US. 'They were cool guys,' he says. 'We went up to Portland, Oregon, where we went out to Quiltman's reservation and ate salmon and bear. And the people there, particularly the elders, were really interested in what was happening socially in Australia compared to America in terms of Indigenous rights and stuff like that. And in most places, Indigenous people would come out and support us, no matter where you went.'

Yothu Yindi members sat down with the elders and residents of reservations in Oregon and Arizona, learning and swapping stories of land rights and Indigenous identity. 'We met all the old people, the kids, it was a connection. It was warm-hearted sharing, meeting these people, Aboriginal families from America,' says Malati Yunupiŋu.

Although Trudell passed away in 2015, Grafitti Man's guitarist Mark Shark looks back on the tour with fondness,

Yothu Yindi's yiḏaki player Milkayŋu 'Milkay' Munuŋgurr and dancer Malati Yunupiŋu rocking aviator shades on their tour bus in the US in 1988. *(courtesy of Yothu Yindi)*

although he concedes it was 'fraught with challenges and craziness'. It was 'very important in terms of solidifying our purpose and commitment to each other and the work', writes Shark from the US. 'John was very encouraged and hopeful that the Indigenous peoples around the world could create a unified movement and enhanced awareness of the issues that bind all of us together in terms of ecology, humanity and the forces that work to divide and suppress us.'

Across the States in 1988, Yothu Yindi were welcomed with open arms and full hearts by Native Americans – a theme that would continue for the band's whole career. 'Everywhere we went, whoever was Indigenous of that place would seek us out. As would every ethnomusicologist on the planet, of which there's at least 300,' says Alan James with a laugh. 'And every didgeridoo player in the world.'

The Oils tour also exposed the lads from the land to a different type of lifestyle – a polar opposite to eons-old Indigenous cultures – one of fast food, fast cars and fast living. The neon shine of mainstream America. And the Australian musicians loved it. 'Stocking up on cowboy boots, the burgers, the Oreos, I mean, we were amazed,' chuckles Stu Kellaway, flicking through old photos from the trip. 'Going to America, I'd been there before, but everyone just felt, "It's just like the movies!"'

In Harlem, a historic black neighbourhood in New York City, Yothu Yindi made a stir when the Yolŋu band members hit the streets, yidaki in hand, strutting the blocks. 'The boys loved it, because all the black women over there were going, "Oh, how cool is your hair!" and touching their hair, because it was straight and not really tightly curly. "How do you do it, what sort of products you using?" and they'd say, "Nah, I'm Australian Aboriginal, that's how we look,"' Kellaway recounts of the good-natured culture clashes in the middle of Harlem. 'So, the boys were loving it, you know, the attention.'

As the tour wound onwards, so did the k's, from city to city, state to state – New York, Detroit, San Diego, Chicago, cutting swathes across the subcontinent. 'You're living on top of each other in this bus; it obviously gets pretty tense sometimes,' says Kellaway. But he adds that any problems on the tour were short-lived and petty – like disagreements over the merits of Elton John's 'Candle in the Wind'. For whatever the challenges were on the road, the nightly shows backing Midnight Oil made it all worthwhile. Those who were there still relish remembering the enthusiasm of those eager early crowds, where venues throbbed with up to 10,000 revellers. 'The audience loved us,' says Malati. 'Every concert we did, we had audiences outside: "Autograph, autograph, autograph!" We were on the move.'

The band's drummer for the US tour was Bart Willoughby, the founder of No Fixed Address. Although Willoughby wasn't yet thirty by the time he ventured overseas with Yothu Yindi, he was already a veteran of the road, having trekked tirelessly around Eastern Europe with his main band – including an unforgettable show behind the Iron Curtain, where No Fixed Address nearly got deported for breaking a strict ban on playing western rock by grinding out a version of AC/DC's 'It's a Long Way to the Top (If You Wanna Rock 'n' Roll)'.

Although he's spent countless months of his sixty-plus years on the road gigging the globe, the Yothu Yindi tour to the

Guitarist Cal Williams, pictured at a gig in the NT in the late 1980s, remembers well the power of his band's live sets on the road in the US in 1988. *(David Hancock)*

US still sticks in Willoughby's mind. 'I reckon the Americans loved the traditional dance, because they'd never seen that type of dancing before. There was a depth there,' he reflects. 'They thought they'd seen everything, but not everything until they saw one of the oldest cultures on the planet. And so, our technique of dancing caught 'em out. They'd never seen the beginning of dance.'

Witiyana Marika agrees that his painted presence onstage, moving like a 'warrior ghost spirit, or a spirit that has woken up from this land', captivated the masses. 'And that's where I drew attention; by my power, by my bilma, and my ochre. It was very different and everyone saw that, right across [the US] ... my fierce and warrior look. A person from out bush coming here in the Big Apple and showing it to the world.'

Cal Williams recalls stepping out each night in Witiyana's wake. 'I quickly realised on that '88 tour, after Witi did his ten minutes, you could walk on stage and play an out of tune guitar, and no one would even give a shit,' says Cal. 'Because he was so powerful. Everyone was just watchin' him.'

The tour wrapped up in the mountainous Mormon stronghold of Salt Lake City, Utah, where Malati Yunupiŋu remembers a blurry final rock-out with the Oils and Yothu Yindi together. It was a tribute of sorts to their comrades who couldn't make the tour – a gut-busting cover of the Warumpi Band's anti-racist anthem, 'Blackfella/Whitefella'. 'We didn't even know the words, but we still rocked it,' Malati grins. 'We rocked Salt Lake City. That was our last concert after thirty cities in thirty-six days. We were all buggered.'

It was nearly time to head home, back to family. But Yothu Yindi allowed themselves a few days off on the way, hanging out on the white sands of the fiftieth American state – they jetted down to Hawai'i, where they cut loose. Malati slaps his knee with evident glee. 'We had a break down in Honolulu, under the sunshine. [Milkay] took a yiḏaki down to the beach, we bought a couple of cartons, and joined the Polynesians. We had a party down the beach in Waikiki.'

From his Gunyaŋara home, Malati is cackling madly about it – his photographic memory bank still cashing out gems from the road more than thirty years since the bus pulled over.

7
The Highway Beckons

Back in their dusty red homeland, Yothu Yindi had garnered some positive press from their tour with the Oils across America. *Time* magazine ran a photo with a trio of the Yolŋu men in ceremonial ochre splashed with the caption, 'It's Not U2, It's Yothu', while the *Sydney Morning Herald* devoted a full page to the band's US adventures, unveiling to its millions of readers what it described as 'a most unusual group'.

'The curtain comes up and the white-bread rock audience is treated to a backdrop of orange light on cloth painted with Aboriginal designs. Three members of Yothu Yindi perform a traditional dance. Milkayngu Mununggurr plays the yidaki, Malati Yunupingu dances and Witiyana Marika plays the bilma ... the audience is somewhat awed by what they see.'

That awe may have fast turned to stunned silence if the crowds had witnessed some of the chaos behind the scenes. One memorable encounter played out in a carpark in Chicago, when Midnight Oil's stage manager – Michael

Lippold, notorious for taking no shit and no prisoners – told Yothu Yindi straight up they wouldn't be getting access to the Oils' drum platform. It's not as if the headliners were lacking resources; as well as state-of-the-art PA and lighting, Midnight Oil's nightly stage set-up comprised an outlandish array of Australiana, from an old water tank and a windmill to a stuffed dingo and kangaroo.

Lippold's refusal to share didn't gel with Malati, the toughnut Gumatj dancer. 'Malati went to the bus and grabbed one of our dancing spears,' says Stu Kellaway. 'And Michael Lippold didn't know it was a dancing prop – all he saw was this angry blackfella chasing him with a spear. And Malati was shouting, "I'm gonna fuckin' kill you unless you give us what we want!" And the next night there was a drum riser on stage.'

As music journos in Australia's main cities started to raise their eyebrows about Yothu Yindi's live shows, their coverage played favourably with the record companies. By early 1989, multiple labels had their pens at the ready to sign this interesting new act. But this hadn't come without some prompting: Yothu Yindi had returned from the US with the wind in their sails, and Alan James was hoisting them high.

'We've toured America and Canada … but we still haven't released an album,' James recounts from the Roma Bar. 'We still haven't got a record deal. So in '89, I was doorknocking record companies around Australia, and eventually we got three offers.'

Of those, the one that stood out was a nod from Michael Gudinski's Mushroom Records – the stable of Australian rock and pop royalty like Jimmy Barnes and Kylie Minogue. The

Mushroom team liked what they'd heard, and agreed to come along and watch the band in action at Sydney Uni. The other interested labels showed up to the event as well, ready to be impressed, according to Stu Kellaway. But with just three Yothu Yindi members reporting for duty that day, the show was poised to be a ramshackle affair.

'Bart Willoughby from No Fixed Address was the drummer,' says Kellaway. 'We only had about five or six songs at that stage. There were more, but they were unfinished. So the labels all showed up to come and see us, see if they should sign us. And Bart was running fashionably late as he always was, he was like an hour late. So, we just started the gig. I had to jump on drums, Cal had to jump on bass and Manda just played the guitar. We were like a three-piece band. All the record companies were there; I'll never know what they thought. Luckily, by the time I'd exhausted my three drumbeats – country, disco and rock – Bart Willoughby showed up, just in the nick of time, and jumped in.'

Willoughby says he doesn't recall the incident: 'I can't remember that much of the '80s. Just bits and pieces on the road.'

But Yothu Yindi's momentary disarray at the showcase did not dissuade Gudinski and his team from bringing this band onboard. Mushroom Records had the 'foresight', James says, to take a punt and sign them before they'd even released a single. (When Gudinski passed away in March 2021, Witiyana Marika was heartbroken at the loss of one of the nation's champions of Indigenous Australian music. 'He shone a light for us to make our way,' says Witiyana. While Yothu Yindi were among the first Aboriginal acts signed to Mushroom, many others would follow. As Gunditjmara Bundjalung musician and national treasure Archie Roach posted on the day of Gudinski's death: 'Michael was a staunch supporter of the work we do. He championed First Nations musicians like Yothu Yindi, Troy Cassar-Daley and Dan Sultan to name a few, along with myself.')

With Gudinski's green light, the Arnhem Land group could finally release the album they'd recorded at Alberts studios during the bicentenary. It would be called *Homeland Movement*, named after the push in the late 1970s for Aboriginal Territorians to head back out bush and live on their tribal homelands, channelling the ways of their forefathers, away from the western dangers of grog, drugs and an erosion of cultural ways in the larger government-run towns. As Bakamana explained in the title track:

> Back in the 1970s, there was movement on the land,
> Yolngu people moved back to their promised land.
> The wheel was a-turnin', and the feelin' was right,
> Dhuwa, Yirritja people, returned to their land.

With the Mushroom deal inked and the album on shelves by April 1989, the band's first official single was released – the song Bakamana had written while he was studying at Deakin.

'"Mainstream" was picked up by the main commercial radio station in Adelaide, which drove it into the charts,' James recollects. 'It wasn't a top-ten hit on the ARIAs or anything, but it started to do the business.'

With these glimmers of success came complications. The Australian media was already struggling with exactly how to grasp this act, and how to properly explain the cultural complexities of Yolŋu life that the band held as their cornerstone. Even pronouncing the singer's name was a linguistic minefield: Barka? Barack? Barry Manna? Bah-kah-mah-nah.

Then a terrible car accident happened in Yirrkala in 1989, which, on top of the community's grief, would make the job of promoting Yothu Yindi and its lead singer to the Jacks, Janes and Annies of southern suburbia even more challenging.

'A family member of Bakamana's with the same name was run over and killed,' explains James. 'And in line with the Yolŋu cultural system, there was immediate avoidance of that name. Of using that name. And so, Bakamana had to start using one of his other names – Mandawuy. And I had the unenviable job of explaining to the mainstream record company in Melbourne and the Australian media, who'd just spent a year getting their lips around "Bakamana", that he was no longer to be called that. He now had to be called Mandawuy.'

Teachers at the Yirrkala School remember being called into an urgent staff meeting by their principal, the man formerly known as Bakamana, to discuss the situation. 'He'd written about six words on the blackboard at the back of the staff room,' says former Yirrkala School teacher Sue Reaburn. 'And he just said, "You can't call me by my name anymore, because my uncle's just passed away. So which one of these names would you like to call me?" And the one that was easiest to say was the one that started with "M".'

The Highway Beckons

A few years after the accident, when the period of forbidding the speaking of the name Bakamana came to an end, the Yothu Yindi singer suggested returning to his original moniker. Alan James said, 'No fuckin' way. I'm not going through that again.'

Time and again, the singer would listen to the advice of his manager. The pair's longstanding partnership remained resilient throughout the band's highs and tragic lows, even if outsiders were at times wary of this white manager's influence over his Yolŋu client. An important part of maintaining trust in this career-defining relationship, according to James, came from each of them understanding the other's clearly defined role. 'His job was intellectual, his job was songwriting, his job was singing and dancing and doing media interviews. My job was logistics. And he was very clear about that,' James says.

By 1989, the manager's task of covering 'logistics' for the Yothu Yindi band was no meander along Mindil Beach. The costs were extravagant, unaffordable, and that was before they'd even left Arnhem Land. Return plane tickets to Nhulunbuy were around $1200 each on Ansett, and with an ever-growing pool of players, a trip to Melbourne to perform wasn't coming cheap. 'Flying three people out of Nhulunbuy and three out of Darwin; we're touring around Australia which involves airfares,' says James. 'We were haemorrhaging money.'

Letters from James in 1988–89, retained by the NT Archives, show the manager was lodging sponsorship requests with Qantas, the Commonwealth departments of Aboriginal and Foreign Affairs, even firing off long-shot pleas to deep-pocketed philanthropists such as billionaire Richard Branson. He did his best to charm them into coughing up some cash to help out. 'Given the burgeoning international interest in Aboriginal culture, it is hoped that you will regard this as a unique promotional opportunity for Qantas, and one that has the potential to develop into a mutually beneficial arrangement,' reads one letter dated August 1988.

The creditors' notices were also appearing. But the Territory-born manager had enough business acumen to make the band's ends meet – if only by a thread. 'I actually had international experience prior to all this. I was in the seafood industry, I was an exporter, and I'd travelled to Japan and Europe and the US in that capacity, which I think was very helpful. You know, for a Darwin kid to have the confidence to just sort of barge around the world, it helps to have actually been somewhere,' says James, laughing. 'The thing about being a band manager is having some business skills really does help … It doesn't matter whether you're selling seafood or whether you're selling rock-and-roll bands, you need to send your invoice in, and you need to make sure you get paid.'

Even if they wouldn't be flying business class for a long while, if ever, the man now named Mandawuy Yunupiŋu and his band were on their way out of the bush and onto the highway – at least when the school terms would allow it. Their label soon got them onto a tour of Australia's capital cities, supporting Canadian folk legend Neil Young. 'Michael Gudinski and Michael Chugg were in partnership with a touring arm called Frontier, and they were touring Neil Young, so we got the support slot,' says James.

The Highway Beckons

Witiyana Marika says the *Harvest* songsmith was a perfect pick by Mushroom Records to further open Yothu Yindi to Australian audiences along the east coast. Young was touring the release of his seventeenth album, *Freedom*, a record that featured one of his strongest commercial hits of the 1980s, the caustic pre-grunge rager 'Rockin' in the Free World'.

'It was something else. Our spirit was the same, connected,' Witiyana says. 'We met him, sat down and talked, he talked with Mandawuy, talked about the dance and customs, culture.' Others say, however, that Young had little interaction with his local support act. 'He was a grumpy old man,' Malati Yunupiŋu says when asked of his memories from that tour.

In the space of a year, between 1988 and '89, sit-in drummer Bart Willoughby says he saw the band transform from an 'idea' and a muck-about with mates to something more cohesive and 'powerful'. They were playing regular shows on proper stages and the practice was paying off. 'Stuey and Cal, they were playing electrified hillbilly music before they joined Yothu Yindi,' the No Fixed Address stalwart says. 'When you mixed that with Mandawuy's version of rock and roll, that's it there. The magic is there, in everything. The dancing, Witiyana's technique of singing … there's a lot in there.'

He says the humming motor of Williams and Kellaway helped Mandawuy keep his confidence under the bright stage spotlights as frontman. 'Cal and Stuey, they would just lock on it, then it begins,' he says. 'Mandawuy, he'd be up in the front, way in the front, and he can't turn around and have fun with us, because now he's on the stage and everybody's looking at him, and he has to focus on delivering the words. But he doesn't have to worry about the music, 'cause we were practised ... he just had to be relaxed while me, Cal and Stuey, we were the guys in the back that were just taking off – boom. From my point of view, it was a big sound. I can still feel it.'

He recalls one night when he saw the singer 'panic and stiffen up' after busting a string. 'Once a string breaks it becomes sort of a nightmare,' says Willoughby. 'But we got through that. He only did it once, but it was still in the back of his mind.'

In 1989, Yothu Yindi weren't seen only by concertgoers – they were also revealed to the world via the big screen, in a documentary about their US tour. *Into the Mainstream* was shot by Sydney filmmakers Ned Lander and John Whitteron and documented the band's hijinks as they journeyed thousands of kilometres across the States with the Oils. Amid footage of the relentless tour-bus kilometres, fast food and cold weather, sits a scene of unbridled bliss: band members pulling out their instruments and playing impromptu in a metre of snow. So far from home, the camera catches Witiyana Marika as he lobs a ball of ice into the air. Arms held aloft, he yells out in disbelief, 'Snow!'

As well as the obvious juxtapositions – traditional men in the big city – the film also carries Mandawuy's myth-busting message: while his Yolŋu people respect their past, they aren't trapped in history, and their culture has a foot firmly planted in the modern age. 'A lot of people sorta tend to see Aboriginal people as the guy with the boomerangs and the spear and whatever, but really deep inside they don't understand that there's a really rich and powerful culture happening, and we've always been there,' Mandawuy says in *Into the Mainstream*. 'And our culture is still very much alive.'

Lander had previously shot and released the 1981 low-budget production *Wrong Side of the Road* – part music doco, part road movie, part social commentary, charting the struggles and songs of South Australian battlers No Fixed Address and Us Mob. When nobody else would, the film gave a prominent platform to some of Bart Willoughby's best early bush reggae tracks, Aboriginal equality anthems like 'Black Man's Rights' and 'We Have Survived'. Willoughby believes Lander and Whitteron's efforts with *Into the Mainstream* captured Yothu Yindi at a pure early moment, before they'd really taken off or been subjected to any of the ugly pitfalls of the Australian music industry. 'It was a pretty amazing document; it captures the innocence. It was more innocent, I believe. We could've just taken over the world with our natural powers,' he says.

Malati Yunupiŋu, who features prominently in the film – often looking particularly bad-arse in a pair of aviators and bomber jacket – says the documentary gave joy to their families back in Yirrkala, who were able to see for the first time the exploits of a Yolŋu band abroad. 'It was cool showing my kids here in Arnhem Land; they'd never seen that stuff,' he says.

As time ticked on, Bart Willoughby floated back to his other bands, and Yothu Yindi were once again left without a drummer. In their early years, holding a live barra was easier than holding onto someone behind the snare. As Kellaway puts it, 'it was real *Spinal Tap*'.

Founding drummer Andrew Belletty had parted ways with the band before the US tour. After years of touring with the Swamp Jockeys, his body was packing it in and he was losing spirit. 'I had my own physical ailments,' Belletty reflects from his home in the Blue Mountains. 'I suppose it's no secret that there was a lot of drugs and alcohol going around, and my body, as the drummer, you know, the bigger the stages got the more animated and energetic you needed to be. And you're on the speed and the cocaine and whatnot, and you're playing these big shows. By the end I was getting home and my ears were just ripped to shreds, they were ringing constantly, I had tendonitis in my arms and legs and I had muscles seizing up, and I thought … it wasn't something I wanted to do.'

With significant international commitments beckoning, the band decided they needed to rope in someone more permanent. Mandawuy enlisted Alan James to track down a player he thought might work: a relative on Elcho Island, another Yunupiŋu, a talented teenage musician who was probably available. He was a Gumatj lad who lived at home with his parents. This boy was notably different from other teens his age on the island; as well as growing up with an uncanny ear for music, he had been born without sight.

'Mandawuy knew of this young blind person at Galiwin'ku who could play drums,' remembers James, still incredulous of the circumstances. 'I was a pilot and I used to fly myself around a lot back in those days, and I flew a Cessna into Galiwin'ku. I tied it down. I walked into town, and doorknocked until I found the blind guy – and his astonished parents.'

James told this eighteen-year-old Yolŋu teen with a wide, earnest face that they wanted to recruit him to join Yothu Yindi. At that point the young man's first name was 'Miltjiri'. James says, 'I didn't know it at the time, but I subsequently came to realise that Miltjiri meant "blind person". So he didn't actually have a name. But I managed to get him a passport. He didn't have a birth certificate either, and that was an interesting battle with bureaucracy in Darwin.'

In November 1989, this Elcho Island teenager took his first international trip to play in Hong Kong as the new drummer for Yothu Yindi. Little did anybody guess that this show would be the first step in his meteoric rise into worldwide solo stardom. This person would later be known as Geoffrey Gurrumul Yunupiŋu, the celebrated singer who would play with Sting, for Queen Elizabeth II, and take Yolŋu Matha music to the very top of the charts. But back in the late 1980s, he was onstage slapping the skins for Yothu Yindi, surrounded by family and having a scream. 'We just showed him a good time,' says Stu Kellaway. 'Basically, just took him on planes and trains and ferries, and went all over the shop. Went to Ocean Park and took him on rides.'

In a high-rise Hong Kong hotel room one night during the tour, Malati Yunupiŋu remembers a knock at his door. He swung it open and had the shock of his life. It was Gurrumul standing there alone. The blind man had navigated his way to his relatives from his own room on a different floor. Lifts, hallways, room numbers. 'I said, "Bullshit!"' Malati cracks up. 'He didn't even ask someone to pick him up. He just found the room. I went outside lookin' for cleaners or someone, but

A backstage pass for a gig at London's Bloomsbury Theatre in 1990, which guitarist Cal Williams described as 'a horrible show', after half the audience walked out. The image came from the cover of their debut album, *Homeland Movement*. *(courtesy of Yothu Yindi)*

there was no one there. He said, "I know, I found it." I said, "You're joking. Your eyes must be good."'

With Mandawuy committed to his day job as school principal in Yirrkala, Yothu Yindi's touring schedule remained limited to term breaks – at least for another year or so yet. Nevertheless there were some memorable gigs, among them a headlining slot at the huge Mount Hagen tribal festival in Papua New Guinea in 1989. The festival gathered colourfully painted rival clans from across the far reaches of PNG's Highlands to showcase their traditional performances in an allegedly peaceful competition. But it was anything but, as James recalls. 'It was wild. After the show had finished, and we'd all finished our stuff, we were warned: "Quick, get on the bus, get to the airport, we're getting you out of here." The mudmen, you know, those guys with the mud masks, they'd come second. And they'd already killed four people from the tribe that had come first. It was time to go.'

In 1990, Yothu Yindi also ventured abroad for their first shows in the United Kingdom, where they struggled to crack the fickle London audiences. During a gig playing the city's Bloomsbury Theatre, Cal Williams says they were greeted by a surly crowd. The punters wanted to see a performance of traditional Yolŋu culture, and weren't impressed when the former Swamp Jockeys backline wandered out to start rocking the venue. 'It was a horrible show,' Cal says. 'Half the people walked out when the electric people walked on. Alan James showed me a review of the show, and they actually mentioned me and Stuey by name: like, "Why the fuck were these people even in the band?" It was a really scathing review. We really struggled with London ... I think we just weren't hooked up with the rock-and-roll people, we were hooked up with the pseudo fuckin' cultural people, and they wanted to come and watch a cultural event.'

But the British snobbery didn't dissuade Yothu Yindi from sticking true to their rocking roots. 'We just cranked it up,' says Cal. 'And 'cause they walked out, they made us play even more rock-y. Like, fucking hell, you're gettin' feedback now! But the mob that stayed went off.'

In Scotland, an arts-council-funded acoustic tour saw the band gig in a Glasgow slum, aged care homes, shopping centres and an old mental asylum. 'The mental asylum was really like [out of] Charles Dickens,' recalls Cal. 'This really cold building, concrete walls, all grey, horrible. The room we played in was like this giant concrete room. We walked in there and we set up onstage, all acoustic, and we had a few percussion things. Before we knew it, within five seconds of us starting, everyone in the crowd just jumped onstage. We were like, "Yeah, come on up!" It was one of the best gigs of the tour. It was unreal.'

The very last show was at a venue in downtown Glasgow called the Third Eye Centre. 'It was electric, and we'd just done a week and a half of playin' acoustic, and we were so pent up,' Cal recalls. 'We just went into that Third Eye place, like, "Sorry boys, but we're goin' it tonight!" And we just smashed it out of the park.'

The band capped off their run on the back of *Homeland Movement*'s release by joining another international star on the road, 'Fast Car' songwriter Tracy Chapman. Chapman

'We play there in one hour': Yothu Yindi singer Mandawuy Yunupiŋu on tour in Glasgow, Scotland, outside the Kelvingrove Art Gallery and Museum in 1990. *(courtesy of Yothu Yindi)*

was well known for her respect of world cultures; she would acknowledge the traditional country she was performing in long before it was common practice. At Chapman's show in New Zealand, the boys of Yothu Yindi decided to give something back. 'That's when I gave her, in Auckland, our last gig, I gave her our yidaki,' says Witiyana. 'Yothu Yindi's yidaki. A present to Tracy Chapman. I hope she's still got it as a memory.'

This souvenir from the band came at the critical juncture just before they rocketed into the mainstream, turning the lens onto Australia's Aboriginal culture in a way that had never been done before.

8
The Brother

In June 1988, in a far-northern community off the Central Arnhem Road – the bumpy, 700-kilometre buffalo track connecting Yirrkala and Nhulunbuy to the Stuart Highway – a celebration was in its opening throes. The Barunga Sport and Cultural Festival, now a mainstay of the Top End's events calendar, was in its early years, but organisers were preparing for a hell of a do. Around 10,000 Aboriginal revellers had travelled in from across the land, from the NT, from South and Western Australia, and beyond. Whitefellas, too, had come in their droves, down from Darwin and from all over the Territory, troop carriers loaded to the hilt with supplies, with firewood, with expectation. Long before the advent of the 24-hour news cycle, the press pack was also on hand for the proceedings. In this bicentennial year they'd all come to the community to dance, to watch and listen, and, chiefly, to commemorate not just two centuries, but more than sixty millennia of continuous human life on the continent.

As well as the myriad clan nations, another visitor was welcomed at Barunga. A silver-haired leader from the south, who had arrived not only to blow into a digeridoo and pitch a spear for the cameras, but also to talk. Prime Minister Bob Hawke had come to promise a treaty. His broad accent echoed through the microphone:

> There shall be a treaty, negotiated between the Aboriginal people and the government on behalf of all the people of Australia. The next step is that you the Aboriginal people should decide what it is that you want to see in that treaty. It's been too long, far too long, in achieving or even being able to think that we will reach that position.

The groundswell from the Australia Day protests on the streets of Sydney had flowed all the way up into the NT bush, through the desert to the tropical north. Aboriginal people were demanding tangible change, and supporters across the country had faith – or at least dared to dream – that this was the announcement that would bring about a better understanding between cultures, and some recognition of Aboriginal sovereignty over a land never ceded by its original occupants, residents who, science has proven, have lived on its soil for more than 60,000 years. Hopes were high that Hawke's planned deal between Aboriginal people and the Australian Government, this treaty, could be the vehicle for change. And as chairman of the powerful Northern Land Council, Galarrwuy Yunupiŋu, Mandawuy's older brother, was poised to help drive it forward.

The Brother

Yothu Yindi, too, would be part of the journey. Although Galarrwuy was rarely up onstage rocking with the band, if you look closely at their work, you'll still see his fingerprints all over it: he sang and arranged traditional manikay, and executed the cultural permissions. But it was his work on the land rights frontier – especially around Hawke's treaty – that was to have a seismic impact on the touring rock and rollers.

These days, as an elderly man in his seventies, Galarrwuy is seldom seen in public, but the Gumatj clan chieftain's family can be spotted on a daily basis, cruising up and down the Gove Peninsula in a silver, flame-covered Lexus sporting the numberplate GURTHA – 'fire' or 'ancestral fire' in Gumatj. He lives in a house outside the peninsula's main communities, down a dirt track and up a hill, overlooking the picturesque Gumatj land of Butjumurru.

In his youth, Galarrwuy was an unstoppable force. To his son, he was also a loving dad, teaching his kids to walk tall in two worlds. 'Dad was always known as a giant in the political world,' says Makuma Yunupiŋu, now in his mid-forties. 'I was pretty close to Dad … Dad loved us all, he loved to balance all his children when he had the time to. Especially when he was home. He went away a lot to Canberra, when work took him away, politics, of course. But comin' back home, he was the happily married husband, the dad, the uncle, to the many people that he proved himself worthy of. And as a dad, he was a very tenderly loving caring dad that we went out hunting and fishing with every weekend. And he would share his influences with us, what he grew up with – westernised music. And of course, Dad was tribally a powerful songman and a true leader in his own right, for which he was outstandingly known for.'

Although Galarrwuy and Mandawuy's father had more than a dozen children from multiple wives, the brothers had the same birth father and mother. And as sons of the esteemed Gumatj leader Mungurrawuy (whose mantle Galarrwuy would assume after his father's death in 1979), they were born into a sacred dynasty. Privately, the pair had their ups and their sideways lurches. Towards the end of Mandawuy's life, they had serious differences – some seemingly irreconcilable. But they were always brothers.

'They're both traditional singing men in their inherited right,' says Ted Egan, now eighty-nine years old, who was close friends with Galarrwuy during the pivotal early years. 'They were both very highly acclaimed as traditional singers, but Galarrwuy was busy on all sorts of other matters, running the negotiations with the mining company and still involved with the land council, so it was Mandawuy who took Yothu Yindi to the musical world.'

Back in the 1960s, Egan was in Arnhem Land working in the 'Native Affairs branch' for the NT Administration, before self-government arrived in the Territory and the place was ruled by bureaucrats thousands of miles away in Canberra. Out there, Egan stumbled across the strapping Gumatj youth who was then known by whitefellas as James Galarrwuy. 'When I got there in '66, he had just come back from Bible college in Brisbane, and the hope in Methodist mission circles was that he would become a clergyman. He came back and he was a very smart, very handsome young man. He spoke his Yolŋu Matha traditional languages impeccably, and he spoke really good English, and could read and write English at pretty well a tertiary level. And so, he became quite important in the negotiations with the mining company.'

Then in his early twenties, Galarrwuy used his skills as a translator for the Gove land rights court case against mining firm Nabalco, acting as an intermediary between the elders and the company's lawyers. 'He and I became very, very good friends,' Egan says of these years. 'His father taught me a few Yirrkala songs, and Galarrwuy and I used to, 'round his family's campfire, sing some Tiwi songs as well as hearing all the Yolŋu Matha songs.' The campfire crooning of these two buddies would soon become something more tangible, in a western sense – they headed into the studio and laid down their track, 'Gurindji Blues'.

Written by Egan, it raised the plight of the NT's Gurindji people, who had entered the national consciousness in the mid-1960s after a group of Aboriginal stockmen sensationally marched off the remote Wave Hill cattle station, demanding fairer pay and equal rights. Aboriginal station workers had been treated abysmally across the Territory for decades, slogging out gruelling days in harsh conditions for little more than rations and pocket change. When a wage increase was flagged for Aboriginal people in 1965, then promptly deferred for three years, the Gurindji workers at Wave Hill, backed by Aboriginal rights activists and unionists, reacted with staunch defiance. On 23 August 1966, the quietly spoken Gurindji leader, Vincent Lingiari, led 200 workers in the Wave Hill

Walk-Off, and away, as historian Charlie Ward puts it, 'from a century of servitude'.

'The Gurindji were not merely protesting about wages,' Ward writes in his book *A Handful of Sand*. 'Lack of pay was one issue. It also emerged that the Gurindji believed they possessed the right to choose the conditions in which they lived and worked, on land they saw as their own.'

The Gurindji returned to their land at Daguragu, more than 750 kilometres south of Darwin, where they stayed, fighting for nine years for their entitlement to traditional country around the remote Victoria River region to be recognised.

Egan recalls how he and Galarrwuy decided to go to Sydney to record the song and asked Vincent Lingiari to accompany them. Once in the studio, Lingiari provided a spoken-word introduction and Galarrwuy sang the lyrics:

> Poor bugger blackfeller; Gurindji
> Long time work no wages, we,
> Work for the good old Lord Vestey
> Little bit flour; sugar and tea
> For the Gurindji, from Lord Vestey
> Oh poor bugger me.

(Later, in 1975, Lingiari would be immortalised when photographed with Gough Whitlam, as the prime minister symbolically filled the elder's hand with the dirt of his own country, at a ceremonial land handback at Wave Hill. Lingiari was later the subject of the 1993 protest song 'From Little

Things Big Things Grow', by Paul Kelly and Bundjalung and Lama Lama artist Kev Carmody.)

On that same day 'Gurindji Blues' was recorded, Galarrwuy laid down the vocals for another song penned by Egan, 'The Tribal Land', which was later altered and re-recorded on Yothu Yindi's *Homeland Movement*. Egan believes the original studio recording marked the first time a yiḏaki was ever used as musical backing in a contemporary western tune. The songs were a mash-up of folk music and traditional manikay, and had a political message at their core – the land rights fights of the Gurindji and Yolŋu.

'A nice end to the story,' says Egan over the line from Alice Springs, 'is that Chicka Dixon, the famous Aboriginal activist, he sold hundreds – I'm tempted to say thousands – of copies of "Gurindji Blues" and "The Tribal Land" as a means of fundraising for the first Aboriginal tent embassy at Parliament House in Canberra.'

'Gurindji Blues' was released as a vinyl single in 1971 by RCA Records with 'The Tribal Land' as its B side. The record eventually spun its way back to the singer's younger brothers in Yirrkala, where it fanned the embers of that Gumatj gurtha. 'I used to sing that song when I was in school,' says Djawa Yunupiŋu, the original frontman of the Diamond Dogs. 'And when I'd say the "poor bugger" section, I would get a clip around the ear from my teacher.' Djawa breaks into song, in time and in tune. *'Poor bugger me, Gurindji*. We listened to it … and we said "Look, this is great. I wish we could do it."'

Witiyana Marika, Galarrwuy's nephew, says his elder uncle was paving the way for other young Yolŋu to find their footing in the western music world. 'When we were boys, we saw our uncle would sing, and we would think, "Ah! Our uncle is smart, ay?"' Witiyana says. 'We'd look up to him. He showed what we could achieve. 'Cause he's been there and he's done that. And he showed that education could change us all.'

As the 1970s rolled on, Galarrwuy's skills saw him in high demand across the south, from the bohemian arts scene of Newtown in Sydney to the offices of Parliament House in Canberra. He took on the starring role in Ted Egan's land rights play, *No Need for Two Blankets*, which ran in Sydney for a month, where its playwright says '[Galarrwuy] and the play got rave reviews'. He had the ear of the day's prime ministers, from conservative William 'Billy' McMahon to Gough Whitlam and Malcolm Fraser, to whom he voiced the ongoing concerns of elders about mining operations in the NT.

In 1977, as the newly elected Northern Land Council (NLC) chair, Galarrwuy gave a National Press Club address where he stunned the gathered journalists by opening in his mother tongue. For the era – just ten years after Aboriginal people were first included in the Census – it was a bold move. Even now, it would no doubt bewilder the nation's broadcasters:

Nhämirri? Dhuŋgarrayyu 1963yu Land Right
ŋurrunyirra Yirrkala wäŋaŋura Arnhem Land, ŋunhi
ŋarrakala bäpayu ga wurru'wurruŋuyu ŋarrakala
Yirrkalaŋura ŋäŋ'thurruna governmentnha Canberra-
lili wäŋawu, wäŋa ŋunhi ŋanapurruŋgu Yolŋuwu.
Ŋunhi ŋanapurru ŋäŋ'thurruna, ŋunhi ŋäŋ'thurruna
ŋanapurruŋgu, government-thu buku-lupthurruna.

The Brother

Ga beŋuru dhuŋgarray 1971dhu, ŋanapurru ŋäŋ'thurruna Justice Blackburn-gala court-ŋura. Ga ŋunhili Justice Blackburn-dhu yaka napurruŋgu gurrupara wäŋa. Nunhi ŋanapurru ŋäŋ'thurruna wäŋawu, yakaŋuwu yätjkunharawu ga midikumanharawu ŋanapurruŋgalaŋaw wäŋawu.

After a minute and a half, he switched over to English to explain his introduction: 'I spoke this in Gumatj – in Australian. In one of the languages of Australia. I spoke it like this for my own people, the Gumatj people, and for the other people of Australia who will be listening today. Now let me speak it again, in English, which is only my second language.'

He then spent much of the next hour decrying the Australian Government's 'laziness and inefficiency' in failing to validate the land rights promises they'd been vaunting. 'In law, we still have no land,' he said. 'We have no title to any land. People we don't like come onto our land and stay on our land, and we cannot get them off. How would you feel if your home was invaded by strangers and you couldn't get rid of them?'

Egan was in attendance that day, and says following Galarrwuy's speech, the 1000-strong audience 'roared with applause'. 'He just slayed 'em,' says Egan.

Not long afterwards, the land council chairman tightrope-walked his way through negotiations for uranium mining on the edge of Kakadu National Park, balancing the very different wants of Kakadu's Mirarr people, the Commonwealth Government and the miners. This toil was widely recognised and he was named Australian of the Year for 1978. 'Governments and mining companies don't normally deal with just any ratbags and radicals,' he famously said in accepting his award.

Inside the boardrooms of Darwin and Canberra, Galarrwuy was a formidable operator. During his decades heading the NLC, he wasn't afraid to take the fight for Aboriginal equality into the corridors of power – particularly against the notoriously pro-business and land-rights-wary Country Liberal Party that made up the NT government of the era. In one instance he was lashed on radio by the NT's conservative chief minister Shane Stone, during a long-running feud, as 'just another whinging, whining, carping black'. Galarrwuy responded in turn, 'Shane Stone is a good-for-nothing redneck.'

One land council member, a Yolŋu man named Yiŋiya 'Mark' Guyula who is nowadays a Territory politician, recalls watching Galarrwuy going at full pace. 'He had authority and control, through Yolŋu Rom,' says Guyula. 'There would have been ups and downs, there would've been struggles, because of issues we had to deal with, with the balanda government and all their policies, bureaucracy and everything else.'

And, of course, there was 1988: the bicentenary. Hawke's treaty.

One of those among the throng watching Hawke speak at Barunga was the then thirty-year-old Guyula. He recalls a mood of elation. Confusion. Hopefulness. 'A lot of us heard that it was just another promise from a prime minister,' he says now. 'People were saying, "We've got treaty now! We made treaty with the government."'

However well-meaning the pledge, there would be no follow-through. By the time Yothu Yindi had returned home to Arnhem Land from their adventures abroad in 1990 and embarked on their second album, it would become clear that Hawke had only been paying lip service to the world's oldest living culture. 'I believe Yolŋu in the Northern Territory were ready for treaty then. We were ready. We had all our different clan groups there,' Guyula reflects of the day. 'The only thing was, Bob Hawke only came up to congratulate everyone … Hawke and his counterparts in government in Canberra weren't ready. They just thought, "This is just a ceremony."'

Nine artists from East Arnhem Land and Central Australia painted an elaborate bark for the prime minister at the festival, called the Barunga Statement, which Galarrwuy Yunupiŋu and Central Land Council chairman Wenten Rubuntja handed to Hawke at the event. Its centrepiece, typed in English, was a list of their demands and aspirations for the future. Galarrwuy laid out those demands in a speech:

> It will be something to remind any government who will run in its power to change policies and Constitution, that Aboriginal people will always be in front of their policy making and decision making. The notice that we will present to the prime minister now will remind not only Bob Hawke but the next one after him, and the next one after him, and the next one after him, and the next one after him, and we can count that for another 200 years.

Galarrwuy's prescient reference to the next prime minister would come to pass just three years later. In 1991, the day after being rolled by his ambitious treasurer Paul Keating, Hawke's last action in government would be to hang the Barunga Statement in Parliament House.

'When Bob Hawke and his government took the paintings, where is it now? It's in an alleyway [in Parliament House] for tourists to come and have a look,' says Yiŋiya Guyula of the Barunga Statement. 'It should be sitting right in the chamber of the Upper House in Canberra. I believe that deserves to be up there. That is Yolŋu Rom at its best from all around the Northern Territory. And that is the treaty that should've been recognised.'

The Hawke era had ended without a treaty. More than three decades on, there still isn't one. Just a reminder of its absence hanging on a back wall of Parliament House.

Galarrwuy Yunupiŋu returned to Barunga thirty years later, in 2018, where he once again spoke to a crowd of his Aboriginal countrymen, concerned balanda and nodding politicians. He said of this so-called treaty: 'It doesn't mean anything to us, really … the word itself means nothing.'

9
Well I Heard It on the Radio

Leaning against the trunk of a paperbark tree, Mandawuy Yunupiŋu slapped at the box of an aged acoustic guitar. An idea was bouncing around his mainframe. He'd been thinking about a broken promise ... one from the highest power in the land.

Two years on from Prime Minister Bob Hawke's pledge to forge a treaty with Aboriginal people, it remained unfulfilled. The affable silver fox had offered an olive branch to the nation's first residents, saying the Australian Government would move to make society more equal through a treaty agreement.

For a while across Arnhem Land, hope had hung in the air. But back in Yirrkala, there was a growing consensus that the popular PM had made yet another empty promise of granting rights to a people who had endured two centuries of their rights being completely disrespected – and worse.

And Yothu Yindi's lead singer wanted to write a song to let Australia know: they weren't gonna let this one drop.

But there were also mudcrabs to be roasted and shellfish to be shucked, beers to be poured and guitars to be picked up and played. It was 1990 and Yothu Yindi had gathered out at Biranybirany to fine-tune some of the titles set to line the sleeve of their second album, *Tribal Voice*. Mandawuy had invited his fellow musos out for a week in the scrub: Witiyana Marika, Milkay Munuŋgurr, Gurrumul Yunupiŋu and Stu Kellaway, plus an assortment of percussionists, random players and relatives.

Kids hopped and hammered around the yards. Elders sat cross-legged in the sand. Dogs sniffed for meat and the men raised their cans and playfully pranked one another. 'There were Yolŋu teachers, kids. It was just a great time. Families just looked after us. We were eating mubcrab every day, and oysters, and getting shown some of the real special heritage spots,' says Stu Kellaway, peering back three decades to when some of his band's most beloved songs were being born.

The residents of Biranybirany treated these visitors to a taste of the fineries from a life lived in the elements. The balanda band members were shown firsthand the rich selection available at the bush tucker supermarket, and fresh seafood jabbed with a spear. 'It was very special for the non-Indigenous band [when they] came here,' Witiyana Marika reflects from Biranybirany. 'They felt it. They felt that power and then it came into them.' Logs were tossed onto the campfire in their heaps and the music blazed on late into the evenings. These boys were having a blast.

Another newcomer had also arrived on the scene at Biranybirany, one who would have a profound impact on a tune Mandawuy was tinkering with. Paul Kelly was firing in his own career, having lit a string of crackers with 'To Her Door', 'Before Too Long' and 'Dumb Things'; stories of suburbia that had become the soundtrack to Australian life on thousands of backyard stereos. Kelly's songbook was growing alongside his pulling power for promoters, with substantial pub tours across the nation and the globe. While crisscrossing the United States in 1988, Kelly and his band the Coloured Girls (called The Messengers in the US due to record-company fears of racial misunderstandings) had the serendipity of bumping into some fellow rockers from the great southern continent.

Kelly's path would intersect with Yothu Yindi's in the windy city of Chicago, home of the soul revolution, bootlegging grog and Al Capone's gangsters. Kelly, with his leather jacket and curious mind, dropped by the Aragon Ballroom to catch the Australian acts. 'We had a night off in Chicago, so I went to see Midnight Oil, and I saw Yothu Yindi then too, and they were awesome – and I don't use that word lightly,' Kelly says. 'Seeing them play, and their traditional dancing, with some of the band in full traditional paint. I think Mandawuy was in jeans and he had that big scarf on his head, red, black and yellow scarf, a big mop of hair and big beaming smile ... they were really rocking.'

Kelly unfurls the memory of this meeting from Queensland, where he's holed up waiting for his own band to be freed from Melbourne's coronavirus lockdown. He recalls how he headed backstage after the gig and had his first ever conversation with Mandawuy. 'I had a song called "Under the Sun", and there's a line in it that mentions "the honey sun",' Kelly says. 'And he said, "Honey sun! That's my Dreaming." That was within the first minute of meeting me. It didn't strike me until later that, "Oh, he's just found this connection between us! A connection between our cultures; between my work, his Dreaming, just like that." I guess that symbolises him for me. He was someone who made those connections, someone who balanced two worlds.'

From this early introduction in the US, a friendship grew between the two men that led to Kelly working with the band in Mandawuy's sacred Gumatj homeland. Out on this stretch of untouched Australia, where tangles of blood-red fire grass skirt the shoreline, this popular songwriter brought his enthusiasm and his bespoke guitar and sat down on the soil. There was much work to be done.

'I'd been asked to come up and work on some of their songs for their second album,' Kelly says. 'We went to Yirrkala first and we spent a couple days there, and then we all came down camping in Biranybirany ... I remember very vividly walking along the shores of Biranybirany, and [Mandawuy] spearing fish that I couldn't see,' he proffers a chuckle. 'Being with someone who was so attuned to their country that they're reading it just like a book, whereas I'm stumbling around blind. That was the feeling I had ... so yeah, it opened my eyes a little bit. But not to the fish!'

The band were chuffed to have Kelly involved. His presence was seen as a positive omen for their new album. But the muggy tropics inevitably toyed with proceedings. 'It

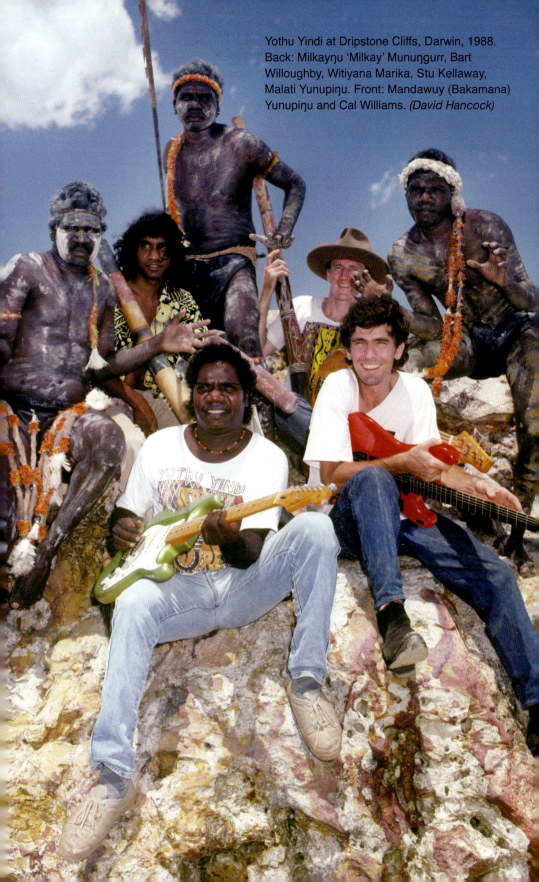

Yothu Yindi at Dripstone Cliffs, Darwin, 1988. Back: Milkayŋu 'Milkay' Munuŋgurr, Bart Willoughby, Witiyana Marika, Stu Kellaway, Malati Yunupiŋu. Front: Mandawuy (Bakamana) Yunupiŋu and Cal Williams. *(David Hancock)*

Witiyana Marika teaches a young man how to remove the barb of a stingray he's speared for tucker, in the remote Gumatj homeland of Biranybirany, in 1987.
(David Hancock)

One of the Yirrkala bark petitions of 1963, painted and signed by Yolŋu elders protesting the advent of mining on their traditional lands on the Gove Peninsula. *(National Museum of Australia)*

A teenage Mandawuy (Bakamana) Yunupiŋu, when he visited the Captain Cook landing site at Kurnell in Sydney on one of his first trips out of Arnhem Land. *(Kevin Kluken)*

Inset: A young Yalmay Yunupiŋu in Yirrkala in the late 1980s. *(David Hancock)*

Witiyana Marika and Mandawuy (Bakamana) Yunupiŋu at a freshwater swamp behind Biranybirany homeland in 1987, playing traditional songs and getting ready to cook up a feed of magpie goose. *(David Hancock)*

George Burarrwanga, Warumpi Band, 1986 (printed 2021), by Juno Gemes. The Warumpi Band's show in Yirrkala in 1986 had a profound influence on the members of Yothu Yindi. *(National Portrait Gallery © Juno Gemes/Copyright Agency, 2021)*

Mandawuy (Bakamana) Yunupiŋu with his daughters and students from Yirrkala School in the late 1980s, when he was the school's principal. *(David Hancock)*

Swamp Jockeys singers Todd Williams and Michael Wyatt onstage with Mandawuy (Bakamana) Yunupiŋu at a land rights gig circa 1987. *(courtesy of Todd Williams)*

Mandawuy (Bakamana) Yunupiŋu graduated with a Bachelor of Arts degree in education in 1988, becoming the first Yolŋu to gain a university degree. *(courtesy of estate of John Henry)*

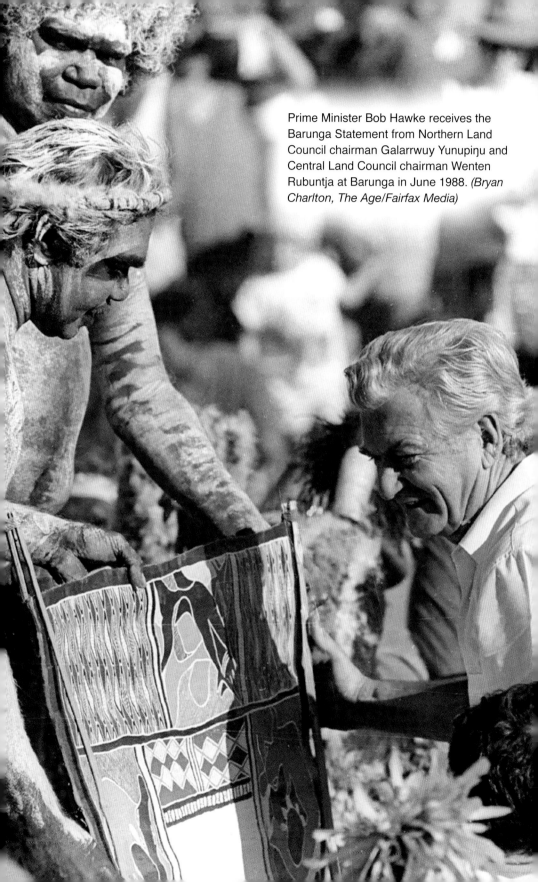

Prime Minister Bob Hawke receives the Barunga Statement from Northern Land Council chairman Galarrwuy Yunupiŋu and Central Land Council chairman Wenten Rubuntja at Barunga in June 1988. *(Bryan Charlton, The Age/Fairfax Media)*

Makuma Yunupiŋu plays yiḏaki while fellow Yothu Yindi members Witiyana Marika, Mangatjay Yunupiŋu and Mandawuy (Bakamana) Yunupiŋu sing and dance with kids from the Yirrkala community. *(David Hancock)*

Dancer Malati Yunupiŋu, frontman Mandawuy (Bakamana) Yunupiŋu and dancer Witiyana Marika, onstage in the NT in their early years, around 1988. *(David Hancock)*

A Darwin pub crowd getting into the vibes of a Yothu Yindi set around 1990, with fans in the front row wearing some of the band's early t-shirt designs. *(David Hancock)*

Geoffrey Gurrumul Yunupiŋu playing guitar and keyboards and hooked up to a vocal mic, onstage with Yothu Yindi at a gig in Nightcliff, Darwin, in 1990. *(David Hancock)*

Dancer Mangatjay Yunupiŋu leaps across the stage during a gig at the Wetlands Preserve nightclub in Manhattan, New York, 1991. *(Steve Eichner/Getty Images)*

Yothu Yindi in a makeshift photo studio at Yirrkala School, 1991. Back: Stu Kellaway, Sophia Garrkali Gurruwiwi, Geoffrey Gurrumul Yunupiŋu, Julie Gungunbuy. Middle: Makuma Yunupiŋu, Witiyana Marika, Mangatjay Yunupiŋu, Cal Williams. Front: Mandawuy Yunupiŋu. *(David Hancock)*

Backup singers Julie Gungunbuy and Sophia Garrkali Gurruwiwi, who were nicknamed 'The Angels of Elcho Island', performing onstage in New York City in 1991. *(Steve Eichner/Getty Images)*

Yothu Yindi onstage after winning the ARIA Award for 'Best Indigenous Record' for their album *Tribal Voice* in 1992. From left: Mandawuy Yunupiŋu, Witiyana Marika, Makuma Yunupiŋu, Sophia Garrkali Gurruwiwi, Julie Gungunbuy and Milkayŋu Mununggurr. *(Bob King)*

was extremely wet,' Stu Kellaway recalls. 'It was moist, it had this fine foggy rain. Paul had brought up one of these fancy handmade luthier guitars with engravings and everything. It lasted about a day until the bridge popped off. And he had to borrow my old crappy one.'

Through the rain, the music continued to bloom. Kelly had hauled a fellow Melbourne-based musician up for the sessions, a renowned percussionist named Ray Pereira. 'My brief was to come up and work with a young Gurrumul ... and show Gurrumul some conga rhythms,' says Sri Lankan-born Pereira, who thinks of the time as an enriching experience – with one annoyance. 'The first night we arrived, they had a bit of a fire and a party on the beach where the boys were jamming, and I brought out my congas and I was playing, and I noticed I was getting bitten by something,' he says. 'The next morning my legs were just covered in sandfly bites.'

A Yunupiŋu elder brought Pereira a bush remedy – a bucket of crushed-up green ants! She rubbed the medicine onto his bites and within five minutes the stings stopped itching. 'That was just amazing,' he recalls. 'I just thought, "Here we have all this Indigenous wisdom, and I've brought this bloody calamine lotion with me that didn't do anything at all!"'

Pereira's beats proved influential in helping Yothu Yindi tighten their material and interweave global grooves with Gumatj manikay and yidaki. A mix of the old and the new. They would be taking a step further than *Homeland Movement* and giving the Australian public a completely fresh sound.

But one song wasn't quite there yet. Mandawuy was still thinking about Hawke's promise. The treaty. He'd been wanting to write a song to express his disappointment, his frustration at the failures of southern bureaucracy for never having properly acknowledged his people.

Kelly says the singer's vision was clear. 'He wanted to write a song about the treaty, and he wanted to write it with a balanda, because he thought it would have more power coming from both cultures,' explains Kelly. 'He wanted to keep that idea and that flame alive.'

Mandawuy pulled Paul Kelly down to the beach and the pair set about penning a dusty first draft of some lyrics. Just a few lines, the embers. 'Brother had quite a few songs already written, so we worked on them,' Kelly explains. 'And in amongst this work on the other songs, we'd come back and pick away at "Treaty", you know, have a go. We had a few lines, some verse lines, and a little bit of a melody.' They returned to the campfire, the sly hints of a song under their belts. Some of the other band members had just the hangover to look forward to tomorrow.

After being tossed around in their troopies along the Central Arnhem Road, the musicians arrived in Darwin to continue their efforts in a rehearsal studio. The room was a makeshift sort of affair, a sweatbox perched above a model aeroplane shop on Bishop Street, in the inner city suburb of Woolner. Kelly and Pereira had limited time before they returned to their busy schedules in the southern states. During a week of rehearsals on the *Tribal Voice* songs, which were coming together, the track about the treaty was left largely dormant. One morning before hitting the studio, Kelly and Pereira were mooching around the backyard of Alan James's house. Kelly was sitting on his back steps, plucking at the still-unfinished 'Treaty', when, Pereira says, he came up with the now famous opening line:

> Well I heard it on the radio …

'He was mucking around with that … and he says to me, "What do you think of this?" and I said, "Hmm, not sure, Paul … you're Paul Kelly! Surely you can come up with something better than that,"' Pereira recalls, laughing. 'It just didn't sound right to me at the time … but he just kept working on that, and he laughed and I laughed, of course I wasn't serious about it, because I know he's an incredible lyricist. But I feel privileged to have probably been the first one to hear that line.'

In the rehearsal room, 'Treaty' remained on the back burner. 'We worked mainly on all the other songs,' Kelly says. 'And on the last day, we were having a break, and the band came back from the break and started jamming on one chord – E minor. They started a funky jam. And I started singing the words we had over the top, and we added another chord, then the manikay, and suddenly we realised we had something.'

This motley crew of Yolŋu and balanda blokes had enough notes to holler along to a basic riff, with a stopgap chorus that they'd invented in the studio:

> Treaty yeah! Treaty now!

The band's bassist remembers feeling something akin to a revelation. 'We went, "Wow!" and we workshopped it more and we put the yidaki in the middle of the groove,' says Stu Kellaway. 'And we went, "Fuck, this is powerful! This is killer." It was the chemistry – we all got on, we had a laugh, some of us were drinkers in those days and we were all just into it, because of the music and the vibe.'

It was raggedy, a bit rough. But it was a start. 'We didn't really have a chorus so we just sang, "Treaty yeah, treaty now!" and we thought, "We'll write a proper chorus later,"' says Kelly.

Not long afterwards, during a show at Darwin's Amphitheatre, Mandawuy decided to chuck the unfinished treaty song into the setlist. 'We just threw that song on anyway, and it wasn't even finished,' laughs Kellaway. 'Manda was like, "Yeah, nah we're doin' it anyway, like, it's got a vibe." I've got a recording of that song, it's absolutely hilarious. A lot of the words were incomplete.' The band was tight and somehow they pulled it off.

'It became a song, right there,' says Witiyana Marika. 'And we said, "One day we'll be powerful, and through this song we'll tour the world and share that message."'

But it wasn't done yet.

The *Tribal Voice* album was a patchwork being stitched together with parts from all over: songwriting sessions and shows in Arnhem Land, Darwin and Sydney. The band had recruited a drummer named Allen Murphy, partly as a way to allow Gurrumul to tap into his myriad other musical skills on keyboards and guitar. You couldn't miss Murphy on the street:

Well I Heard It on the Radio

tall and black with a booming baritone, the unmistakable tones of an East Coast American. Born in Queens, New York, Murphy was notably the ex-drummer for outlandish disco pioneers the Village People.

'Those guys were songwriting and I was kind of assisting,' says Murphy of joining Yothu Yindi. 'I had a little recording portable rig, and we'd just record stuff. We went out to Ski Beach and we recorded out in this old house on top of a hill, and then we'd come back to Darwin, and then we went to Sydney to do a couple of gigs, and we were staying out at this hotel at Bondi Beach and we set up in a hotel room … I remember those songs being worked on all over the place. They would just gradually start to take shape.'

Eventually Yothu Yindi headed into RBX Studios in Melbourne to begin tracking the album. They'd handpicked a producer named Mark Moffatt, a Queenslander who'd previously produced '(I'm) Stranded', the formative single of Brisbane punk pioneers The Saints, and Goanna frontman Shane Howard's solo record *River*. Moffatt, speaking from his home in Nashville in the US, grew up knowing few Aboriginal people, and says jumping into the Melbourne rehearsal room with Yothu Yindi quickly became a crash course. 'Just hearing them talk to each other, hearing all the language, they were as exotic as French people or something to me,' Moffatt says. 'It felt like that pretty quickly.'

These Yolŋu men effortlessly blended cultures – the city and the bush, trendy fashion and tradition, country music and rock – leaving the producer amazed. 'Witiyana walking around in a Slim Dusty t-shirt and reggae driving gloves, and an Elvis belt buckle. It's like, "Okay?"' Moffatt says of his first impressions.

He says the Yolŋu were initially shy of the foreign environment, this whitefella world of quiet booths and serpentine cords, a multicoloured space station of switches, panels and panes. One of the yidaki players on the album, Galarrwuy's son Makuma Yunupiŋu, was just sixteen years old and remembers being bewitched by this daunting new universe.

'We were introduced to state-of-the-art technology,' Makuma says. 'It was very new, very fascinating – mind-blowing. Like, "If I can blow this didge into this mic, it will sound like this." I was very fascinated by it, I really treated studio time seriously … the studio was a place of discipline, knowing your art. It was like stepping into a classroom. A time of expression … through music and through your instrumentation.'

Whatever divides existed to begin with, the music soon bridged the gap. Moffatt brought his friend and percussionist Ricky Fataar – a former Beach Boy – in for the session, whom he describes as 'beyond an amazing drummer' and a 'musical source'. 'I'll never forget, when we were recording the original version of "Treaty", when it got to the manikay in the middle, the [musicians] just went crazy,' says Moffatt. 'Suddenly, [Ricky] hit this groove, and [yidaki player] Milkay; it just locked into this amazing thing. You could see all their ears prick up, like, it was some other real thing that they hadn't sensed before … that was the sort of, "Oh crap!" moment. "This is really amazing."'

On tour in Europe, with new drummer Allen Murphy (third from left), formerly of Village People, with Malati Yunupiŋu, Mandawuy Yunupiŋu, Stu Kellaway and Witiyana Marika. Murphy was on deck for the recording of the band's second album, *Tribal Voice*. (courtesy of Yothu Yindi)

The song was coming together and its improvised, stopgap chorus – 'Treaty yeah! Treaty now!' – was staying in. Mushroom Records thought it was hot and had the potential to be a hit.

Some well-known Melbourne musicians were called into the studio to add some backing vocals for 'Treaty', including Archie Roach, Tim Finn of Split Enz and Rose Bygrave from Goanna. 'It was pretty cool,' says Moffatt. 'I'd called Tim up and said, "You want to come by and hear this!" because we'd worked together a lot … so he came in and jumped out there and sang on that part. And obviously his voice really cuts through [on the chorus].'

The sessions in Melbourne were solid progress, but the band and their producer were well aware that 'Treaty' wasn't quite finished. They left space for a bridge and the lyrics remained a work in progress.

Not long after, at Moffatt's Sydney home studio, The Vault, in a warehouse by the water in the suburb of East Balmain, Yothu Yindi knuckled down to knock over their outstanding parts on *Tribal Voice*. 'They were staying in an apartment complex in Glebe and taxied over every day. We'd get a few bits done then the rest of them would go up to the Commercial Hotel at East Balmain, and Gurrumul and I would stay there and soldier on,' Moffatt says. 'It was pretty evident how much talent he had then; they left me for days with him doing parts and singing.'

At The Vault, Gurrumul had to be guided by Moffatt to use the outdoor toilet. 'He'd wanted to have a pee one day, so we went out, and there was only a handrail on one side of the staircase,' the producer recalls. 'Below it, about six feet down, was this garden bed. And I moved to the right, to the side where there was no stair rail, to push this tree fern frond out of the way.'

In step with his guide, Gurrumul veered to the right as well. He leaned for a rail where there was none, and plunged over the side, six feet down into the garden bed. 'I thought, "Oh shit I've killed him!"' Moffatt says. 'And he got up and said, "Jesus saved me!" and brushed himself off. What actually saved him was the fact they'd just mulched the garden. He was okay. Then we went up and got some chocolate cake, because he liked getting chocolate cake every day.'

With the album nearly done, 'Treaty' needed to be completed. Back at his base in Victoria's capital, Paul Kelly picked up the phone to Alan James. In Kelly's memory, the conversation between the bewildered band manager and Melbourne muso went as such:

James: 'The band have recorded this song, "Treaty". Mushroom want it to be the single. But the thing is, I can't understand what [Mandawuy's] singing!'

Kelly: 'Oh well, I don't think we've finished the words yet, so maybe he's sort of just mumbling something?'

James: (Pause) 'Can you get up to Sydney?'

Kelly was flown in from Melbourne, reuniting with Mandawuy at Yothu Yindi's rental place in Glebe to thrash out the final lines. 'I remember going to the hotel and sitting around with brother and writing the rest of the lyrics,' says Kelly. 'Because they had a recording session booked the next day, we finished the lyrics pretty quick – nothing like a deadline.'

But before they signed off on it, Mandawuy sought Midnight Oil frontman Peter Garrett's input. 'The Midnight Oil offices were not far away. We went there with a guitar, we sat down and played the song to Peter, just to sort of get what I jokingly call, "the royal nod",' laughs Kelly.

Peter Garrett looks back at his unique role in the song's creation. 'It was in the office in Glebe Point Road, and then that night or the night after, actually in the studio itself,' Garrett says. 'Essentially the song was pretty much done, not completely, but more or less done. Manda and Paul Kelly had written it, so the architecture of the song was pretty much there. So, they brought it in ... saying, "Look, this is as far as we've got, what do you think? And how can we take it further, and what, if anything, what can we do together just to lift the song up an extra notch or two?"'

The trio talked through the track and Garrett made a couple of suggestions for linking lines. In Midnight Oil's office, the blank bridge section was finally realised as a rising refrain:

Promises disappear! Priceless land! Destiny!

Garrett had sorted out the final piece of this pop music puzzle. 'I thought the song had a lot of potential, and I thought it was a really strong song, and I thought once we'd finished with it, it was even stronger,' says Garrett. 'And if you like, that's partly what I saw my role to be. Just to sort of get the rivets in place and strengthen it up as it went through.'

There was nothing further to do but hop into the booth and polish off the track. Garrett headed down to East

Balmain and into Mark Moffatt's studio by the harbour. 'It was pretty relaxed, he just came in, and got out of there,' says the producer.

With *Tribal Voice* wrapped, Makuma Yunupiŋu recalls a sense of excitement and energy. 'It was a very busy time for us,' Makuma says now. 'It was a challenging time, a fun time as well, and a time of changing Australia. It was totally like riding a wave. And some waves are longer than others ... and Yothu was determined and we wanted to make it out there. We had the heart to make it to the people of the land.'

With a meritorious single featuring two of the nation's most prominent songwriters, the band took stock of what they had up their sleeve. They'd all worked on it, so band democracy came to the fore. The songwriting credits for 'Treaty' feature not just Mandawuy, Paul Kelly and Peter Garrett, but five other members of the Yothu Yindi family: Gurrumul, Witiyana, Milkay, Stu and Cal. These extensive credits show the optimism around this release, if only for the hope of a few bucks to filter through in songwriting royalties.

Witiyana says he felt something in the air after 'Treaty' was recorded. 'We knew it was going to be a hit song for Australia, for Arnhem Land,' he says. 'We knew. Manda reckoned it could be a best version of Yolŋu balanda mix, contemporary and traditional. When I saw the kids were dancing, it was something. A new revolution had come. An era. It was something really powerful. The lyrics hit people and made them get up and dance right across [the nation], which is something beautiful.'

Treaty

(M Yunupiŋu, P Kelly, P Garrett, G Yunupiŋu,
W Marika, S Kellaway, M Munuŋgurr, C Williams)

Well I heard it on the radio
And I saw it on the television
Back in 1988
All those talking politicians

Words are easy, words are cheap
Much cheaper than our priceless land
But promises can disappear
Just like writing in the sand

Treaty Yeah, Treaty Now
Treaty Yeah, Treaty Now

Nhima djat'paŋarri nhima walaŋwalaŋ
Nhe djat'payatpa nhima gaya nhe marrtjini Yakarray!
Nhe djat'pa nhe walaŋ, gumurr-djararrk Gutjuk!

This land was never given up
This land was never bought and sold
The planting of the Union Jack
Never changed our law at all

Now two rivers run their course
Separated for so long
I'm dreaming of a brighter day
When the waters will be one

Come on!
Treaty Yeah, Treaty Now,
Treaty Yeah, Treaty Now
Treaty Yeah, Treaty Now,
Treaty Yeah, Treaty Now

Nhima gayakaya, nhe gaya'nhe
Nhe gaya'nhe marrtjini walaŋwalaŋ, nhe yä!
Nhima djat'pa, nhe walaŋ
Nhe gumurr-djararrk yawirriny

Nhe gaya, nhe marrtjini, gaya'nhe marrtjini
Gayakaya nhe gaya
Nhe marrtjini walaŋwalaŋ
Nhima djat'pa nhe walaŋ, nhe gumurr-djararrk, nhe yä!

Promises disappear! Priceless land! Destiny!

Treaty Yeah, Treaty Now
Treaty Yeah, Treaty Now

Well I heard it on the radio
And I saw it on the television
But promises can disappear
Just like writing in the sand!

Treaty Yeah, Treaty Now,
Treaty Yeah, Treaty Now
Treaty Yeah, Treaty Now,
Treaty Yeah, Treaty Now

Come on!
Treaty ma! Treaty ma!
Treaty ma! Treaty ma!
Come on!
Treaty ma!

10
Into the Mainstream

Out at beach camp in Yirrkala, a Yothu Yindi player is tending to a glowing pit of coals. Chances are, if you saw the band live during the 1990s, you would remember this man. He became the group's star dancer after Malati left around 1991. He was a captivating presence at the front of the stage – graceful, lank and athletic, with chest-length hair like a hippie savant. One of his trademark moves was to leap the entire drum riser in a single bound. The flight of the brolga. He channelled the brolga deeply in his spirit.

His name is Mangatjay Yunupiŋu.

On this late wet season evening, he's placing cut milkwood into the fire – the traditional method of softening the wood before shaving the branches into gara. 'In the ancestors' days, they would've just picked up the coals,' Mangatjay, now sixty-one, says, his hands gloved, turning the wood on the fire. 'Since the balanda came and gave us all these new things, we've gone soft.'

As the fire burns, Mangatjay reflects on one of the wildest years of his life, between 1991 and 1992. A period during which his band jetted to the frontline of popular culture, their songs spinning on hit radio stations and in nightclubs around the world. They picked up a swag of ARIA awards. They nailed down a US record deal and had their first serious crack at the overseas market. They toured with the Grateful Dead; played the first Big Day Out straight after Nirvana. Huge audiences flocked to the front-row fences at their shows, hooting joyfully, wanting more.

'It never really ceased to amaze me that wherever we went there were crowds just as excited as we were for getting up onstage – excited to see us,' Mangatjay says. 'This new thing; rock and roll combined with traditional stuff. This was out there. For Australia, this was out there. Everywhere we went, people were just exploding, going off.'

It was an exciting time to be in Yothu Yindi. As Alan James says, 'Treaty', which had dropped in late 1990, 'was out there doing its job', giving Mandawuy's voice a bigger platform than ever before. 'When you take Mandawuy's philosophy, he was using music as a vehicle to essentially be working in a national and international classroom,' says James. 'His music had messages and "Treaty" had the obvious message.'

Mandawuy wrote with the depth of a philosopher, sprinkling his songs with metaphors for his people and places. He gave constant nods to his ancestors, like Baywara, and to spirits, like the Bayini. Like few others could, the bilingual singer interlaced languages seamlessly, weaving English choruses into Gumatj manikay. But ironically, it wouldn't

Yothu Yindi onstage at the huge Concert for Life in Sydney's Centennial Park, in March 1992, where the other billed acts included INXS and Crowded House. *(Bob King)*

be Mandawuy's songwriting that sent Yothu Yindi and its frontman soaring into the musical stratosphere – that push would come from an unexpected source.

DJ Gavin Campbell was running Melbourne's hippest nightclub; a grungy hang for artists, actors and musos, the likes of Michael Hutchence, Bono and Kylie Minogue. It was called Razor. In 1990, it was the place to be. 'It was a pretty cool underground venue, very inhabited by all of the arts and entertainment industry,' says the warm and garrulous Campbell from his digs in St Kilda. 'When I announced that this cool little club in Melbourne was going do some dance music, a lot of the record companies wanted a piece of it, because there wasn't a big scene for dance music in Australia.'

Capitalising on the popularity of his nightclub, Campbell had started up an independent dance label called Razor Records. When Michael Gudinski wooed him, Campbell hitched his label to the Mushroom Records wagon. 'Lo and behold, one day I'm in the Mushroom A&R office, and I saw a photo of what looked like a ceremony – a corroboree, if you like – with a logo on it that said "Yothu Yindi". And I went, "Oh wow." I'd always had a little bit of a fascination with the Dreamtime and movies like *The Last Wave*, the Peter Weir film from the '70s ... so when I saw the Yothu Yindi photo I thought, "Wow, let me hear their stuff, maybe we can remix it for the dance label!" They showed me two albums from Yothu Yindi, and of course, "Treaty" instantly stood out.'

Campbell says upon hearing 'Treaty', he 'knew exactly what he wanted to do with it'. He would grab two mates – DJ Paul Main and Robert Goodge (the founder of 1980s funk-pop band I'm Talking) to help him rework the track. They'd call themselves Filthy Lucre.

Unfortunately, Mushroom couldn't immediately see the vision. 'They wouldn't let me remix it at first, the company bosses,' he says. 'But you know what, I just knew they needed to hear what I heard in my head – so we did sneak the tapes. We snuck the master tapes out of the building, and worked on it, and when we presented it, it was a complete surprise to them. They weren't expecting it.'

They didn't *steal* the tapes as such; Campbell insists a couple of key people inside Mushroom knew what was going on. But they did feel a growing uncertainty about their secretive actions. 'We did something very inappropriate, and probably disrespectful too,' Campbell says on reflection. 'We took it without permission and we pulled the song apart, including the traditional elements, and reworked it, put it back together ... and when we actually finished making it, we just looked at each other and said, "We've messed around with their traditions. This is actually not cool." So, we didn't play it to anyone for about three months. We just sat on it, and I waited for the right moment.'

That moment would arise at a record-label Christmas party at the home of Michael Gudinski. The Mushroom boss was chatting to *Countdown* guru Molly Meldrum in front of his flash new stereo. Campbell leaned over and pulled Meldrum into his plan. 'I had handed the tape to Molly. I told him what it was and was whispering in his ear, and he pulled away and looked at me and said, "Really?" And I went, "Yep. Put it on and turn it up."'

The cowboy-hatted Meldrum chucked the cassette in the player. Gudinski's sound system boomed with this new mix: Yolŋu manikay laid down on a gangbusting dance beat.

> Clap your hands and dance!
> Treaty yeah, treaty now!

The industry crowd huddled around the speakers. It was Christmas, and this was the gift they'd been hoping for. They could hear the hints of a hit. Campbell was promptly forgiven for sneaking the masters out of Mushroom without formal permission. 'Everybody loved it,' he says. 'And on Monday, it was like, "Okay, let's get cracking on this!"'

Once they knew of its existence, Campbell says the band also received the remix with 'love and gratitude'. 'It was just pure happiness that "Treaty" was sounding so jumpy and raw and authentic,' he says. 'I just think for some reason everything was aligned and we nailed it. It sounds like a perfect protest song from an Indigenous Australian act, I reckon, the funkiness and rawness of it. So, [Yothu Yindi] absorbed it immediately into their hearts. And I never looked back; I never again thought about the inappropriateness of what we'd done … it was made very easy by being accepted by the band and the company.'

Witiyana concurs. He'd first heard Filthy Lucre's dance version in a Sydney hotel room, and says the band twigged to its potential 'straight away'.

'We heard that Razor remix, me and Manda, after AJ told us about it – it was something special. I knew it was something that will move the whole of Australia.'

Into the Mainstream

One of the song's most powerful aspects is the Gumatj chanting weaved throughout:

Nhima Djat'paŋarri nhima walaŋwalaŋ,
Nhe djat'payatpa nhima gaya nhe marrtjini Yakarray!

This manikay in 'Treaty', while resembling an ancient songline, the land being sung to life by an ancestor, doesn't really have any deep meaning. 'The *Djat'paŋarri* section is actually a composition, a dance step invented by my two *maris* [grandmothers],' says Mangatjay Yunupiŋu. 'They came back from a trip into Central Arnhem Land [around the 1930s] and they had this Djat'paŋarri … and this Djat'paŋarri manikay has been incorporated into one of our songs, into "Treaty". Djat'paŋarri was a Johnny-come-lately invention. It was for fun. It's not in the deep cultural understanding. It was just invented for people's mind pleasure.' Mangatjay says it's the Yolŋu equivalent to Hanson's 'MMMBop' or MC Hammer's 'U Can't Touch This' – basically a nonsensical creation.

'I don't know what kids these days are thinking which is the best song, or what song's being followed, but it's just for fun. It's gone off the deep end, for the better. Djat'paŋarri is immortalised now [in "Treaty"].' He loses himself in a chuckle.

According to the Australian Institute of Aboriginal and Torres Strait Islander Studies, Djat'paŋarri 'is a form of song that is about fun and entertainment which dominated the popular music scene among Yirrkala youths from the 1930s through to the 1970s'. 'It doesn't translate to anything,'

Mandawuy's wife, Yalmay, confirms. 'Djat'paŋarri is just something that someone made up,' she says. 'It sounded really catchy, then they wanted to keep that thing in "Treaty".'

The remix had a sluggish entry into the Australian charts but found an opening elsewhere. Gavin Campbell says it first became a chart hit in Belgium, France and South Africa. While its birth nation took a while to catch on, it was eventually embraced with gusto. The song cemented itself in the ARIA charts for twenty-two weeks, peaking at various times in the different states and territories.

Campbell knew it was primed to be a dancefloor sensation – he'd already road-tested 'Treaty' at club Razor and had seen its transformative effect on pumped-up punters. 'It was extraordinary. There was one fellow, a well-known jewellery maker, quite a bohemian type of character, and from the dancefloor he climbed up the wall of the DJ booth and was pretty much hanging over, trying to give me big a kiss on the cheek.' Campbell laughs at the memory. 'He was just screaming "Wow!" and he looked like he was crazed. He was completely blown away by it. And it was stuff like that that made me realise it wasn't just a song to dance to, it was really rocking people's worlds.'

The producer of the song's original cut, Mark Moffatt, says not many people are aware that one of main voices that cuts through in the remix's chorus is none other than Tim Finn's. 'The [vocal] track that the remix guys used was the one that Tim Finn was the loudest on,' says Moffatt. 'On the "Treaty yeah! Treaty now!" ... If you listen to that, you can hear Brian Timothy Finn all over it. Which I thought was funny.'

Into the Mainstream

Those who had been part of the Yothu Yindi universe since the beginning twigged that this new mix was a blast-off point for the band. 'When the time came for the "Treaty" remix to happen with Gavin and Filthy Lucre, it just blew people's minds,' says former Swamp Jockeys singer Todd Williams. 'It was just a confluence … it was out of the box. I don't know if it would be a hit these days, but at the time it was just right. And what an amazing sound, what an amazing remix of that song. The whole thing was just beautifully done … some [bands] do something clever, and suddenly *zhoop*, they're up to the next level. And that's exactly what Yothu Yindi did. They did the remix of that song, and they went *zhoop*, to the next level. It just caught on like wildfire and really launched the band nationally and internationally. People were clamouring to see them and to know what else they had to offer.'

One of those who quickly realised what the 'Treaty' remix could do for Yothu Yindi was wild-haired Darwin boy Stephen Maxwell Johnson, the English-born filmmaker who would later go on to direct feature films *Yolngu Boy* and *High Ground*. Johnson was tight with the band, having already shot the film clip for the original 'Treaty', which spliced concert footage and Arnhem Land buŋgul with archival tapes of Bob Hawke at the Barunga Festival.

It was a cool clip, but the remix was another beast entirely. Johnson recalls the first time he heard the Filthy Lucre remix blaring through car speakers. 'I'll never forget, we were in Sydney and AJ said, "Come here, you've gotta listen to this, listen to this!" And he smashed it on in the car. We just listened to that song, we just looked at each other and I just

Darwin filmmaker Stephen Maxwell Johnson, pictured here with his camera in the early 1990s, re-shot the 'Treaty' clip for the Filthy Lucre remix, which ended up winning Best Video at the 1991 MTV International Music Awards in Los Angeles. *(David Hancock)*

said, "That fuckin' rocks. We have to reshoot. We have to go and reshoot." And he said, "Absolutely."'

Johnson and Yothu Yindi promptly returned to Arnhem Land, where they shot new sequences and completely reassembled the video to match the remix. 'We did that very quickly, and before you know it, we'd remade the "Treaty" clip and kind of the rest is history,' Johnson says. 'It hit a nerve.'

Johnson had made magic. The video's final cut shone with the energy of East Arnhem Land: fast edits of Milkay hopping one-legged, blowing his yiḏaki; Witiyana on the beach with his biḻma; and Mandawuy singing through smoke like a fire-eyed spirit. Kids backflipping on the white sand of the spectacular Yalaŋbara homeland. 'We all really felt that we'd connected to a fabulously fresh energy,' says Johnson. 'We'd really tapped into something that celebrated Yolŋu culture in a way that had never been done before. Turned it into just a complete dance and a celebration.'

Michael Wyatt, the piloting former frontman of the Swamp Jockeys, counts working on the 'Treaty' film clip among his life's proudest artistic accomplishments. It wasn't like it was a pampered company production: it was out in the heat, the mozzies were biting and their lighting rig was often limited to Johnson's Toyota headlights. But something clicked. 'There was just a feeling that came out,' Wyatt says. 'Everybody that I was ever around that saw that clip, it affected them in a way that was different from watching other video clips. It was almost like people tapped into something primal within themselves, watching that footage. Because it was so new.

I don't think anything like that had ever really been shown at that sort of calibre in a music video in Australia.'

It stormed the Saturday morning *Video Hits* parade and, in today's terms, went viral.

Wyatt believes the clip also had a profound effect on the Yothu Yindi band members. 'I think seeing themselves in such a powerful set of images, I think that actually affected them in a big way,' he says. 'To see themselves in such a way actually changed their attitude and motivation to what they were doing. There was that moment where they were like, "Jesus, that looks fantastic. We look great, we look powerful, we look magnificent, and we look cultural. We are representing our ancient knowledge and stories in a very powerful way." And I think the clip itself helped the band members actually take onboard that what they were doing was so important culturally, and they could actually see the power of it themselves. Even today, I still don't think that anyone's really brought out the intensity of the culture in that short amount of time, that short four-minute clip. Something was so rich in there, and the Yothu Yindi guys saw it and just went, "Wow."'

Riding the sensation of 'Treaty', the band's second album, *Tribal Voice*, was released to the world late in 1991. It slotted into the ARIA charts respectably and peaked at a laudable fourth place. Things were happening and happening fast.

Yothu Yindi scooped the pool at the ARIA Awards in 1992, winning song of the year and single of the year for the 'Treaty' remix, along with best engineer, best cover art and best Indigenous release for *Tribal Voice*. This group of blackfellas and whitefellas from remote Arnhem Land had weighed in at Australia's flagship music industry awards, bagging five shiny pyramid statues alongside the other big artists of the day such as Jimmy Barnes, INXS and the Baby Animals.

As if they'd stepped directly off the buŋgul grounds, Yothu Yindi strode onto the ARIAs stage, painted and proud. Among them were two young, newly conscripted touring back-up singers and dancers, Julie Gungunbuy and Sophia Garrkali Gurruwiwi (whom bandmates had affectionately dubbed the 'The Angels of Elcho Island'), rocking miniskirts emblazoned with earthy Yolŋu *miny'tji* (designs). Before joining Yothu Yindi, the girls had never sung in a band in their lives; at whiplash speed, they were under the spotlight on national television.

'I was about sixteen; it was a great experience for someone my age, coming from a small island. All those bright lights!' says Sophia now. 'It was scary to realise that people hadn't really known that our race existed before … you just felt like, "This is why we're here, to share our culture with the world."'

Dancer Mangatjay Yunupiŋu was also up on the podium that night. 'All those big nobs in the crowd – I was not very comfortable, just cautious,' he says. 'Don't overdo things, don't overreact. I was very excited – but thought, this is stuff for big nobs, not us,' he chuckles. 'We're from the grassroots.'

Sitting by the beach in Yirrkala, Mangatjay remembers the moment when Yothu Yindi's name was read out as the winner that first time. 'Holy crap. It was excitement. We were over the moon. The achievement – we'd achieved something. It felt great. And it wasn't just for us, it was for our mob back here, our families. And eventually, for the nation. The song would be a stepping stone to better living here in Australia. Which is still coming. Recognition for the black man of the land.'

Mandawuy Yunupiŋu got up onstage that night and spoke in both his mother Gumatj tongue and in English, where he called *Tribal Voice* a 'truly Indigenous album', an 'untold story, a story for the future, a story for all Australians to enjoy the privilege of this country'.

'Treaty' had knocked off releases by Crowded House, Daryl Braithwaite and Deborah Conway to win ARIA's song and single of the year. The remix had a booty-shaking beat, for sure, and thanks to Milkay's yidaki it rang out with the deep sound of Arnhem Land – of the real Australia – like no other song had before it.

It was pop brilliance. But it was also a Trojan horse. Inside this funky package was a fist held high for Indigenous rights; a message about a nation's inability to properly recognise the first people of the land. A clarion call for better understanding of Yolŋu Rom, which has always existed in the north-east of Arnhem Land.

And it wasn't just 'Treaty': the whole album cried out for cultural equality, religious freedom and unity in the great southern land: *you better listen to your tribal voice!*

```
     There's a wakening of a rainbow dawn
        And the sun will rise up high
     There's a whisper in the morning light
        Saying 'get up and meet the day'
```

Into the Mainstream

> Well inside my mind there's a tribal voice
> And it's speaking to me every day
> And all I have to do is to make a choice
> 'Cause I know there is no other way
>
> All the people in the world are dreaming
> (get up, stand up!)
> Some of us cry for the rights of survival now
> (get up, stand up!)
> Saying c'mon, c'mon! Stand up for your rights
>
> While others don't give a damn
> They're all waiting for a perfect day
> Better get up and fight for your rights
> Don't be afraid of the move you make
> You better listen to your tribal voice

'There was optimism. We were happy that our voice was being heard,' says Mangatjay Yunupiŋu now. 'But on the other hand, there was still the negativity there. In the media, you look at the newspapers, and there was nothing relating to what the band was preaching. It just still seemed like opposition, everywhere really.'

Johnson's 'Treaty' clip claimed a coup at the MTV International Music Awards in Los Angeles, winning video of the year for Australia in 1991. His breakthrough work with Yothu Yindi, which culminated in a 1994 documentary on the band, *Tribal Voice*, set the path for Johnson to eventually become a feature filmmaker, directing his two landmark NT movies, both of which stayed true to Mandawuy Yunupiŋu's Both Ways vision for Australia.

'It was always talking about how we go about things, always a collaboration, always a time of listening and learning and getting it right,' says Johnson. 'I was always completely committed to that process and allowing time for that to take place with everything we did.'

The magic touches on the 'Treaty' clip helped make real inroads for Yothu Yindi into America. Just a few short years since the band had toured the States with Midnight Oil as a nearly anonymous 'ethnic group', as US papers had declared them, they were ready to storm their way back to the world's biggest music market on their own terms.

11
Hollywood Calling

A handsome and blue-eyed balanda man stood in the backstage green room beaming a 1000-megawatt Italian smile. He had a look about him of success. Of celebrity.

It was Witiyana Marika's thirty-first birthday, and Yothu Yindi had just finished a showcase set at The Palace theatre, a historic venue in Hollywood, California. The crowd was thick with music industry types and LA personalities. But there was one bloke, pure Hollywood, who was blowing the birthday boy's mind: A-list actor John Travolta.

'We had a birthday party after the gig, and he shows up,' Witiyana says of this meeting between two dancers, two showmen from opposite worlds. 'He goes: "I came here to see the man who could do that great dancing, that movement." And I said, "Oh, me!" and Travolta says, "Ah, you! The dreadlocked one. You've got that great movement, you were good onstage you know, it's different! Different to what we do."'

Witiyana stood there with Travolta, the dancefloor lothario from *Saturday Night Fever* and *Grease*, comparing moves. His fellow Yothu Yindi dancers at the scene, Malati and Mangatjay Yunupiŋu, both light up when recounting the moment. 'I said "John, in my school days, you were my hero,"' Malati recalls telling Travolta. 'He turned around. "No, you are my hero!" He reckoned my moves were a bit fast.'

Mangatjay says he was floored by the silver screen icon's casual demeanour: 'To my amazement, this guy, John Travolta, he was just an amazing guy. He just blended in with us really, and we talked like old friends.'

Witiyana says the touring Territory band had been given a welcoming present by the Australian Embassy in the States: a carton of VB. A frothy taste from home. Someone reached into the fridge and handed one to Travolta. 'They brought it in from the Australian Embassy, to celebrate my birthday,' Witiyana recalls. 'The American beer, we didn't like it, and we wanted to celebrate with our own beer at that time.' He throws back his head and laughs at the memory. 'It's a different kind of beer, Aussie beer, but [Travolta] thought, "Why not?"'

Yothu Yindi had flown to the States to firm up a lucrative deal with Hollywood Records. Driving through the boulevards of Los Angeles, the band was stunned to find the burned-out husks of buildings and an eerie quiet through the city. They'd arrived in the aftermath of a traumatic event for LA: the police arrest and bashing of an unarmed black motorist named Rodney King. This brutality had been captured on camera, yet the cops had walked free from court, acquitted of all but one charge. It'd been the catalyst for the violent LA Riots in 1992 – a chaotic six days of civil unrest in the streets.

'We were driving through the part of town where Rodney King was bashed by the cops, and the remains of the burned houses were still there,' says Mangatjay Yunupiŋu. 'It still amazes me to think that we had been through the area where someone had been assaulted, and all coming down to racism. [We thought] racism is everywhere, even here in the United States.'

Mangatjay hadn't been on the 1988 tour with Midnight Oil across the US, and so the extravagant landscape of palms and neons flooded his senses. 'Nothing is familiar. All you remember is the landscape that you've seen in the films, gangster films and all that,' he reflects. 'Different, different, vast areas of taken land. Areas where there should've been… you know when you see the old cowboys and Indians movies? Those plains. Taken over by houses, houses everywhere on the plains …' Mangatjay pauses for dramatic effect, '… and up on the hills, a sign saying "HOLLYWOOD". And the Yothu Yindi band rocks in.'

The sensation of 'Treaty' and *Tribal Voice* had carried over into America, with the band's second album pegged for US release in March 1992. Yothu Yindi were in outer space. 'Hollywood Records was just crazy,' says Witiyana.

According to their press material from the time, they'd become the first Aboriginal band to sign a 'worldwide' record deal with major distribution. The deal was inked after they'd impressed US crowds at a new music seminar in New York City the year before. Amid brawling gangster rappers and

Californian post-punkers, these unique world-music performers had offered up something entirely new, as the *Washington Post* reported: 'In a week in which musicians and attendees alike tended to have distinctive looks, Yothu Yindi still stood apart. Two of the loincloth-clad singers had covered their bodies with traditional clay and paint designs, made more unusual by the Madonna-style headset microphones.'

As Hollywood Records signees, they were in the mix with the who's who of LA royalty. They rubbed elbows with musician Jackson Browne and *Splash* mermaid Daryl Hannah at the Felt Forum in Madison Square Garden. They chatted to infamous 'Sugar Man' singer Rodriguez. But it was meeting Little Richard that proved an epiphany for the men from Arnhem Land, who had been influenced by this black trailblazer who first took rock and roll to the world.

Mangatjay says Yothu Yindi spent hours yarning with the 'Lucille' singer in a hotel opposite LA's House of Blues on Sunset Boulevard. 'Little Richard sat with us for like three hours, and we were just amazed at his stories,' the dancer says.

According to Witiyana, he and the man with the towering black bouffant swapped tales of their childhood rock idols. 'He said, "Who are you a fan of?"' Witiyana's voice deepens, imitating the singer's southern rasp. 'I said, "I'm a fan of Elvis Presley." And he goes, "Oh, the man! The real man." Little Richard was the man who introduced rock and roll and built up the relationship between black and white, and put black Americans onstage. America couldn't do anything about it ... he broke through with spiritual gospel songs later, he was the first guy. He's amazing.'

Witiyana, Malati and Mangatjay held out their autograph books, which Little Richard and his band members duly signed. For Malati and Mangatjay, those keepsakes were lost long ago, but Witiyana believes he may still have his somewhere.

America was a concrete wilderness and these boys from the Territory bush went hunting through its streets without a spear at hand. They had some real-life *Crocodile Dundee* episodes out there; their equivalent of the 'that's not a knife' moment. 'In New York, Stuey went to buy ganja from this African American guy – he gave him his money and the guy just took off.' Malati Yunupiŋu roars with laughter. 'Stuey went chasing him. We were in this nightclub, an underground nightclub, with dancing and lights everywhere, and Stu comes in puffing. He goes, "Fuckin' bastard just stole my money." I told him, "This is not Humpty Doo! This is not Darwin! This is New York!" Me and Cal started laughing. "This is not Swamp Jockeys days! This is New York, haven't you seen the movies?"'

On one occasion while strolling a New York sidewalk, a Yothu Yindi band member was mistaken for an actual star of the Paul Hogan franchise – the Yolŋu actor David Gulpilil. 'I was walking with Mangatjay and this guy pulls up on a pushbike next to us,' says Michael Wyatt, the former Swamp Jockey, who worked as a stage manager for some of the band's performances in New York. 'And he goes, "Hey man, are you from *Crocodile Dundee*?"' Wyatt puts on his best broad American accent. 'He thought he was Gulpilil. And Mangatjay was happy to be a hero, and goes, "Yep, mate, that's me!" The Americans just loved it.'

On tour in Chicago, 1992. Back: Witiyana Marika, Stu Kellaway, Sophia Garrkali Gurruwiwi, Mangatjay Yunupiŋu, Makuma Yunupiŋu, Malati Yunupiŋu, Milkay Munuŋgurr. Front: keyboard player Michael Havir, drummer Huey Benjamin, Mandawuy Yunupiŋu, Cal Williams. *(Paul Natkin/Getty Images)*

Also accompanying the band in NYC was another freshly recruited Aussie drummer, a long-term session muso named Huey Benjamin, who'd worked with everyone from Cold Chisel's Ian Moss to Dragon. Benjamin had been called in as a last-minute replacement for Allen Murphy, who'd been forced to pull out of the 1991 US tour due to other commitments. (Murphy would return to the band for a second stint around 1993.) Benjamin ended up staying with Yothu Yindi for a colourful stretch during the early 1990s. He recalls walking through a Manhattan supermarket deli after a show, alongside Witiyana and Mangatjay, both still streaked in full white body paint and rocking feathers in their hair. 'The looks these guys were getting was hilarious,' Benjamin says. 'Like, "Where are you fuckin' guys from? Outer space?" They looked amazing. The funky New York black dudes were looking like, "What the fuck?" Jaws hangin' open, tongues out. And [Witiyana and Mangatjay] were completely oblivious, just walking the aisles and doing their shopping, and leaving this trail of aghast and agog people behind them as they walked around.'

The main output from Hollywood Records in those days was Hollywood Pictures movie soundtracks, and the band's deal saw them score a spot in an upcoming comedy. Released in 1992, the movie *Encino Man* was a silly teen romp about a prehistoric caveman who thaws out in modern-day California and is forced to come to terms with the changes. *Encino Man*'s million-year-old main character was played by Brendan Fraser, of *George of the Jungle* and *The Mummy* fame. Yothu Yindi's 'Treaty' features in the film.

From his yard in Yirrkala, Witiyana explains the scene like a scriptwriter pitching to a studio. 'Brendan Fraser gets up, he's very, very hairy and bushy and everything, he goes around, he's hungry, he's looking for meat. He goes into the fridge. Then he sees a television. And then he goes BANG! Hits the television; the screen comes on. Then BANG! Another channel, he sees some heavy metal music. He doesn't want that, switches the channel and BANG! He hits Yothu Yindi. Ah! That's the one he wants! "That person is like myself," he thinks. Then he tries to imitate my movements,' Witiyana laughs. 'Just three or four seconds. Then we went to the red-carpet premiere too. It was just bloody awesome, crazy. You know what Americans are like? So enthusiastic, always there, just screaming.'

The release of *Tribal Voice* in America was a triumph by Australian standards, breaking through to reach number three on the US Billboard world-music albums chart. But it wasn't just the number of discs being sold; acclaim was coming from unexpected places. Yothu Yindi's press releases shared news that punk rocker Joey Ramone – the leather-clad lead singer of New York City punk pioneers The Ramones – was among the new fans.

'Yothu Yindi is an electrifying molten of tribal tradition and Aboriginal freedom,' said the now-deceased Ramone. Another US fan quoted in the blurb, whose band Yothu Yindi would soon support on tour, was a singer and guitarist named Bob Weir, a founding member of San Francisco counterculture icons the Grateful Dead. 'Yothu Yindi builds what they do on a bed of timeless, ancient Aboriginal music and dance,' said Weir. 'To this they add their interpretation of today's popular music. But it's more than just music. It's more than just a performance. It's magic.' Later in 1992, Bob Weir would venture to East Arnhem Land, where he stayed with Mandawuy, recording sounds and researching a children's book he was working on called *Baru Bay*.

Arnhem Land's Yothu Yindi and acid rockers the Grateful Dead may seem like an unlikely double bill, but a US tour did happen – and some of the band even remember it through the haze. 'It was an absolute trip,' recalls Stu Kellaway, sitting by the sand at Yirrkala. 'Those guys were absolute trippers. I don't know how it got set up. But it sort of works, you know? The mystical Yothu Yindi and all the Deadheads [the affectionate name for diehard fans of the Grateful Dead]. They loved it.'

'There would be like a thousand people in every carpark at every Dead gig,' says Kellaway. 'People who couldn't get in. There'd be stages set up, bands playing, they'd just follow the Grateful Dead. The Dead themselves, they had a travelling primary school, secondary school … they even collected all their gaff tape from every gig, and had a whole truck that was just filled with giant balls of gaff. Remember that ball of gaff on the side of the stage?' he asks his bandmate Mangatjay sitting beside him. 'Their roadie told me they had ten more of those back at their warehouse. Every member had their own spiritual healer or whatever you'd call it, they were all doing meditation with some orange guy or some other guru, there were candles, Tibetan bowl action, whatever.'

Yothu Yindi's shows with The Dead culminated in an expansive arena called the Oakland Coliseum, in California, more commonly used for Major League Baseball matches.

Environmental warriors Greenpeace International were also on site for the concert, where they created a special solar-powered recording of some of Yothu Yindi's live songs. 'They had a solar-powered studio, like an OB [outdoor broadcast] van, I think it was in the Coliseum itself; it was that huge that venue,' says Kellaway. 'They were boasting it as one of the very first ever solar-powered recordings.'

A live version of Mandawuy's song 'Yolngu Boy' eventually made it onto a Greenpeace compilation album titled *Alternative NRG*, which also featured U2, REM and Sonic Youth. The Greenpeace project hit a chord for solar power, while the Deadheads had filled the Oakland air with a hazier kind of green energy.

Back at Yothu Yindi's show at The Palace in Hollywood, John Travolta wasn't the only person watching. A young Aussie singer named Natalie Gillespie was among those in the crowd. The Arnhem Land band was performing as part of an Australian music showcase called Wizards of Oz, alongside other antipodean acts like The Angels and Kate Ceberano. Gillespie had also been onstage that evening, gigging with an outfit named Beatfish, featuring members of Mental As Anything and Models. She says the showcase was largely 'a flop' due to the city's eerie mood so soon after the LA Riots: except, that is, for the final act.

'The night that Yothu played was packed,' says Gillespie. 'I'd played my gig and then came to the front of house to see Yothu Yindi play, and it was just mind-blowing. I couldn't believe what I was seeing onstage. It was so dynamic and powerful that none of us were talking. Our mouths had dropped. It was wonderful, it was such a great gig.' Later that night in her hotel, Gillespie received a message from Yothu Yindi's manager, Alan James: they needed another back-up vocalist and would she like in? 'I dropped everything and jumped on their tour, because I thought it was just an incredible opportunity, but also a very meaningful opportunity for me being a black woman,' she says. 'Having some purpose around what I was doing and what I was singing about.' Surrounded by the glitz and bright lights of Hollywood, she says she saw the significance of Mandawuy Yunupiŋu's philosophy and the cultural vibrancy of the other boys in the band. 'I just felt like it was a really important time,' she says. 'And I felt like I was a part of it.'

After Gillespie's chance meeting with Yothu Yindi in LA, she stayed for the next four years, travelling the world and hopping onto its most diverse stages, from heaving music festivals to foreign embassy openings and schoolyards in outback Australia. After Hollywood, the band decamped on a 1992 tour across Europe and played the gigantic Roskilde festival in Denmark, where some of the members watched grunge icons Nirvana going full throttle in their prime.

'Some of the most memorable shows were in Europe ... [on] the summer outdoor festival circuit,' says Huey Benjamin. 'The band had really great energy. The crowds started off intrigued, but then ended up being caught up in the beauty and the power of the performances, which were really something.'

Mandawuy and Yothu Yindi were putting the Yolŋu voice on the international stage. The singer was educating the rest of the world about the cultural power of his people in a spectacular way and, in doing so, was helping to correct the one-way flow of western culture into his homeland. As he wrote in the autobiographical paean to his people, 'My Kind of Life':

> We have lived here now for a long, long time
> Even to this day
> And the going's been rough but our feelings flow
> Like the honey from the mayku tree
> It's my kind of life, it's our right
> That's what we write on the wall
> Well I've been to New York, I've been to BC,
> And I've seen Hollywood too
> And our oils were burnin', shinin' like the sun
> From the land of the kangaroo
>
> This is my, my kind of life
> This is a Yolngu, Yolngu way of life
>
> You see that old man taught me things I should know
> From the memories of the past
> And the situation is the bottom line
> Between illusion and reality
> We have always thought of making things right
> Right from the beginning
> It's a big proposition from the Yolngu of this Earth
> How about you come too
>
> This is my, my kind of life
> This is a Yolngu, Yolngu way of life

The group's other backup singer on the 1992 tours, Sophia Garrkali Gurruwiwi, says tears would well in her eyes each time she sang 'My Kind of Life' onstage, making the ochre run down her cheeks. She'd fall homesick for Elcho Island, but held strong in the knowledge she was helping to impart a potent lesson. 'Before I joined the band, I knew so little of my people's struggle, and what we'd been through with land rights, the Yirrkala bark petitions and all of that,' she says now. 'But in Yothu Yindi, I grew up pretty quickly.'

Mandawuy's message of a brighter day for Aboriginal people was cutting through at exactly the right moment. The United Nations had announced that the next year, 1993, would be the International Year of the World's Indigenous People. Yothu Yindi were invited to help launch the celebrations in December 1992 by playing 'Treaty' at the UN headquarters in New York. The hall was packed with Indigenous peoples from across the globe, and among the diverse audience were Oscar-winning Indigenous Canadian-American performer Buffy Sainte-Marie and family members of jazz royalty Miles Davis. 'That blew my mind,' Natalie Gillespie says. 'And I just felt that was a really significant gig. I don't know what it was about that particular gig; we were shuffled in and shuffled out, it wasn't like we had a lot of time there. But it was pretty poignant.'

It felt like someone was finally paying attention; Indigenous issues were out of the shadows and on the front page. And it wasn't just in the US – Australia was in the grips of its own awakening. The new year would be interesting.

12
Australia Tunes In

For Yalmay Yunupiŋu, it was all fairly overwhelming. The cops had blocked traffic through the centre of Sydney, as she and her husband whipped through the streets on their way to Admiralty House. It was the first time Mandawuy had asked his wife to accompany him to such a glamorous interstate event, and the Rirratjiŋu teacher's nerves were abuzz. They were on their way to meet the prime minister.

'There was big, huge traffic, and they made way for us to go through.' Yalmay tells the story from Yirrkala, nearly thirty years since that Australia Day in 1993. 'It was so interesting. I just went, "Wow, they're here to make way for us?" The cops were in front, telling people to make way for us.'

Mandawuy Yunupiŋu was to be announced as the Australian of the Year for 1992, for his reconciliatory role in remote education and as the visionary frontman of Yothu Yindi. He'd first found out about it while touring the States, via a phone call to his hotel. 'He came to my room and took the call,' says

Alan James. 'And afterwards, in a bit of a state of shock, he said that the call had been from the prime minister, Paul Keating, asking him if he'd accept the role of Australian of the Year if he was nominated. And in true Mandawuy fashion at the time, he said, "I'll have to ask my brother," who was his leader, the leader of the clan. As polite as that was, I think he'd probably made the decision to say yes, because it would've been some time before he had the opportunity to ask his brother.'

The National Australia Day Council had voted to hand Mandawuy the gong for 'building bridges of understanding between Aboriginal and non-Aboriginal people'. He'd been dubbed an ambassador for Indigenous Australians, and as such was helping put the issue of land rights – the fight his fathers began – back on the table. 'I think that this year's going to open a lot of avenues, it's going to open a lot of eyes, for realising Indigenous people and realising we can build Australia together if the opportunity is given,' Mandawuy told the television cameras after receiving the recognition in Sydney.

The award made him the second of his parents' sons to be handed the title, after Galarrwuy before him in 1978. 'To be able to get Australian of the Year with my brother is something that has never been done before,' he told Darwin reporter and artist Chips Mackinolty for *The Age* between songwriting sessions for Yothu Yindi. 'It's history for us, something that I am proud about. It'll lay the foundation for my family, but also for the future of this country.'

Prime Minister Paul Keating presented the Australian of the Year award to the Yolŋu songman, a moment captured in news photos of Mandawuy and the prime minister sharing

'Dancing him home': Mandawuy Yunupiŋu (centre, wearing ceremonial bathi) with friends and family, who had gathered at Gove Airport in 1993 to celebrate the singer's return to Arnhem Land after his Australian of the Year award. *(courtesy of Kathy McMahon)*

a laugh, a trophy between them, the iconic Sydney Opera House in the background. It was a fitting image for the mood of the moment.

Keating had laid out his own agenda for Aboriginal justice just weeks earlier, delivering the moving 'Redfern Address' to launch the impending Year of Indigenous People: 'Isn't it reasonable to say that if we can build a prosperous and remarkably harmonious multicultural society in Australia, surely we can find just solutions to the problems which beset the first Australians, the people to whom the most injustice has been done,' Keating told the Redfern crowd that December day in 1992. 'The starting point might be to recognise that the problem starts with us non-Aboriginal Australians. It begins, I think, with that act of recognition. Recognition that it was we who did the dispossessing. We took the traditional lands and smashed the traditional way of life. We brought the diseases. The alcohol. We committed the murders. We took the children from their mothers. We practised discrimination and exclusion. It was our ignorance and our prejudice. And our failure to imagine these things being done to us.'

They were stirring words – admissions seldom uttered by an Australian leader of such stature. Keating's speech was a notable shift in the political discourse, a positive, respectful pledge for a more inclusive Australia, and it left the door open to hope. There was no mention of Hawke's treaty; the momentum for that idea had lost traction since 1988. The term was instead replaced by 'reconciliation'. By early 1993, the creation of a reconciliation council and the Aboriginal and Torres Strait Islander Commission (ATSIC) were still recent developments; they'd not yet yielded any concrete outcomes for bettering the lives of First Nations Australians.

But one ruling had made a difference. In June 1992, as Yothu Yindi's 'Treaty' was wriggling its way into eardrums across Australia, a Torres Strait Islander from Mer (Murray Island) was forging history. After an uphill legal battle that dragged on for a decade, Eddie Koiki Mabo and his fellow plaintiffs had finally proven through the High Court that their Meriam people had held traditional, inherited land rights to their island home for hundreds of years. The ruling thereby extinguished what Keating described as the 'bizarre conceit' of terra nullius: the notion that before the British invasion, Australia had belonged to nobody.

'*Mabo* establishes a fundamental truth and lays the basis for justice,' Keating said in Redfern. 'It will be much easier to work from that basis than has ever been the case in the past ... *Mabo* is an historic decision. We can make it an historic turning point, the basis of a new relationship between Indigenous and non-Aboriginal Australians.'

Eddie Mabo was a national hero. Yothu Yindi released a tribute track, 'Mabo', about Koiki's journey, on their album *Freedom* in late 1993:

> We were right
> That we were here
> They were wrong
> That we weren't here
> Liya balkurrk bapa-lili, Liya waltjan bapa-lili
> Liya waltjan bapa-lili, Liya balkurrk bapa-lili

> Meriam people are dancing
> Pastime heroes are dancing too
> Mabo's spirit is sailing,
> Telling the world a story
> Terra nullius, terra nullius,
> Terra nullius, is dead and gone

The *Mabo* decision was a landmark for the land rights movement, and paved the way for the *Native Title Act* to be passed in 1993 – thirty years since Yirrkala's bark petitions – through which clan groups could officially claim ownership of their traditional country throughout Australia. It was a bittersweet moment for Mabo's people. The man himself hadn't lived to see what his struggle had achieved, passing away from cancer five months before the High Court win.

At Admiralty House on 26 January 1993, Yalmay Yunupiŋu remembers a sense of pride in her own husband's achievements, but also the awkwardness of hobnobbing with the officials and VIPs in that hallowed house in the shadow of the Harbour Bridge.

'He got that because he deserved it. We knew that he'd been working very hard for Yolŋu people, in music, but also through education,' says Yalmay. 'It was good to recognise him for the work that he did ... I was just overwhelmed by it.'

It was a steep learning curve for Yalmay. In the years to come, she would also become a prolific and public advocate for Yolŋu education, meeting with powerbrokers of every ilk, from government ministers to high-flying foreign officials and academics. 'The experiences with my husband gave me strength in my own *djäma* [work],' she says.

Mandawuy's recognition was a breakthrough in many ways, but not everybody would see the positives. After the fanfare of the Australian of the Year ceremony was over, the fireworks began. And the fuse was lit on talkback radio. One of Sydney's top-rated shock jocks, whom Yalmay remembers as 'the bald headed radio guy', had his opinions on Mandawuy's recognition, and they weren't particularly nice.

Broadcaster Alan Jones described Mandawuy's Australian of the Year win as an 'insult' and suggested he'd only received it because he was black. 'To promote people because of their colour or their history, rather than their merit, is the most intolerable form of racism, which givers of such an award say they oppose,' Jones told his listeners, ignoring the singer's years of hard work for Both Ways education.

News of the slur reached Mandawuy's room in the InterContinental at Circular Quay. In a moment of anger and confusion, he barrelled into the neighbouring room of Alan James. 'We'd had a pretty big night. And I was woken up by this *bang, bang, bang!* on the door,' recounts James. 'And I opened the door, and in stormed a furious Mandawuy. Someone had just rung him up and said that, what he'd heard, was Alan *James* had said it was "a disgrace" for him to be Australian of the Year. I was totally bewildered, like, "What are you talking about?" I had to go get the papers and then bring the paper up to his room, and go, "Mate, it wasn't me, it was this guy." And now anytime anyone mistakes my name and calls me Alan Jones, I react quite strongly.'

Mandawuy's former Yirrkala School colleague and friend Kathy McMahon says Jones's insult cut the singer deeper than it may have seemed publicly. She recalls him returning to Nhulunbuy with a disconsolate slope – walking around in the same depressed state as he was after being branded a 'coon' at that NT principals conference years earlier.

'He came back and he looked dejected,' McMahon says. 'And I said, "Congratulations and all that ... but what's going on?" And he said, "Do you know Alan Jones?" And he told me he'd heard this vitriolic rage against him personally. Jones saying, "He only got it because he's an Aboriginal, what's he ever done to deserve it?" And of course, I just said, "Oh, he's just horrible, don't take that to heart." But that's what he heard in the taxi on the way back from winning the award. Just no matter what, someone is going to come and smack you.'

Witiyana Marika remembers hearing of the Jones broadcast about his uncle. He says while his family had been 'offended' by the comments, the Yolŋu chose not to weigh in publicly. 'It was bad, but we didn't want to hit that road with Alan Jones,' Witiyana says. 'All we wanted to do was fight for our rights, and live, and go on and move on for both races, people of both colours, Yolŋu and balanda. That's what we're fighting for, that's what we're singing for. Be equal. Be one people and stop fighting, we go on, live on.'

Even if others had missed the significance of the moment, back home Mandawuy was a hero. His family and friends gathered at the old Gove Airport to dance the Gumatj man back onto his country. There were tears and there was ceremony. 'Everyone was there, all lined up, and us dancing him home,' McMahon says. 'He had his bathi on, and people were proud. But he was having to find the balance, really, of his community really loving it and being proud, and having this guy on the radio, and saying, "Why does he hate me? I can't understand it."'

The Jones radio slag-off wasn't an isolated incident. The year before, the Yothu Yindi singer had landed on the front page of Melbourne's *Herald Sun* after he was refused service at Catani Bar in St Kilda. The staff had claimed it was due to how he was dressed. Mandawuy couldn't cop that as the real reason. 'I was wearing lean jeans, Doc Martins and a shirt I bought in London for twenty-five quid,' the singer wrote in an opinion piece about the incident for *Rolling Stone*. 'So we started arguing about their supposed dress standards and started talking about other guys there who were dressed in t-shirts and that. And they just wouldn't budge at all. I thought I was the odd one out there. It was just a feeling I get from balanda when I'm not wanted. I gave up and walked away.'

The incident created headlines across the country. There was widespread outcry, and the manager of the venue quickly gave a public apology. It all ended with Mandawuy offering to buy the bloke a beer. 'Unfortunately, not all such incidents are settled so amicably,' Mandawuy wrote in *Rolling Stone*. 'It saddens me to think that this level of racial discrimination is still so prevalent in our society. I thought things were changing … elsewhere, racism is an everyday experience for Aboriginal people. Many of my countrymen don't have the kind of capacity that I have had in terms of exposure at a national level where the media took an interest in my case.'

Tribal Voice producer Mark Moffatt recalls a similar incident taking place not long after the Catani Bar episode, at a Sydney rock club where Yothu Yindi was hanging out with UK-Jamaican reggae vibers Steel Pulse. 'We rocked up at the door and the doorman said, "These guys can come in, but the Abos can't!" pointing to the West Indians,' Moffatt shakes his head. 'Someone piped up and said, "Did you read the paper the other day about this club in St Kilda?" And the guy knew about that, so he backed off pretty quickly. But it was a pretty wild moment. I think that's a pretty stunning indictment of racism in Australia.'

Moffatt says he was often required to arrange taxis after a studio session, especially if it was late in the evening. 'After the sessions I always had to go out and hail the cab,' Moffatt recounts. 'And then when the cab stopped, I'd have to explain, and then call them over and put them in the cab. Because they wouldn't stop if it was me and a bunch of Aboriginals hanging around outside Festival Records in Pyrmont at two in the morning. No one's gonna stop. That happened a fair bit.'

There were memorable exceptions, moments that suggested Australia was growing up and away from its racist roots. Moments that suggested Mandawuy's mission to build bridges between cultures was working – especially with the youth.

'We were all sitting at Melbourne Airport, Tullamarine, the whole band and myself in a departure lounge. "Treaty" was out, the clip was out. Then all these white schoolkids came up and were asking for an autograph,' Moffatt says, still audibly amazed. 'I thought, "This is something else."

That was pretty hard-hitting for me to see that happening, because you know, that would have just never happened before.'

In 1993, a year when the glare of the media and government had turned abruptly onto Indigenous affairs, Mandawuy's message was suddenly in much higher demand than ever before. Yothu Yindi's drummer at the time, Allen Murphy, says he watched as the singer's commitments jumped tenfold after winning the Australian of the Year recognition. And it wasn't like the band had been twiddling their thumbs before that – Yothu Yindi had already been shuttling across the seas touring Europe, the US and back home in Australia, where, Murphy says, some of the shows became akin to a 'cultural ambassadorship'. 'Once he became Australian of the Year, the demands on him were even greater,' says Murphy. 'Like, we were in Melbourne and he'd have to do like twenty interviews in a row, before we even played.'

Less than two months after presenting Mandawuy with his Australian of the Year trophy, Paul Keating was up for re-election. He went to the polls in March 1993, and against the predictions of pundits, he won. Suitably for the moment, his team chose Yothu Yindi to play at Labor's victory dinner party. 'We played at Parliament House, just when Paul Keating became prime minister,' says Allen Murphy. 'We did a set and at the end of the set we were all standing in the front, and Mr Keating came up to the stage and went right down the line and shook everybody's hand in the whole group. And there were a couple things like that that were really great memories, that you felt like, "Wow ... this is special."'

Yothu Yindi played at Prime Minister Paul Keating's re-election victory dinner in the Great Hall of Parliament House, in March 1993. Keating (third from left) thanked the band after their performance: Witiyana Marika, Allen Murphy, Mandawuy Yunupiŋu, Makuma Yunupiŋu, Banula Marika and Natalie Gillespie. *(Roger Foley-Fogg)*

From their ramshackle beginnings camped on the floor of Andrew McMillan's Camperdown squat, this band from the Territory bush had now been granted an all-access pass to play the country's most revered stages, from Parliament House's Great Hall to the Sydney Opera House.

They were becoming something of a household name.

Twelve months since they'd dominated at the ARIAs, they picked up three more gongs in 1993 for their single 'Djäpana', a new version of the song penned by Mandawuy a decade earlier when he was a homesick assistant school principal sitting on a veranda on Elcho Island. Now he was a rockstar who had become, whether he'd pushed for it or not, the face of reconciliation for a nation.

'He had a higher vision than all of us,' says bassist Stu Kellaway. 'Because he'd been a principal and worked his way up in education – he saw that as an amazing way of spreading the message of bilingual education and Indigenous rights. So, he obviously had a bigger vision. We were out there just playing music and enjoying it. But then when you're touring the world and getting accolades and human rights awards and stuff like that, you go, "Well, we must be doing something right."'

It was a vision and a voice from Aboriginal Australia that the country was finally tuning into. The sun was shining down and the wave was cresting – how long before it crashed was anyone's guess. All the band could do was ride it hard and hope for the best.

13

Freedom

In a somewhat conservative suburb of Auckland, New Zealand, Mandawuy Yunupiŋu rocks up at the home of Neil Finn. The Yothu Yindi and Crowded House songwriters exchange warm greetings and words, then it's made pretty clear that Mandawuy's hankering for a toke.

'The idea was that he would come over to Auckland and stay with us for a few days and we'd write a song together, which is exactly what happened,' recalls Finn over Zoom. He's speaking over the wires from his pad in Piha, a scenic seaside village west of Auckland. 'He turned up … and one of the first things he was keen to get was something to smoke. And I wasn't far away from that at that time, generally. So we went on a mission straight up.'

The floppy-haired New Zealander responsible for writing some of the Antipodes' best loved tracks, from 'Weather With You' to 'Don't Dream It's Over' and 'Fall At Your Feet', has just hopped out from a swim in the chilly Pacific. He's thinking back to those 'memorable' few days in the early 1990s of Mandawuy crashing at his place, which began with the pair lighting up a nicely wound spliff. 'I just remember him totally educating me over the course of a night about the way he looked at the world,' the Crowded House songman says. 'It was quite an amazing thing. I think he felt he had to give me a perspective about how people look at things up north and his people and the different realities that people refer to and how we should try and evoke those … it was a real fun night. And he was really on one, he was really talkin' up large, and telling me as much as he could about the way he looked at the world and the way his people looked at the world and his family. He gave me an education, really.'

At some point during the evening, Finn and Mandawuy got onto the subject of nature and 'the dots on the shells, and the way the shoreline goes on forever, and the way the animals and wildlife relate on a daily basis to the way [Yolŋu] conduct their lives'. That conversation became the catalyst for the song they would write together, a moving ode to home and nature named 'Dots on the Shells', alive with imagery of the sea and sky:

> And the water's edge goes on
> Always rolling into the horizon
> We'll go down where the octopus plays
> Changing colour with the incoming day
>
> Like the lines on your face
> The answer is here

Freedom

> And the light in your eyes
> Don't hide it away
> Like the dots on the shells, they shine

'The next day we sat in my studio for a whole day, just kind of jamming around, as you do with another musician,' says Finn. 'And it's kind of humble to start with, in many cases, a few chords. He started to come up with some words which became a verse of the song. I came up, I think, with "the dots on the shells, the answer is here", those lines, and the chorus came through and a little melody to accompany them. We just were strumming guitars, and he was sittin' around and throwing asides in and little perspectives and actually having a really good laugh. And he was in top form.' By the end of the day, the musicians had the skeleton of the song. There was still work to do, but as Finn phrases it, 'the song had a sense of itself'. They called it a night.

When morning hit, Finn and his wife, Sharon, awoke to a low, rumbling drone. They hauled themselves out of bed, trotted downstairs and found Mandawuy outside, blowing into his yidaki, and giving the neighbours something to think about. 'There he was with his didge, out on the porch,' recalls Finn. 'It was a beautiful sunny morning, playing his didge out to the valley. We were sort of on the edge of a park. It was a reasonably conservative neighbourhood, and I just remember looking over to the neighbour's, and there was a woman in a brunch coat standing on her balcony looking at him playing the didge with her mouth wide open, like, "What is that?"' He's still chuckling about it from across the Tasman.

'She really didn't expect to see that on a Saturday morning. It was really funny. I think he found it quite funny too. He was attracting people out from their houses all around the neighbourhood. In Australia maybe it isn't so unusual, but in New Zealand, not a normal way to start a Saturday morning.'

They spent the rest of the day tidying up their track, and Mandawuy eventually bid Finn farewell with a demo in his pocket. They only ever played 'Dots on the Shells' once together live, Finn says, 'a spirited performance' at the Sidney Myer Music Bowl in Melbourne. Like two rivers, the musicians would flow their separate ways after that song, making it their lone collaboration. But Finn still looks back fondly on those few days together. 'He was just a great presence,' he says. 'He was in really good form, and I like the fact that he came in and tried to pass on as much as he could about the different way that he saw the world, and we were very receptive to it. It was a lot to grasp. But it's the great resource that Australia has and is only, in many cases, dimly aware of. A whole world view that is super connected to natural rhythms and the conscious living state of the world.'

Since his days as an educator, Mandawuy had been trying to encourage others to look deeper into the Yolŋu way of life, and to see that, by doing so, Australia would be a richer country for it. A land where culture could be a two-way street: western and Yolŋu societies coexisting and coming together, like two rivers that meet and form one body of water.

One of the key planks in his philosophy was the metaphorical concept of *ganma*: a Yolŋu term loosely meaning 'converging currents'. 'Ganma has many meanings,' Mandawuy wrote in 1986. 'The one we wanted to communicate to others is "a place where two knowledge systems meet". In the context of unrestricted Yolŋu knowledge, it refers to a special place at which fresh water meets salt water. At this special place two systems of knowledge handed down from the ancestors meet: a whole "fresh water" system of knowledge and a parallel system of "salt water" knowledge.' The meeting of two waters: black and white. Yolŋu and balanda. From out of the foam, new knowledge, new culture and society could form. Mandawuy's former lecturer Helen Verran says it was 'a very deep sort of metaphor': 'It was about changing the mainstream, changing Australia.' Through this idea of ganma, Yunupiŋu saw a path to his people's cultural survival. A society run on shared ideas rather than one dominant culture calling all the shots.

With 'Dots on the Shells' in the can, the singer flew back into a busy time preparing for a new album. Even before his Australia Day honour, life had been a whirlwind for Yothu Yindi, who little more than two years earlier had still been a relatively obscure rock group from the NT. By early 1993, they'd been hard at it, writing and prepping for the follow-up album to *Tribal Voice*, which the breakout band aptly titled *Freedom*.

As Andrew McMillan would observe of his Yothu Yindi mates in *An Intruder's Guide to East Arnhem Land*, they'd been head down thrashing out the tracks for it in a house by the bay at Butjumurru, which looked out towards the smokestacks of Nabalco's alumina refinery. The main room of the place was strewn with musical gear, cords and recording equipment, as band members worked to the hum of ceiling fans spinning overhead.

Freedom would include some of the group's catchiest offerings, like the upbeat title track, written by Mandawuy during the Oils tour in 1988, about the changes happening to Yirrkala School's curriculum. It simultaneously seemed to capture the band's ethos and their singer's vision for a stronger Australia:

> Making money can be one thing
> Building bridges can be the other one
> All it takes is understanding now
> To make that dream come true

It also featured the hooky 'Baywara', alongside high-profile co-writes 'Dots on the Shells', with Finn, and 'Our Generation' with Andrew Farriss, a co-founder of INXS. *Freedom*'s lyrics were heavily influenced by two events that impacted the lives of Yothu Yindi in 1993: the death of the Rirratjiŋu clan leader and Father of Land Rights, Roy Marika, in January, and Mandawuy's participation in 'Djungguwan ceremonies' out on his tribal homelands.

'The Djungguwan ceremonies, which may best be described as the Yolngu equivalent of earning a degree in cultural education, served as the inspiration for two songs on the album, "Back to Culture" and "World of Innocence",' read their press material of the day. During the creation of *Freedom*, the band also decamped from Arnhem Land to the Blue Mountains, on the outskirts of Sydney, for a songwriting retreat in the Megalong Valley. The musicians began each morning on horseback, riding out into the valleys and exploring the myriad caves and natural wonders of the area. Here, some of the record's most enduring music came to life, including the singles 'Timeless Land' and 'World Turning'. Witiyana remembers it well. Midnight Oil's newly released 'Truganini' thumped on the radio as he rode in the back seat of a hire car along the winding mountain roads on his way to the sessions. 'It was out at that time as we were going into the Blue Mountains to write "Timeless Land",' he recalls. Stu Kellaway had come up with a groove for the track, and a title inspired by a tourism signpost at the old Gove airport that read something akin to 'Arnhem Land: a timeless land'. Witiyana, who added a traditional Yolŋu manikay into the mix, says the English lyrics were partly inspired by a monolithic rock formation, sacred to the Blue Mountains tribes and named the Three Sisters in English.

'It was gonna be called "Wild, Wild Dog Mountains",' Witiyana says. 'Because all the wild dog mountains are everywhere, the Blue Mountains. And then we twisted it into "Timeless Land". Because of the shape and the rocks that stood there; the mountains, the high ground, the low ground and the valleys – it was just awesome. It just takes you back.'

The lead singer of Not Drowning, Waving, David Bridie, also had a hand in polishing 'Timeless Land'. Its other author, Mandawuy, explains in Aaron Corn's *Reflections and Voices* how the song 'reflects our own Yolŋu ties to land and how there are fundamental ways of understanding the land in Australia that can be appreciated across different cultures'.

Writing in the Sand

> I feel the spirits of the great sisters
> Calling on me to sing
> This is the learning of the great story
> I'll tell you about this place
> From the edge of the mountains, fly down the valley
> Down where the Snowy River flows
> Follow the water down to the ocean
> Bring back the memory
>
> This is a timeless land
> This is our land

Keen to add extra layers of harmony to their sound for the record, the band put the feelers out for some new female back-up singers. One of those who got wind that Yothu Yindi was recruiting was a talented teenage singer from Far North Queensland named Jodie Cockatoo. 'I had to do a demo tape and send it away, and yeah, they got back to me,' Cockatoo says from Cairns. 'I suppose the rest is history. But my life changed at that present moment. And then next minute, like two weeks later, I was in Sydney. I'd never been to Sydney and never been into a studio, and then ended up in the studio doing vocals. Then the manager, Alan James, has gone, "Would you like to come on the tour, Jodie?" and I was like, "Yeah … yeah!" and two weeks later after that I was doing my first gig at the QEII [Centre] in London for Indigenous week. And man, was that a blow-out.'

Jodie Cockatoo has now racked up nearly thirty years belting out tunes with the band. At live gigs, she's an electric presence, whirling and shimmying, beaming confidence. But back then, rocking up in Australia's biggest city to meet these tribal NT men was 'confronting'. 'Being a shy, naïve girl from Cairns, where my grandma was Stolen Generation … we didn't get to grow up culturally and by tradition and our ceremonies,' she says. 'I'd never seen proper dark Aboriginal people before; like, [who] knew their culture, knew their language, knew their traditions, their ceremonies and they were singing about it as well. And mixing the two together. Which was to me, that was fascinating and scary at the same time.'

When she journeyed down to Sydney on that first trip, she'd only just turned nineteen. Now in her forties, she says joining Yothu Yindi made her want to explore her own Aboriginal ancestry, even though she'd grown up largely disconnected from bush culture. 'It made me aware, I got curious as to, where's my language? Where do my bloodlines go? My songlines? What have I missed out on? And it made me envious,' says Cockatoo, whose surname harks back to her grandfather, a Yupanguthi man from south of Old Mapoon, on Cape York in Far North Queensland. 'I was very envious of it, because you know, they lived the best of both worlds, bilingually. And that was inspiring.'

Most of the songs on *Freedom* were recorded at Festival Studios in Sydney, where among the recently recruited musicians on deck was Natalie Gillespie. She recalls an incredibly busy period, where everything was happening all at once, in a blur. 'It was really full on, there were all these tours and shows, and there wasn't much stopping,' says Gillespie, now an established solo singer-songwriter based in

Perth. 'It was a really beautiful album, lots of great songs, good fun making it, but the moment we finished it we were out touring again. We didn't even know how it was received back in Australia.'

Their world was turning: off they flew on frantic tours across Australia, Europe and Japan. Out on the road, Gillespie says she watched as the band's frontman was pulled every which way by his long list of commitments. 'He was stretched thin,' she reflects. 'We had this touring schedule and it was just brutal, and he couldn't be everywhere at once. So, he was Australian of the Year, but we were out touring for the next however many months. I think he had to do phone interviews from wherever we were in the world back to Australia, and it was really brutal for him. Just keeping that momentum going, I think it would've been really, really tiring to be honest.'

In spite of the punishing regime of concerts, interviews and kilometres touring for *Freedom*, Gillespie says Mandawuy always managed to maintain a smile. Where others would've gone to water, he kept a composed balance and a sense of purpose. 'He was grounded, man. He was very grounded in who he was and what he was about,' she says. 'His message and his narrative were always the same; and it was a deep philosophical message. But I think physically it took a toll on him. It was taking a toll on all of us. And I think, those fellas being away from home so long, I don't think it felt natural. Their life is about Mother Earth and it's about groundedness, and it's about their homelands, their spiritual homelands where their energy and their spirit is safe. I think running around New York and running around these big cities on buses and planes ... I know how displaced I felt, and I'm not deeply connected with my Earth. So, I felt like it would've definitely placed a toll on his physical and spiritual capacity. But in saying that, he coped with touring better than anyone I've ever seen. They all did, because they were still based in their family values, their message. Every time we got onstage it was profound.'

Decades since *Freedom*'s release, Gillespie says she can still feel the power of Yothu Yindi's shows. 'Their live gig was unbelievable, because you had the deeply cultural element to it,' she says. 'Live, the band just totally killed every gig. No matter how tired we were or hungover or whatever, the minute the band hit the stage it just absolutely blew out. It was amazing. There was something really beautifully spiritual about that gig, which I loved. I felt it every gig ... totally joyous, and sometimes, it almost transcended the band as such. It became something more than the band. It was an energy.'

Another muso from the *Freedom* sessions was Makuma Yunupiŋu, the talented singer and yiḏaki player. Makuma has never forgotten, and never will, the thrill and thrum of the audience in that split second of stepping out onto a stage, at a time when Yothu Yindi was at the very peak of their popularity. 'It was just mind-blowing. To stand onstage and look out towards the crowd was amazing. It was the single most amazing feeling ever,' recalls Makuma, sitting in the front yard of a house at Gunyaŋara, where he's just been attempting to sell a battered ute to a mine worker. His granddaughter skips around his feet. The sun blazes down on his dusty home community by the sea. It's a far dimension from the extravagant world he once straddled.

'To see countless heads of people, people of all walks of life, colour and race. Oh, mate. The emotion that's triggered within yourself – from a big open-air concert to a personal nightclub venue, I always felt it, always felt the same,' Makuma says. 'It was personal. You were connected with the people. That in itself was its own force.'

Out on the stage with an audience of thousands screaming in unison. A crate of new tracks and a message to share of education, family and culture. A practised group of musicians, dancers and mates playing their souls out. For that moment at least ... a sense of freedom.

14
Raypirri

From nation to nation, city to city, Yothu Yindi were zipping between continents like a honeybee across a picnic spread. The early 1990s became a movie reel flicker of hotel rooms and concert venues, tour bus bunks and rectangular trays of semi-edible airline food. Band members estimate that during their career, their passports were plastered with the stamps of more than thirty countries, from Asia to Africa and across the Pacific. 'We were living out of a suitcase,' says Yothu Yindi dancer Mangatjay Yunupiŋu. 'We'd have a shower after the show in every city we pulled up, and drove on straight after. We'd just wash off the paint from our bodies, put the same clothes on, and off we'd go. Or maybe another shirt from the suitcase which you'd worn the other day.'

While the road could be a slog, wrapped in stinky threads and barrelling across borders, for members like Mangatjay, who had spent most of their lives in a single remote postcode, it was also 'really new and exciting' stepping into the lobbies of luxurious hotels and seeing for the first time what each new city had to offer.

The men and women of East Arnhem Land felt like they'd stepped onto another planet. 'We thought this would happen to other people – not us,' Mangatjay says with a chuckle. 'But it did. We were all music lovers from back here, listening to Slim Dusty since we were knee-high to a grasshopper, and getting into the bands like Rolling Stones and whoever else, Elvis Presley. That really excited us, because we were in the realms of these idols we were listening to back home … we were in their country.'

Back-up singer Natalie Gillespie remembers shooting between scenes at a rapid rate, one day in Nhulunbuy, and off to Frankfurt, Germany, the next. 'It was just heaving with excitement, and pretty fast, man, pretty fast paced,' Gillespie says. 'It was quite magical. I loved those contrasts; finding myself in another city, another country, another space, then the tour bus life, then the plane life, and then the Nhulunbuy life, then the Sydney life.'

Amid those years of hurtling around the planet, one particular tour stands out in the memories of Yothu Yindi alumni – many of them still cite it as a highlight. It was in 1993 and was a tour like no other. One that reconnected the band members to Aboriginal country in the Northern Territory and had them on the same stage as one of their greatest childhood heroes. It was also, as filmmaker Stephen Maxwell Johnson puts it, 'riddled with logistical nightmares'. 'It was a big show to have on the road,' he says.

Picture this: Yothu Yindi's performers streaked in ceremonial clay, hollering out an ancestral chant with a floodlit

Uluṟu – Australia's monolithic red heart, stars burning in the sky above – as their backdrop. Each night, for nine shows, a different corner of the ancient Territory was lit up and an international-quality stage erected, to play free concerts and spread a message of self-respect and discipline across the NT bush. It was called the Raypirri Bush Tour: Yothu Yindi with their 'special guest' Slim Dusty. The prized exports of Arnhem Land alongside the king of country music, with his battered Akubra and guitar at his side. Raypirri translates to 'a matter of being sensible', and the tour was sponsored by the NT and federal governments as an anti-grog, anti-drug initiative.

'We started at Uluṟu and we zigzagged all the way up to Bathurst Island,' Natalie Gillespie recalls of the tour. 'Our backdrop each night was some incredible sacred site. They were our backdrops. And we actually had full crew, full stage, full lighting. So, what would happen is, there were like two buses and the crew would go on up ahead, set up this stage which would take hours and hours ... then we would come in and maybe do some workshops with the folk in that town, then do the gig at night where the big lights would shine on these backdrops. Then we would sleep in swags. It was unbelievable.'

The tour wound along some of the nation's bumpiest highways, from Mutitjulu in the shadow of Uluṟu, to the Red Centre community of Hermannsburg, Yuendumu in the Tanami desert, Kunjarra in the Barkly, Wadeye in the west, then on a Douglas DC-3 over to the Tiwi Islands, and back to the mainland for final shows in Kakadu, Katherine and Darwin.

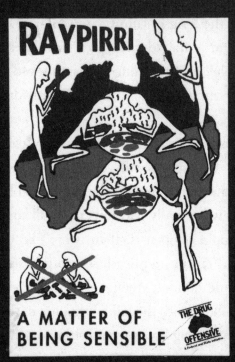

A poster advertising Yothu Yindi's Raypirri tour with Slim Dusty, which delivered large-scale concerts to remote corners of the NT outback in 1993 and was sponsored by the NT and federal governments as an anti-drug initiative. *(Alex Nelson)*

Raypirri

For the Yolŋu from Yirrkala, this tour was special. Touring with Slim Dusty truly meant something to the Yothu Yindi singer, to the dancers and yidaki players, to their families. Although the man born David Gordon Kirkpatrick's coolness factor had diminished somewhat in the southern cities with the rise of rock, Slim Dusty's star remained undimmed in remote Aboriginal Australia. 'Manda was a huge Slim Dusty fan, and his brothers, and all of the old crew from here,' Stu Kellaway offers from the shoreline in Yirrkala. 'They'd grown up listening to his music, you know? And Mandawuy knew how to play at least a dozen of his songs.'

The singer's favourite of Slim's vast repertoire, Kellaway recalls, was the tune 'By a Fire of Gidgee Coal' – a melancholy tale of a retired drover pining for his youth, rolling across the mustering plains and stretching out by a scrubby campfire at night. 'Because it was that fire, the Gumatj fire, that Manda identified with,' says Kellaway. 'And not just here, but all over Australia, [Slim] identified with Indigenous people. Even though he was an old whitefella bush balladeer, they just loved him … Every community we went to, people just followed Slim. Particularly the older generation, they all just loved him.'

Eyes cast to the campfire in Yirrkala, dancer Mangatjay thinks back to the Raypirri tour. 'It was a great experience for me,' he says. 'Growing up listening to Slim, it was very heartwarming to me, particularly being with Slim. My father, who I grew up with, played Slim's music on guitar, listened to his records. Everyone could play and sing it. Everybody here could play Slim on their guitar … being with Slim was an experience I would never have imagined would have happened in my lifetime.'

Musically, Slim's strumming was simple. But the text was rich – songs and stories of heartache and travel, family and hardship, living rough and getting by in the Australian bush. Along with his wife, Joy McKean, who wrote many of his most beloved songs, including 'Lights on the Hill' and 'The Biggest Disappointment', Slim Dusty spent decades travelling to far-flung remote communities where other musicians would rarely make the effort to go, before he passed away in 2003, aged seventy-six.

'Raypirri was probably a very significant tour for him as well,' says Mangatjay.

Joy McKean came along for the Raypirri tour but opted against slumming it in a swag; instead she brought a motorhome. Speaking over a landline from Sydney, the grand lady of country music chuckles when asked if the roads on Raypirri were too rough. 'We're used to rough roads,' McKean, now in her nineties, sets the record straight. 'We had no problems, we've been used to doing that since the 1950s. We got caravans and everything across the dry gullies there going into [remote NT community] Areyonga and all those places,' she laughs. 'And got them in and out of those places. We went cross-country to some of those communities. I'll tell you, if you wanted to get yourself somewhere on a bad road and you wanted to hire a bloke, I would've suggested you hire my husband.'

McKean says she and Slim agreed to do the Raypirri tour because of its anti-drug agenda. 'Slim enjoyed it, he really enjoyed the companionship,' she says. 'And Mandawuy and Slim were dead serious about the message that they were trying to get out.'

The country singer says she took special notice of one of Yothu Yindi's musicians during the tour; the band's blind guitarist, Geoffrey Gurrumul Yunupiŋu. 'He'd be sitting on either an old chair or a box or something like that, and just singing softly and playing guitar, during the day,' McKean says. 'And I remember, always, all the children from the communities would cluster around him … I used to sit down somewhere and watch him and listen to him, sitting on that old box. I was intrigued, he was a left-handed guitarist, that's the first thing that made me look. I didn't realise at first he was blind.'

Natalie Gillespie says Slim and Joy's long history of touring the outback acted as a guide for the younger players on the tour (who among them included an up-and-coming Christine Anu, before she'd found fame covering Warumpi Band's 'My Island Home'). '[Slim] was the most professional out of everyone,' Gillespie says. 'He was the one who had all the life experience, and he was the one we turned to, to see how it was done. He was humble; he just got up and did his gig then went to bed early, got up early. He was the true star, and I looked at him with utmost respect and I watched him to see how he did it.'

Slim was renowned as the quintessential country gent, but there was one moment that band members recount with a degree of surprise: when he lost his cool with filmmaker Stephen Maxwell Johnson. By some accounts, he even threw his famous hat to the ground. A film crew headed by Johnson was on the Raypirri tour to capture the shows with the plan of cutting a doco. One morning, there was a hullaballoo. 'I don't know what actually happened, but all we saw was Slim Dusty just losing his shit, shouting at Johnson and pointing his finger a lot,' says Stu Kellaway.

Slim Dusty had, as Stephen Johnson now describes it, 'chucked a tantrum' at not being featured in the previous night's concert footage. 'I was just lying in my tent in the morning and AJ came to me and said, "Slim Dusty's about to leave the tour and it's your fault." And I went, "What do you mean?" and he says, "Because you didn't shoot him last night, you shot all the other guys."' The filmmaker says he'd only had limited film stock left and had decided to shoot just Yothu Yindi that evening. Slim wasn't happy that he'd been neglected, and there were words.

'AJ said, "Do whatever it takes to make him stay." So, I rock up to his campervan and they're packing up in a big huff ... I said, "Slim! Mate, honestly, please understand, this is what happened." And he kind of started to listen to me,' Johnson says. He managed to sweeten Slim's mood by promising to shoot some video clips for him later in the trip. All was made good and the great man stayed.

From her side, Joy McKean says she doesn't remember any sour grapes during the tour. 'Everyone seemed to get on and enjoy themselves,' she says. 'It was a happy tour.'

After each show on the Raypirri tour, Kellaway recalls, Yothu Yindi would spend 'hours and hours around the campfire' with the members of Slim's Travelling Country

Band, or TCB, jamming, riffing jokes and swapping stories. At one concert in Kakadu National Park, the stage was being swarmed by huge beetles, lured in by the beaming lights. Kellaway says the divebombing bugs were flying into Slim's mouth and face as he played, and torching themselves in wild kamikazes into the lighting before plopping frizzled onto the stage. 'It was just this stink of burning insects,' the bassist says. 'But it was this amazing backdrop of Cannon Hill, where they'd lit up the whole escarpment.'

Slim's keyboardist Alistair Jones wrote in *The Age* following the tour of this strange phenomenon: 'night bugs that had never seen floodlights hailed down as martyrs to the electric flame – their fried husks burying the stage in a crunchy black shroud'.

Out in the middle of Kakadu, it wasn't just the beetles that kept the crew alert. With an abundance of snakes and sandflies, not to mention a nearby floodplain swamp teeming with saltwater crocodiles, the nights were spent on edge, pondering the whereabouts of the myriad bitey inhabitants of the Top End bush.

And, as usual, it was hot. Territory hot. 'There were so many sandflies where we were sleeping, and I found this derelict house,' Kellaway recalls. 'And I turned the switch, and I heard this grunt, and went, "Oh shit, we have power here!" I found something to stand on and unbent the fan, it had been bent by vandals or whatever, straightened it out enough for it to turn, and I just put my swag under there.'

The remote community spirit is the enduring memory of the Raypirri tour for Natalie Gillespie. 'It wasn't about how big the gigs were or the capacity, it was about that community. Like, "We're here, let's come together and just celebrate,"' she reflects. 'I know we were there for a political message around alcohol and drugs, but I'm not a believer in telling people what to do. I'm there to play music and it was a big celebration. To take those large-scale gigs to those small communities was really important, maybe even more important than the message, really, because they weren't able to get to the cities and the big shows Yothu Yindi was doing all around the world.'

There was an element in the messaging Yothu Yindi was delivering to those communities – the government's anti-grog campaign – that felt a tad hypocritical to Gillespie considering some of the band members' late-night recipes of the road. 'I had to laugh, because Raypirri was about no drugs, no alcohol ... but anyway,' she says.

However, others there say lead singer Mandawuy took the obligation seriously, and swore off booze for the tour. As Alistair Jones offered in *The Age*, 'To paraphrase Manda, when it comes to grog "it's a matter of being sensible". And while Manda seems to be able to drink without experiencing much change in his personality, he took the pledge for the Raypirri tour and so did the rest of us ... Manda's enthusiasm for reaching out to young people with his knowledge never seemed to wane.'

Tour drummer Allen Murphy says the singer would often take the time to explain to him why each gig was culturally significant. 'It was all about Yolŋu Rom – knowledge and being sensible, and your sensibility as a person. They were really universal messages, but told from his perspective,'

Yothu Yindi members with family and crew about to board a Douglas DC-3 plane to fly to the Tiwi Islands, during the Raypirri tour with Slim Dusty, in 1993. *(courtesy of Yothu Yindi)*

Murphy says. 'That's how I saw it, and I felt just really lucky to be around that.'

In his New York accent, Murphy describes what was physically a 'really tough tour, because we were all camping out' but one that had a special significance for everyone involved. 'To have Yothu Yindi and Slim Dusty together just made this kind of legendary vibe around music and culture,' he says. 'It was great, I remember that being just a really special tour.'

It wasn't long after the Raypirri tour that alcohol caused a horrific, bloody accident for one of the Yothu Yindi band's co-founders. In the months following the death and funeral of his father, Roy Marika, Witiyana was gunning it towards the East Arnhem community of Ramingining to go to another funeral. It was night time, he had his own son in the vehicle and he was blind drunk. Not far from the turn-off, the inevitable happened: a violent swerve and a tailspin in the dirt.

'I missed the corner, braked, and then rolled over six times,' Witiyana revisits the scene. 'I had my boy with me when he was about five years old. We weren't wearing seatbelts.'

The car thudded to a disgusting halt, a mess of strewn glass, half-eaten food and fluids. Witiyana still has thick scars atop his head as lifelong reminders of the moment. 'My skin was filled with pebbles, gravel, leaves and everything, blood all over. And I was dead, I think. And the boy, he cried out, "Oh father, father, help my dad to come back!" He was just crying, yelling in the wilderness, where there was no car, no one around.'

On the side of a remote dirt road in the middle of Arnhem Land, Witiyana lay with death knocking. Somehow, a passer-by did appear, and the alarm was sounded. The crash victims were shuttled to the nearest clinic before being rushed to Gove District Hospital. The Rirratjiŋu songman's dreadlocks were shaved off by hospital staff so they could properly assess the impact on his skull and brain.

In spite of their injuries, father and son had survived. But for both of them, the journey of recovery took months. In the hospital there were drugs and procedures, and eventually, back out on country, there was traditional healing – bush medicine – to help them mend. 'The ladies, my mother and five of her elder sisters … they wrapped me completely in paperbark, herbs and rushes from the lagoon. I couldn't walk,' Witiyana says. Mud had been heated on coals then, scorching hot, placed on his wrapped body. 'It was burning, and the herbal medicine was just going in, right through everything, and I was burning, crying, with my son … it was powerful way, powerful healing.'

A crumpled Land Cruiser and the bloodied son he could've killed: these images became the catalyst for Witiyana to walk away from the grog, and, for a long period, the band. 'After this accident, I just quit. Drink and everything. That's it, no more,' he says now. 'Through the accident I met [the spirit of] my father, he said, "Quit – I want you to become a leader for your nation and for this community. You've got something special, there's something special in you, so please be strong."'

Witiyana Marika had an awakening of his own raypirri – a matter of being sensible. 'A big raypirri for me,' he reflects. Just no Slim Dusty to come along for this ride.

15
A Global Nation

Amid the whirl of 1994, Yothu Yindi touched down on the tarmac of Port Moresby Airport, skirted by the mountainous surrounds of Papua New Guinea's capital. The NT group had already played twice in the former Australian territory, and this time they'd landed to play at a basketball stadium in PNG's main city, where one of those in attendance was a lumbering, dreadlocked drummer with a calm spirit named Ben Hakalitz.

He was among Yothu Yindi's passionate PNG fanbase – as was his father before him. 'My dad was one of the greatest Yothu Yindi fans. He was the one that introduced me to the band by buying the album, when I was still back in PNG. I kept hearing this music that he played, it was one of his favourite bands. It was the only thing he played in the house, was the Yothu Yindi cassette. That's how I came to know the band,' Hakalitz says. 'When "Treaty" went out and "Djäpana" came out, they were a band that was really hitting the radio

A Global Nation

waves in Moresby, in PNG ... and I thought, "This is a great band!" but I didn't give a second thought about it until they turned up in Moresby in '94 to do a show.'

At that concert, Hakalitz was drumming in the local support for Yothu Yindi – one of PNG's most popular acts named Sanguma, a hotpot of tribal beats and electric noise. Hakalitz struck up an instant rapport with the Australian musos, particularly the band's bassist Stu Kellaway, who himself grew up in PNG in the wild northern township of Wewak, where his father worked as a vocational school teacher. 'It was funny, Stuey at that time was wearing the latest Michael Jordan sneakers,' Hakalitz says. 'He had these shoes, and I said, "Listen, man, I really like that pair of sneakers you got." And he said, "Well, let's do a trade. You give me a kundu drum," which is one of the traditional drums I was using at the time, "and then I'll give you the shoes." And I said, "Fair deal." So I gave him the kundu drum, and he gave me his black Jordans.'

The PNG musician thought nothing further about it until one night, about three weeks after the show, while he was working in the studio, the phone rang. It was Stu Kellaway calling from Australia. 'He said, "Listen, mate, you might have to come over and buy a new pair of Jordans yourself." And I said, "What do you mean?" and he said, "Well, we've just had a meeting with the band, and we've decided to have you as a full-time drummer in the band."' Hakalitz still feels a certain disbelief about this moment. 'I thought it was April Fool's Day.'

It wasn't a gag; it was a legitimate offer to join this outfit that he'd been loving from afar for years. In the same swoop,

Yothu Yindi also picked up another member from Sanguma, a multitalented keyboardist (and musical legend in his home country) named Buruka Tau.

'Alan James called me and says, "Your visa's ready and your ticket's at Qantas, so go down and get your ticket and get on the plane." I thought, "What?" So, everything was coming together,' Hakalitz reflects. 'My dad found out about it, and I think he was one of the most proudest men ever. He said, "Man, that was my favourite band, and my own son is going to go and tour with this band." He was rapt.'

The introduction of the two PNG musos would provide extra layers of love and musical diversity to Yothu Yindi for many years; they would also at times prove to be a boggling bureaucratic challenge for the band's management. 'The two guys from Papua New Guinea in the band needed a visa for every country in the world, except the UK. And that was a battle,' says Alan James. 'Somewhere along the line, Ben and Buruka's passports went missing, and so then we're bluffing our way through border control with photocopies of their passports,' he laughs. 'I think we got away with it mainly because when you fronted with this group, this quite diverse group of people, it was like, "Get out of here!"'

Yothu Yindi were preparing for another barrage of tour commitments and sent Hakalitz a tape of their performance in Port Moresby and a copy of their latest album, *Freedom*, which he studiously memorised through a Walkman as he shot over the sea towards Nhulunbuy.

Once he arrived in Arnhem Land and checked in to his hotel, he mooched about awhile without a clue as to what was happening, before he was picked up and delivered out to Mandawuy's house at Gunyaŋara. He was ready and expecting a chance to hone the tunes. 'All the band were there, just having a few quiet ones on the beach,' he laughs. 'I thought, "Okay, this is a very interesting rehearsal." I arrived and it was like an initiation process with the VB, the good old VB. Straight into it.'

The band performed a concert in the Nhulunbuy town hall that week with no prior rehearsal for their new drummer. For Hakalitz, he'd had just his Walkman to learn an armful of tracks and then it was straight out onto the stage. 'I thought, "Man, these guys really trust me!",' he says. While he acknowledges 'it was a sink or swim situation', the Papua New Guinean had arrived equipped to tread water. Soon it was onwards to Byron Bay, the Gold Coast, New Zealand, and far beyond the southern hemisphere. He'd passed the initiation.

Cal Williams laughs about this induction of the PNG players: 'Those poor bastards ... They flew to Australia, flew to Nhulunbuy, did a show in the town hall, that was their practice ... They did the show in the town hall then did the tour. Ah, I love how we threw people in the hot water. Just no practice. Good luck!'

The big man from Bougainville was strapped in for the ride as Yothu Yindi took off around the globe, discovering fanbases in nations they'd only ever heard about from headlines. 'We were doing 3000-seaters in Europe, and when we turned up in Brazil, it was then like 10,000-seaters. It was amazing. We didn't realise Yothu Yindi was so huge in Brazil until we turned up there. It became one of our favourite places to tour.'

Hakalitz flashes back to a swaying ocean of fans in front of the stage. South America was a surprise: Yothu Yindi were selling out shows in a country where they didn't even speak the language.

'The adrenaline is just something else with that crowd,' Hakalitz says of the Brazilians. 'Because the people loved the band so much, the venue couldn't fit everybody in, so they had to book another show the next day. And the promoter was really worried, she came up to us and said, "Listen, can you guys do another show?" And as [Mandawuy] put it, he said, "Yeah, let's just do another show." So we put on another show for the people, and it was still packed. We could've done two or three shows in one venue, and no problem, we'll still pack it in.'

From Asia to Europe and the Americas, on buses, on planes, on ferries, on floodlit international stages, Hakalitz could still hardly believe he was physically there. 'It was incredible. I sat in the tour bus, and I was pinching myself to wake up. I was saying, "Is this real? Am I finally doing this, am I finally living the dream that I wanted to do, touring the world with a band?" And not just any band, but one of the greatest Indigenous bands in Australia.'

Mandawuy's message of human rights was cutting through and the band's polished live act – with or without rehearsals! – was pulling in the numbers. Yothu Yindi had long been branded with the genre of 'world music', and by 1994 the band was owning that tag, jumping boundaries of countries, of colours, of mother tongues. As Yunupiŋu sings in 'Our Generation':

A Global Nation

>Cultures fuse in a global nation,
>Human rights for Indigenous people,
>Learning life's lessons of old,
>You can't take it away, from our generation
>Last chance for freedom, for our generation
>
>In our generation, it's our generation
>In our generation, it's our generation
>
>Sending a message of hope to the world
>Love sees no colour in everyone

'There was something about this band that really brought people together,' Hakalitz says. 'Loving the vision that Old Man [Mandawuy] had and what the band had. There was a great respect for him on the road. We were working for him. We loved working for him. And I think for me, I came to fulfil the vision that he had, to work with him to achieve what he wanted to achieve. But the amazing thing is just the shows, and the feeling to just get out on the stage with the crowd roaring ... when Old Man walks onto the stage, it's just like the whole place roars like somebody's scored a try in the State of Origin.'

The singer's deft ability to cross cultural barriers is often remembered with awe by his former bandmates. Allen Murphy recalls a trip where he and Mandawuy mashed cultures together like potatoes. It sounds like the opener of a bad comedy routine: a tall New Yorker and an Aboriginal Australian from Arnhem Land walk into a German pub run

On the road: Mangatjay Yunupiŋu, Witiyana Marika and the newly recruited drummer, Papua New Guinean musician Ben Hakalitz, on the streets of Paris, circa 1994. *(courtesy of Yothu Yindi)*

by two Chinese people. 'We were in Essen, Germany, and I think we were about mid-tour. We had a big show that night.' Murphy paints the scene: a cavernous concert hall, sound check already completed. Lunchtime. 'It was like eleven o'clock in the morning ... and just the two of us, we went out for a walk. We ended up walking about three or four kilometres away, and we ended up in this German pub, right? Which is probably not too far of a stretch. And this pub was owned by this Chinese husband and wife – this German pub owned by this Chinese couple. And we're sitting there, and we start talking to them, and we say, "Oh yeah, we're playing at the so-and-so thing tonight," and they said, "Oh really! Please, come have lunch with us."'

The beers began flowing and the hours ticked onwards. 'We ended up spending the whole afternoon with this Chinese couple in their flat above this German pub,' recalls Murphy. 'They cooked us a combination of German and Chinese food, and Manda's talking about culture and this and that, and we're having a few beers, and all just having a grand old time. Then we look at the watch, and we realise that our show starts in like ten minutes. And we're on the other side of town, with no clue which direction we were walking in. So, we jumped in a taxi and fortunately we managed to get back to the gig, which ran a little bit late. The management tore strips off of us that night, but it still ended up being a pretty good gig.'

Murphy uses the story to sum up something of the singer's character – the Yolŋu man's rare ability to engage with people from all walks of life, in spite of his prominence. 'I guess the point is that Mandawuy, he always took time with people,'

Murphy says. 'Not just us, who he saw all the time. People would ask him things, strangers, "Hey, how come you're wearing this yellow thing or that?" He'd take five minutes and talk to them, or sit down, and tell them, "Oh, that's the colours of my clan, the Gumatj clan". I always admired that greatly about him.'

The tours for *Freedom* began to last months, and then eventually, years. 'I can say, this band is one of the hardest working bands ever in Australia,' says Hakalitz. 'Normally bands would release a new album, go out on tour, and fill the venue. Yothu has something … that's just magical. Just turning up and filling the venue still with the same album. People still flocking to the shows. And it was such magic with the shows.'

The band had a few methods for dealing with the hectic nature of their touring lives. One of which, as Hakalitz describes, was to roll up a few herbal supplements to help calm down from the elation of the evenings out in front of the teeming throngs. 'I don't really do drugs, but I seemed to attract drug dealers. Because I had these long dreadlocks and everybody thinks I take drugs.' He laughs. 'So, every night, we'll finish the show and the band is walking off, and people are yelling out for something: for a drumstick, for a pick, just anything so they can remember the concert.'

As the punters hollered out for a souvenir, Hakalitz would stride up to the stage barricade. 'I ended up giving drumsticks every night. I just kept giving sticks to those kids. I'd walk up to the front and give them the sticks … and as I'd do it, they'd exchange it with drugs! They'll give me a handful of marijuana and I'd give them the sticks. I'd look at the bag and go, "Okay!"'

It was a perfect transaction between performer and audience. The dreadlocked Papua New Guinean would then appear backstage, where his bandmates were hungrily hanging out in anticipation of a session. 'I'd walk back into the dressing room, and I'd throw the big bag in front of them. And they'd go, "How'd you get that?" and I said, "Well, you guys want to be thanking me, because I'm always the last person to leave the stage; I give my sticks to the audience and they give me the drugs!" … The boys do it just to relax, because we go on the road for so long.'

Hakalitz's talent for scoring weed through barter would become a running theme. In another episode, the band was scheduled to play the House of Blues in Los Angeles, for the final show of an exhaustive American tour. They rocked up at their Sunset Strip hotel, the same Hyatt where Keith Richards once threw a television from his window. In the lobby, Hakalitz was greeted by the hotel restaurant's Jamaican sous chef. The two men had a brief chat, bonded over their shared island heritage, and, 'that was it': 'He became my good mate, and I gave him some tickets to the show. And he said to me, "Listen; if you need anything in this hotel, you let me know, and I'll sort it out for you."'

Early the next morning there was an unexpected rap at the drummer's room door. 'I thought, "Oh no, who's this?" and anyway, I opened the door, rubbing my eyes. And there's my friend from Jamaica, the head chef, standing there with a tray full of breakfast, hot food, all the things you can think of. And then right at the bottom there's a bowl of marijuana. I said, "Who paid for all this?" He said, "It's on the house, bro."' The rest of Yothu Yindi were swiftly invited up to the room to indulge in the spoils of the drummer's latest rock-and-roll transaction: a banquet scored by the Bougainville bandit.

Many jet-lags later there was a show in Amsterdam. The show after Yothu Yindi had spent the day sampling the legal delicacies available in the Netherland capital's infamous 'coffee shops'. They played a venue that night called Melkweg (the Milky Way), and, according to Yothu Yindi's long-serving tour manager, Geoff McGowan, the band was blasted about that far out. 'I was out there mixing the band that night and everything was really slow. And I was kinda lookin' around going, "Why is everything so slow, but all the audience are enjoying it?" Everyone'd been out to the cafés that day, the audience as well,' McGowan laughs. 'It was a pretty interesting gig. I just thought, "Geez, it's gonna take about three hours to get through this set tonight," because it was so laid back.'

Over the years, Yothu Yindi's globetrotting was punctuated by moments of extreme confusion. Lost in translation, lost in transit. Steering Gurrumul through the busy streets, airports and train stations of foreign cities was undeniably challenging. Throughout the early 1990s, band members would take turns guiding him, including dancers Julie Gungunbuy and Merrkiyawuy Ganambarr-Stubbs (the Yirrkala School principal, who did a stint as a touring member of Yothu Yindi). On one occasion, Yothu Yindi had arrived at their digs in the baroque Austrian capital, Vienna, tired and worn out off a tour bus at two in the morning. Gurrumul was checked into a room. 'Everyone was given keys and then someone's led him to his room, but it wasn't on any of the lists. And this hotel had like 1200 rooms,' Stu Kellaway replays the incident. 'And it was in the middle of Vienna. So, the next morning we were waking up and having breakfast, and ringing the rooms, "Where's Gurru?" No one's heard from him all day. We couldn't find him.'

The sun crept across the sky and still no sign of Gurrumul. The band was growing alarmed. 'The hotel staff searched so many rooms, like 200 rooms, and still nothing,' says Kellaway. 'We notified the police and they were on the lookout for a blind Aboriginal guy in Vienna. It was one of the sound guys who ended up getting a master key and basically just checking every room. And then there he was – just chillin' out listenin' to some tunes, and an empty mini bar fridge.' The bassist laughs, his relief still palpable. 'He'd been in there a day and a half. So, he was probably wondering where the hell we all were, and if he'd been abandoned.'

Gurrumul's family on Elcho Island at times worried about how he was faring so far from his home. But those in the band's orbit say his fellow musos did their best to watch over him. Joy McKean describes watching the relationship between the Yothu Yindi players and their sightless bandmate on the Raypirri tour. 'One of my fondest memories is of the affection and care they took of Gurrumul,' McKean says. 'I used to watch them … they used to be so careful of him, and I'd often be sitting there just watching and listening … and I just took special notice of the love and care that all those band boys had for him and how they looked after him.'

The frantic life of an international touring band wasn't sustainable for everybody. While Merrkiyawuy Ganambarr-Stubbs remembers 'exciting' trips in Europe – London, Amsterdam, Germany – and around Australia, overall, she didn't love it. 'The crowds were amazing, but in my mind, we always had to perform,' the school principal says. 'We had to entertain the crowd so that they would like the show. Later on, I thought, "This is not for me. I don't need to be up there entertaining all the time, I'm not an entertainer." I just wanted to go home and work and earn money in a stable place to live in.' She says she stayed 'buried in books' to kill time during the long journeys into new lands. 'On the tour buses, I just read and read.'

On the highway there were hardships, cultural complexities, homesickness, occasional blow-ups. But there was also a bonding, a family togetherness. 'It was a once-in-a-lifetime opportunity for me to travel the world with family,' former dancer Julie Gungunbuy said in the award-winning NT podcast *Birds Eye View*. 'It gave me a good insight into the world, because I saw myself not [just] as a Yolŋu person but a human being. And it [showed] there is people out there of different races, and we all human beings and we all family when you get to know them.'

Many of those in the band were actual blood relatives, or at least related in the gurruṯu sense. But for those who came later into this brother and sisterhood, like Ben Hakalitz, there was still that same feeling of close camaraderie. 'We were not just a band, we were a family on the road,' he says. 'We had so much fun together, and I think, that respect that they had for me to be able to do my job without trying to take anything was the greatest thing. I felt so free.'

The PNG drummer who was initially signed on for a three-month contract – thrown in at the deep end without a rehearsal in Nhulunbuy – has found himself keeping time in the Yothu Yindi family for just shy of three decades. They'd become a global gumbo of musicians who would travel to the far corners of the Earth, from tropical Bermuda to the arctic circle of Norway and poverty-stricken South Africa, just to play for people. A band beyond borders, beyond races; world music in its truest form.

16
One Blood

From his farmhouse in the NSW countryside, one of the founders of INXS is thinking back to the time he accompanied Yothu Yindi into Abbey Road Studios. They were headed to the London birthplace of The Beatles' famous album to record a new track. Since the 1930s, Studio Two at Abbey Road has hosted some of music's most popular names, from John Lennon's mates to Pink Floyd and Ed Sheeran. But it was the enthusiasm of an Elcho Island musician inside those famed walls that stuck in the mind of INXS's Andrew Farriss. 'I can remember Gurrumul getting really excited because they still had The Beatles' organ in that room, and getting to use a piano they used to use,' Farriss says. 'It was pretty cool – it was all in really good condition, I mean, Abbey Road is one of the best studios in the world.'

Yothu Yindi drummer Ben Hakalitz was among those there for the sessions. 'The day we were recording the drums, George Harrison was upstairs, mixing some Beatles remasters,' says Hakalitz. 'They were remastering or remixing something, and we were there in the studio working downstairs. Abbey Road's still the same as it was in the days when The Beatles were recording – there's something about it when you walk in there. There's just me with the drumkit in this huge studio … it was a great experience, wonderful experience – that was one of the little boxes I ticked for my bucket list.'

It was 1995 and a central gang of the Yothu Yindi family had hunkered down at Farriss's farm in rural England to hammer out their impending album. Lush paddocks, cobbly roads and low-hanging clouds threatening to douse the scenery with cool drizzle; it was a far cry from Yothu Yindi's comfort zone on the Gulf of Carpentaria. But there they were. 'We ended up in England after the European tour and the rest of the band flew back,' Hakalitz remembers. 'We started writing there, and recording most of the backing tracks at his farmhouse. We've worked with different producers all throughout the life of the band, and Andrew was such an amazing producer.'

Farriss, who nowadays plays as a solo singer-songwriter, had first connected with Yothu Yindi when they joined the bill alongside INXS, Crowded House and Ratcat at the Concert for Life in Sydney's Centennial Park in 1992. Dancer Mangatjay Yunupiŋu recalls sipping a couple of schooners with the stadium rockers – who were then still in the grips of international superstardom – after the gig. 'We stayed in the same hotel in Sydney, and we drank at the same bar after the show,' Mangatjay says. 'Michael Hutchence, he thought I was skinny! I saw him in person and I thought he was thinner than me, true god! He was a great guy. They were one of the first bands to go against racism in Australia.'

Not long after, Farriss teamed up with Yothu Yindi's singer to co-write a track for *Freedom*. 'Mandawuy wanted to write with me, so we worked on a song that I'd already sort of started called "Our Generation", and we tracked that,' Farriss says. 'I just clicked with Mandawuy, in particular, and Stuey Kellaway, those guys, I just got them, and hopefully they got me, as a person. And that was how it started.'

These would be the early threads of a friendship that would eventually weave through more than a decade of work together, on and off, and one that would help dig Farriss out from one of the most traumatic upheavals of his life; the sudden death of his close mate Michael Hutchence in 1997. But at this point in the mid-1990s, the task at hand was finishing off the new tune he'd written with Yunupiŋu. 'Mandawuy got excited about this song that we wanted to put out called "Superhighway", about the internet,' says Farriss. 'So, we worked on the song.'

'Superhighway' was to be the lead single off Yothu Yindi's forthcoming album, *Birrkuṯa – Wild Honey*. Yothu Yindi headed into Abbey Road Studios to lay down the track:

```
          Planet earth - is spinning around
          Make the earth - one big highway
         People are yearning - don't understand
          Can't eat money - there's no more land

              Missing my home, missing her love
       Missing the land, missing her touch, out on the road
```

One Blood

> Superhighway – around the world,
> Children of the earth, you and me
> Superhighway – across the sky
> Children of the earth, wanna be free, wanna be free

In a jarring juxtaposition to the swish gear of Abbey Road, the bulk of the band's fourth album was recorded in a warehouse, The Tin Shed, in Darwin's industrial area of Winnellie. A US producer, Lamar Lowder, had been flown in for the project, but according to Alan James, only so much could be done with the facilities at hand. 'It was this rundown, ramshackle thing that we just hung lots of blankets and stuff to do acoustic treatment,' says James. '[The album was recorded] between the shed and the downstairs room at my house … because that got set up as a studio for a while. A lot of the mixing was done under my house. Unfortunately, if you listen to the different albums, you can pick up there's a drop in production qualities with that album.'

Despite this perceived dip, the band remained tight, adding in freshly honed vocal harmonies over sweet reggae grooves, like the Stu Kellaway–penned 'Stop That'. The introduction of the PNG players brought more of a Pacific flavour to tracks like 'Spirit of Peace' and 'Timor', written largely by musicians Buruka Tau and Ben Hakalitz. Mandawuy's songwriting brought standouts to the new setlist, like 'Yirrmala', which, as always, combined his hopes for the cultural survival of his people with a western pop sensibility:

Sometimes I think we're poor boys here,
Got no money, got no job,
And at times when I might turn to drink,
I lose my head but then I start to think
Miyamala matjala, Ngathiya Djaŋala,
Liyawayma Marŋarrŋura, Numbernydja Buwakurru

By the time *Birrkuṯa* was released, Yothu Yindi had morphed into a multimillion-dollar operation, a busy business with numerous staff running finance and global logistics. Alan James had hired two full-time employees who were kept flat-strap securing visas, booking hotels and keeping concert promoters and debt collectors at bay. 'Lots of logistics: flying people in from PNG, flying people in from north-east Arnhem Land … it was quite a big administrative effort,' says James. 'Keep in mind, mobile phones had only just been invented, emails were still not really a thing, everything was being done by fax. So, my upstairs loungeroom was the sort of front office for quite some time.'

In spite of the hard work and high-profile INXS collaborator, *Birrkuṯa* barely nudged the ARIA top 100 albums upon its release in 1996. The Australian charts were jostling with a saturated race field of both local and international artists, and Yothu Yindi were evidently battling to make fresh headway above the ruckus.

'Nothing did the business like the *Tribal Voice* album,' Alan James says. 'We kept investing in subsequent albums, but probably made the mistake … certainly I know from the musicians' perspective there was an assumption it was always going to be like the *Tribal Voice* album. But that wasn't the case. In hindsight, if you looked at it from an accountant's perspective, we probably should've stopped recording music. But if you looked at it from a creative perspective ...' he pauses over his thoughts for a moment. 'Do I regret that they kept writing songs and we kept recording them? No, I don't. But if we'd just put that money into buying houses or put it into super or something, we'd probably be a lot better off at the moment.'

After their efforts in Abbey Road, the band would soon have another crack at recording overseas, jumping on the long-haul back to Europe for sessions in Ireland and Germany. This new project was seeded during an unlikely collaboration between the band and German rockstar Peter Maffay, who in 1997 had travelled to the Arnhem Land homeland of Dhanaya to work with the group on his ambitious concept album, *Begegnungen (Encounters)*, which also featured jams with musicians of various cultural backgrounds from Israel to the US. Maffay recorded a version of Mandawuy's track 'Tribal Voice' and in 1998 took Yothu Yindi on tour across his home country, where his lavish nightly show set-up included multiple stages which represented different corners of the world, and were brought together during the concert using high-tech hydraulics.

'I was blown away with this bloke! Here's this bloke who wants to sing "Tribal Voice", a non-Aboriginal person, I've never had any bloody request at all like that coming to me,' exclaims Mandawuy, laughing, on the *Begegnungen* documentary, about the album's creation and shot during

Maffay's visit to Dhanaya. 'So I thought, "Well, this is a new idea, why not run with it?"'

This encounter soon evolved, with musicians from Maffay's band stepping forward to produce Yothu Yindi's fifth album, *One Blood*, a reworking of older hits with a couple new cuts thrown into the mix and traditional manikay sung by Mandawuy and Galarrwuy.

In Dublin, members of Yothu Yindi wandered the River Liffey and sampled stout in the famous Temple Bar district. Between such sightseeing, they were joined in the studio by collaborators Jim Kerr, the frontman of famous Scottish rockers Simple Minds, and Irish musician Liam Ó Maonlaí of Hothouse Flowers, who surfed a wave of popularity in the early 1990s, including a number-one album in Australia, *Home*. An Austrian film crew captured the band's recording process in Ireland and later in Maffay's studio in Bavaria, and included it in the documentary *Yothu Yindi: One Blood*, which was released on videocassette in 1999.

'We've been to Ireland before, this is something like our third trip,' Mandawuy says in the doco. 'It's kind of interesting to be involved, recording here in Ireland. Thing is, we've chosen the wrong time to come here. It's pretty cold.'

Liam Ó Maonlaí recalls dropping into Yothu Yindi's Dublin digs to find the Arnhem Land band not coping entirely well with Ireland's notoriously 'miserable' climes. 'The wet cold of Ireland, it takes a different mindset to get used to,' says Ó Maonlaí from Dublin. 'And if you're used to the warmth and the heat and the humidity of the Northern Territory, I can well imagine [how cold it would feel]. The lads were staying

After the release of their fourth album, *Birrkuta (Wild Honey)*, Yothu Yindi took off for a tour of Europe in 1997. *(courtesy Yothu Yindi)*

in a house quite near me, and I went to visit, and they had the house kind of heated up and the curtains closed. Kind of cocooning themselves, really. Which I can well understand.'

The Irish singer added some folk touches to a retooled version of the track 'Mainstream'. 'I sang a verse on that, and it was very emotional actually,' says Ó Maonlaí. 'I just remember feeling a surge of emotion listening to that melody as I was standing there in the studio. Mandawuy was there ... it was so exciting to see this vision. This "under one dream" vision.'

Despite the seas separating Ireland from Australia, Mandawuy still found connections between the two lands: primarily in how their Indigenous populations had been treated by the Brits. 'People where I come from have had some connections with the Irish people, and I think it's something to do with the cultural background in which we come from,' he says in the *One Blood* doco. 'There's common areas in which we share ... where the English, the major power, they did the same thing as far as oppression is concerned. So that's something that we relate to, even though we come from different backgrounds. Those common areas can only help in people trying to contrast the two situations.'

Ó Maonlaí agrees with the comparison: 'We have an Indigenous language and we have a story where that language was forbidden. And we were starved and we were corralled and we were hunted.'

Mandawuy was acutely aware of the damage the invading English had inflicted on Aboriginal people across Australia post-1788, including frontier massacres in Arnhem Land, in Gangan and even in his own homeland of Biranybirany. But from the time he was a young man, his bandmates say he always managed to maintain an open mind towards the colonial power.

'People call us a political band, but I think we're not as political as Midnight Oil,' says drummer Ben Hakalitz. 'A lot of [our music] was about Manda's voice about unity, living together, working together. One thing I want you to know about him, in my experience with him, I have never heard him speak badly about white Australia. He never spoke against it. He's always talking about unity, talking about living together. Most of his songs are about, "Let's do this together, let's work together, we can do this together." That's really what it is ... he was a very diplomatic man.'

Mandawuy wasn't afraid to call out Australia's shortcomings. But he often did so wearing a smile. In this spirit – a gentle nudge to the ribs of those in power – Yothu Yindi reworked their biggest hit as the funky final track on *One Blood*. It had been ten years since Hawke's promised treaty, and there were still just crickets chirping when it came to any action.

> Now it's 1998, all you talking politicians,
> Words are easy, words are cheap,
> Much cheaper than our priceless land,
> All your promises have been broken,
> Just like writing in the sand!

'Treaty 98' was a reminder, a sequel of sorts: there were outstanding debts to be paid.

But while the band remained on message, the mood in Australia's Parliament had turned recognisably darker. A conservative government run by John Howard had been elected in 1996, and, as Alan James (a Labor stalwart) believes, an old strain of negativity had begun to seep back into the nation's discourse. 'When we first got into the business, no Aboriginal band had ever made any inroads in a mainstream sense,' James says. 'And racism was institutionalised. People didn't even think of it as racism. It's a bit like that stuff that's coming out now about *Hey Hey It's Saturday*, and the jokes that they used to make to Kamahl and things like that. That was just so normalised that anybody who complained about it at the time was on the road to a hiding.

'But with "Treaty", the amazing thing was we were playing in pubs and clubs all around Australia, with packed houses, and the audience going off. But within two or three years, it felt like there was a backlash to that. And I don't remember the year, but when that became pointedly so was after John Howard became prime minister. And that normalised everyone to be able to go back to being good ol' racists in Australia.'

Perhaps the most visible sign of Australia reverting, at least to an extent, to its divided past was the election of former fish-and-chip shop owner Pauline Hanson, the future One Nation party leader, to federal parliament in 1996. Hanson won her Queensland seat after, and in spite of, comments she'd made about Aboriginal welfare benefits, which had seen her scratched from the Liberal Party ticket and forced to run as an independent.

In her maiden speech after victory she doubled down. 'I have done research on benefits available only to Aboriginals and challenge anyone to tell me how Aboriginals are disadvantaged when they can obtain three and five per cent housing loans denied to non-Aboriginals,' Hanson told the parliament. 'This nation is being divided into black and white, and the present system encourages this. I am fed up with being told, "This is our land." Well, where the hell do I go? I was born here, and so were my parents and children. I will work beside anyone and they will be my equal, but I draw the line when told I must pay and continue paying for something that happened over 200 years ago.'

It was a long way from the reconciliatory rhetoric of Keating's Redfern Address.

Mandawuy was once asked in a *Guardian* Q and A: 'Which living person do you most despise?' to which he answered: 'Pauline Hanson'. 'She's disrupted development of the Australian way of thinking,' the singer added.

'[It] was very disappointing,' says James of the shifting era. 'When you're on the wave of something, where you can feel actual significant change happening, and then you're actually part of the backlash afterward. The only way I've been able to console myself through that over the years is to believe that we made some incremental change. Initially it was seismic, and then after it swung back, it was still a step forward.'

Yothu Yindi responded to the nation's changing political climate in the way they knew best: by urging a sense of unity through their songs. Paul Kelly reunited with Mandawuy to pen the standout title track on the new album, 'One Blood'. Like 'Treaty' before it, 'One Blood' would dream of a more equal future in their scarred brown land: beating one blood.

```
Can you see it? See it in the haze
Moving shadows, race against time
Different colours — one blood
```

And as with 'Treaty', the collaboration between the two Australian songwriters who had two completely different approaches to the artform wouldn't come easily. At least, not for one of them. Alan James tells the tale. 'They were back writing at Paul's house in Melbourne. Paul, at some point, I could see he was really frustrated. And I said, "What's the matter?" and he said something along the lines of, "Look, when I write a song, I start off with a word, then it turns into a line, then it turns into a verse, then eventually I get to the end of it and I've got a song. This guy, he starts off with a book, and he's trying to jam it into a song."'

Kelly laughs when told of the anecdote. In his mind, writing with Mandawuy wasn't so much a 'frustrating' process, but rather just a 'complete opposite' to his own way of doing it. 'He saw his songs as spreading a message, he saw his songs as a way to teach,' says Kelly. 'Whereas my songs don't come from any sort of coherent philosophy or world view, they just come more from the bottom up, I guess, from images or scraps of ideas or phrases, and I don't quite know what's happening in the song until I'm well into it.' But Kelly also notes that the songwriting pair had their common ground: 'His songs are full of imagery, that's how he comes at the world too. He's a visual songwriter, and so am I.'

Yunupiŋu always remained the educator. Ever the school principal, delivering a message. 'I think that was the thing about Mandawuy,' says Alan James. 'He would think long and hard and deep about what message he was trying to get across. And often that was a message to all Australians, in fact the global community, and at other times it was a message just for his own people.'

As the turn of the millennium neared, Mandawuy, along with other clan elders, could see clear ways to turn those messages into something tangible for Yolŋu. As he wrote in *One Blood*'s liner notes: 'We are moving toward the establishment of the Garma Cultural Studies Institute and the Yirrnga Music Development Centre near Nhulunbuy in order to facilitate a sharing of traditional Yolngu and contemporary western knowledge.' If these plans were realised, there'd be no need to travel abroad to record their tracks in the future – there'd be a way to do it much closer to home.

17
Garma

It was the late 1990s and the blueprints for a grand plan were coming to life. The land had been cleared and construction was nearly finished for a new recording studio by the sea at Gunyaŋara. The studio had been designed with an outdoor stage, and Yothu Yindi were painted up, ready to head out and hit this newly built platform for opening night. It was a celebration: the Yirrnga Music Development Centre was ready to open its doors.

'There were hundreds of people there,' says Alan James. 'Michael Gudinski and Michael Chugg and the assembled forces of the Mushroom empire were there. And I was on the side managing a bunch of crazy rock-and-rollers from Melbourne and Sydney.' Some of the Oils were there, a Chisel, maybe even an Aztec. Out on the bay, a small flotilla of sailors had anchored close to shore to catch the spectacle.

'It was really, really amazing,' says drummer Ben Hakalitz. 'All the yachties from around there had sailed their yachts over to the little bay, and they had their barbecues there and their beers. We faced the PA right out towards the sea, so you had the crowd on land, then you had the crowd on the boats as well. It was just an amazing sight.'

The studio was part of a long-term dream being brought into reality. A dream that also gave birth to the vibrant annual Garma Festival of Traditional Culture, a celebration of Yolŋu life, education and music that is today seen as Australia's hallmark event for sharing Indigenous ideas. The groundwork for these developments had been laid years earlier, way back in 1990, when Mandawuy and Alan James registered an Aboriginal Corporation called the Yothu Yindi Foundation. A pathway to helping find real outcomes to better the lives of Yolŋu.

'Right from the beginning, in the late '80s, [Mandawuy] was urging me to help him start a foundation,' says James. 'Right from the beginning, he recognised that he wanted to do something to put something back into his community, so [the Yothu Yindi band] wasn't just seen as an external exercise. Because both he and I had an unerring confidence that we were going to be successful,' James laughs, adding the disclaimer: 'Based on what science, I have no idea. But on a gut feeling. And at the time, I must admit, I was a bit aghast at the idea of starting a not-for-profit foundation before we'd even made a dollar. But we did.'

It was steered by a Yolŋu association comprised of leaders from five clan groups of the region – the Gumatj, Rirratjiŋu, Djapu, Galpu and Wanguri. By 1997, they'd focused in on what the foundation could achieve. They released an

Yothu Yindi's Yirrnga Studio was opened in the late 1990s near Gunyaŋara, mainly as a way to help Arnhem Land bands access musical equipment and resources close to home. *(Peter Eve/Newspix)*

expansive proposal for what they envisaged would one day be built, called the Garma Cultural Studies Centre. 'For several years the Yolngu community leaders and Yothu Yindi band members have discussed and planned for a Cultural Centre,' the proposal reads. 'Their principal aim at the moment is to realise this community dream.'

This would be developed in two stages. The first was to construct the Yirrnga Studio at Gunyaŋara, the proposal explains, while the second was for a separate Garma Centre. In Mandawuy's mind, according to close friends and family, this centre was to be a 'bush university' – a hub for learning on country, for connecting back to culture, and for balanda to gain insights and lessons on Yolŋu life from the Yolŋu teachers themselves.

'Dedicated to both research and teaching, [the Centre's] focus will be threefold: on Yolngu visual and performing arts, Yolngu language and linguistics and Yolngu culture and law,' the 1997 proposal reads. 'The Centre would, desirably, be affiliated in a formal way with more than one Australian university, to encourage scholastic interaction between the staff and students of the Centre and other relevant areas of scholarship.' It was to be built on the site of a defunct school called Dhupuma College, by an escarpment spot called Gulkula, a special place overlooking the waters of Waṉuwuy (Cape Arnhem).

'After a few misfires, one year we decided to hold a gathering of, essentially, architects – we invited architects from all over Australia to come in, to talk up and think up ideas of what this would physically look like,' says James, who was the founding chief executive of the Yothu Yindi Foundation. 'And what was originally going to be a gathering of probably twenty or thirty people turned into a gathering of a couple of hundred.'

This gathering went for three days. There was family, food and a confluence of creative ideas. At its conclusion, Alan James says the Gumatj clan leader Galarrwuy Yunupiŋu made a call. 'Galarrwuy, to his credit, said, "This has worked. This has been really interesting. We could wait for twenty years to get the money to build that [cultural centre]. Why don't we just do this every year?" And that was the start of the Garma Festival,' says James.

The early years of the Garma Festival, from 1998, saw the creation of a *mulka* (a culturally safe place) out in the scrub of East Arnhem Land. Word travelled and the event reeled in a wide spectrum of guests, from academics to musicians, to learn from Yolŋu on Yolŋu land. 'It started off as a small group,' says Yalmay Yunupiŋu. 'Then after the next year, more and more came. News had spread about the foundation, and then we made [Garma] into a yearly thing. And then since then, it ran successfully.'

There was a good-natured vibe, a campfire camaraderie, at these festivals. 'At that time it wasn't too political,' says Yalmay. '[Mandawuy's] vision was to bring people in, to share knowledge, to give and take. That's what his vision was. But also run forums for Indigenous people and invite stakeholders to listen to us; what our needs are, what we want for our community … just sharing and giving and taking. Getting to know each other.'

Those in the Yothu Yindi band universe remember fondly

the first Garmas. 'They were fun, I loved it,' says Jodie Cockatoo. 'Just seeing and meeting all the Yolŋu families, all my *yapas* [sisters] and *wäwas* [brothers], my *mukuls* [aunties] … you know, all of 'em! I never had to worry about anything when I went there, I was always looked after by all the families … and just camping at the Garma grounds, on that escarpment – there's something really special about that place.'

One of those who felt the power beaming from Garma was Oils singer Peter Garrett. 'For people who'd never visited into Yolŋu country, it was an utter and absolutely transforming revelation,' says Garrett. 'I think for those of us who have had associations over time, it was a confirmation of the strength and the depth and the urgent issues that are facing First Nations people … and for someone who's been in most of the big stadiums in the world, and been lucky enough to see a lot of fancy, flashy stuff, I think particularly in those early days, the Garma Festival was another level altogether.'

The festivals were also infused with a spirit of playfulness, where pranks were pulled and laughter carried through the grounds. Yothu Yindi's tour and production manager Geoff McGowan remembers returning to his campsite one year to find his tent had been hoisted up a tree. 'I came back and went, "Where's my tent?" and thought, "Ah, it's up in the air." So I looked straight up, and it was up hangin' out of the tree, and everyone was pissin' themselves laughin' about it,' he recalls, also pissin' himself, years later. 'So I thought, "Okay, yeah, no worries!" and so, later on I went back when no one was around, and I totally went into Stuey's tent, who was the main perpetrator on that one, and I disconnected his tent from the fly, and took his tent out. I just left the fly standing up. So when he came back and opened it up there was nothing in there, just dirt!'

The seed for these big philanthropic projects like Garma began to sprout when the band toured to South Africa, Zimbabwe and Vietnam around 1996 for a series of shows in collaboration with eyesight charity the Fred Hollows Foundation. Yothu Yindi travelled into poverty-hit corners of these countries, where they played small-scale shows and ran acoustic workshops for kids in schools. In Zimbabwe, the group strummed for communities in Harare and Bulawayo, and in Vietnam they had a rare glimpse of a nation still suffering post-war. 'We did concerts in Ho Chi Minh City and then also in Hanoi, and in the mid-'90s, Hanoi was still pretty closed,' says Alan James. 'Sometimes in Yothu Yindi's career, it's fair to say that it wasn't a commercial path we were following. We did what felt important, and we did what we felt right, rather than "this is a vehicle to make lots of money".'

One of the band's shows in Vietnam was inside a concrete Russian circus tent, where Ben Hakalitz says there were 'monkeys running around everywhere'. 'You gotta play drums and keep an eye on monkeys jumping all over the joint!' He laughs.

In Vietnam, Yothu Yindi also visited patients suffering from eye disease in regional hospitals. 'There was this one old man, and his eye was not good,' says Jodie Cockatoo. 'And he had a family of eight, and had a farm. He was the farmer, and he was in hospital, and he didn't have enough money to have this operation. And how much he needed was like how

Mandawuy Yunupiŋu singing with musicians in Soweto, South Africa, in 1996, where Yothu Yindi had travelled for a series of shows in collaboration with charity the Fred Hollows Foundation. *(Michael Amendolia/Newspix)*

much we got for per diems. So, we gave him the money. We gave him the money, because, you know, far out, he's got his livelihood, he's got his family to look after.'

Cockatoo says some of the band were overcome seeing the burden of disease firsthand. 'It was hard to take,' she says. 'Because when you're in situations like that, you realise what you've got, what we have and how lucky we are, where we're from … and all I found is, at the end of the day, in all of those third-world countries, they've still got a smile on their face. For everything they go through, they've still got a smile. That was amazing to us.'

Yothu Yindi also saw parallels in these countries to the increasingly dire situations in their communities back home in the NT, where petrol sniffing was ravaging youths, and preventable disease was claiming the lives of Aboriginal adults at dizzyingly high rates. Alan James says working alongside the Fred Hollows Foundation, a relationship that dated back to 1993, taught him and Mandawuy how to do something positive for Aboriginal health outcomes and about 'the art to philanthropy and fundraising'. 'Which was how we got the initial money to build the recording studio at Gunyaŋara, and the money that started off the Garma Festival,' James says.

During some of the early Garmas, Yothu Yindi band and crew members would camp in swags on the floor of the Yirrnga Studio. It was an opportunity to put the facility into its prime use – recording the music of community bands and giving them access to resources and expertise that wasn't previously available on their remote Aboriginal land. In the Yothu Yindi Foundation's 1997 proposal, they laid out what the studio's construction would mean for Arnhem Land: 'Many bands, at a range of levels and often in remote areas, are working extremely hard at their music against all odds – poor conditions, instruments needing repair, lack of music information and little support outside their communities ... young musicians, songwriters and dancers in the Yolngu communities are well-placed to benefit from the experience of Yothu Yindi band members who have struggled with these problems and continue to do so in some areas, for many years.'

Geoff McGowan says in the studio's early years there was a steady stream of musicians and other visitors rolling through the doors. 'Local bands, and bands from other communities, they were all coming through, and we were all in there helping them record songs.'

One of Mandawuy's nieces, a young Yolŋu leader named Rarrtjiwuy Melanie Herdman, was in a Yirrkala School band called Wild Honey that went into Yirrnga to lay down some tunes. 'We had opportunities to go and record music and eventually have an album,' says Herdman. 'It was beautiful. I remember ... we had a school camp out there, and we would go fishing, and then in the afternoon we would have songwriting sessions with Uncle, who would come and talk to us about music.'

In their downtime, the Yothu Yindi crew would swim in the waters of Melville Bay out in front of the studio and just pray they wouldn't be gobbled up by a passing reptilian resident. 'We actually seen one, one day; when we got out of the water and we were sittin' on the rocks, a big bäru came by,' says Geoff McGowan, lucky to still count all his limbs.

The first Garma festivals saw an influx of invited musicians, from Australian performers like Billy Thorpe and Paul Kelly, to overseas attendees like British Indian muso Nitin Sawhney. But the centrepiece was always the traditional Yolŋu cultural activities, with buŋgul at the heart. The events were brimming with positive energy. 'The whole effort was because a bunch of motivated people with goodwill put in a lot of time and effort and energy,' says Alan James. 'I'm really proud of what we did. We used to bring together an amazing cross-section of the Australian community each year, and anyone who was involved in those days has lasting memories of it. It was genuinely an effort to try and do good. And it just kept going.'

A close friend and artist for the band, Trevor van Weeren (who did the band's original logo and painted the sign on Yirrnga Studio), says the early Garmas set the scene for the festival to continue growing into the nationally recognised event of today. 'It was just fantastic,' Van Weeren says. 'We were all just buzzing off each other, and lots of creative ideas were happening. It really formed the whole concept of Garma.'

The two Yunupiŋu brothers, Mandawuy and Galarrwuy, brought their different strengths to the festival. The Yothu Yindi singer contributed ideas, contacts and a creative energy while the elder brother brought his political clout to try to effect change for their people.

Those who were there stress that the gains made in Arnhem Land during this era were by no means the result of a Napoleonic crusade by one or two leaders. It was always a whole community effort, steered by the advice of strong elders and educators, including – but far from limited to – Galarrwuy and Mandawuy's sister Guḻumbu Yunupiŋu, Witiyana's sister Raymattja Marika, Dr B Marika, Yalmay Yunupiŋu and Yirrkala bark petition signatory W Wunuŋmurra.

In Yalmay's terms, the first Garma festivals tapped directly into the Yolŋu philosophy of the fresh water and the salt water 'coming and joining in the middle'. '[Mandawuy's] using that philosophy for Garma,' says Yalmay. 'In the beginning. The meeting of the two waters. He wanted to see the people like that.'

Yothu Yindi and the Yolŋu leaders weren't going to wait around for politicians to change things. With Garma, they'd taken matters into their own hands. Even if they didn't have a treaty, by the end of the 1990s, they'd created something to bring Australians together.

18
The New Millennium

In Yirrnga Studio, the rapid-fire gunshot of tom-toms filled the booth. The opening bars of Yothu Yindi's new album, *Garma*, were booming out. The year 2000 had arrived and, with the record nearing completion, the band had entered the new millennium on a positive beat. They'd reunited with INXS's Andrew Farriss as a producer, who'd travelled up to the Gunyaŋara studio to assist with writing and tracking the tunes. For Farriss, the opportunity to collaborate couldn't have come at a better time.

'I was kind of still in a bit of shock and depression because Michael Hutchence had killed himself,' says Farriss. 'It was a pretty tumultuous sort of time. And it was Mandawuy who called me, kinda out of the blue, and said, "Look, I hope you're okay. I just wanted to know if you'd be interested in producing an album for Yothu Yindi, for the millennium changeover and for the Olympics." And I said "Well, sure! I'd be very interested in that."'

Under the blue sky and standing on the bauxite red earth of the Gove Peninsula, Andrew Farriss was able to leave his turmoil behind. 'It was quite cathartic, almost a healing thing,' says Farriss. 'Going from a big city with a tragic suicide experience with a close friend and a work associate of mine, to go right out bush, to one of the most beautiful, natural areas in Arnhem Land ... I was able to get outside of my mind and my heart for a minute and just look at life from a different perspective.'

The creation of the *Garma* album, their sixth and what would turn out to be their last release of completely new material, was an epiphany for some of the members of Yothu Yindi as well. Jodie Cockatoo holds the experience close to her heart, as it marked the first time she'd been invited to be fully involved in the songwriting process. '[Mandawuy] gave me the opportunity to spread my wings in the *Garma* album,' says Cockatoo. 'He opened the doors and let me write with him, Stuey and Andrew Farriss. And we wrote for like two weeks ... and I'd never been involved with a songwriting session like that before, for an album. It was an honour and a privilege for me, and I loved it. And he trusted me ... I felt that I had his respect.'

Jodie's soulful voice cuts through *Garma* in her co-writes, including 'Fire' and 'Good Medicine'. Mandawuy described the latter as 'a celebration of womanhood' amid the usually 'male dominated' Yothu Yindi line-up:

> So stop what you're doin',
> Put your soul on the ground,

> We can run this place, out of space,
> Only so much land.
>
> I have been told I am a lucky child,
> And respectfully, I can say,
> It's cause I'm a woman.
> Can you dig it, in a woman's world?

The songwriting on *Garma* also sparkles with history lessons of Arnhem Land, like 'Macassan Crew', which tells of the centuries-old trade partnership between the Yolŋu and Macassan people of Indonesia, long pre-dating English colonisation. With the 2000 Olympics in Sydney impending, these were lessons the band hoped all of Australia would hear. 'Working on the *Garma* album ... there was a sense of excitement about it,' says Andrew Farriss.

Yothu Yindi's audiences had also responded well to the band's new *Garma* setlist – even before the songs were fully formed. 'You had to be a really spontaneous player to work in Yothu Yindi,' says Cal Williams. 'Because sometimes Manda would go off cue. Quite often. Me, Stuey and Ben, [we'd go] "Oh fuck, Manda's just gone into the chorus early! Oh, Manda's just added an extra line to the verse!" Bang, skip a beat. We became masters at smoothing things over.' One time in a downtown Darwin nightclub, Mandawuy miscued the *Garma* track 'Silver Owl'. The band hadn't rehearsed it and things looked like they were certain to go swiftly awry. But the rhythm section wasn't to be beaten. 'Our only option was to make up a whole new song on the spot,' says Cal. 'We made up a whole new song and played it through and it worked. The crowd went off. And Geoff [McGowan] was just crackin' up, 'cause he knew what was goin' on.'

The couple of years leading up to the Olympic Games had been a creative boomtime for the band, with accolades and opportunities coming from all sides. Among these was recognition for Mandawuy's lifelong work as an educator, in the form of an honorary doctorate from the Queensland University of Technology. Up on the podium and dressed in academic regalia, he held a fist in the air. In western terms, it was another milestone in a decorated education career. From becoming the first Yolŋu to gain a university degree in Arnhem Land, to leading Yirrkala School as its principal, to helping create the Garma Festival, here he was now, as Dr Yunupiŋu.

'I wanted to deliver education to my own people because I realised that if Aboriginal people could read and write we could influence people all over the world,' he said on receiving the honour. 'I also recognised the power of music and the ability to reach people around the world through music.'

His wife, Yalmay, was in the audience, as were his bandmates. However, a couple of the lads stayed outside. Geoffrey Gurrumul hadn't wanted to go in, so Stu Kellaway sat with him, killing time in a wombat-shaped hire Tarago, smoking ciggies in the carpark, and waiting for their mates to return. By Kellaway's account, the conversation soon turned to a challenge:

Kellaway: 'You ever driven a car before?'
Gurrumul: 'No.'

Dr Mandawuy Yunupiŋu receives his honorary doctorate from the Queensland University of Technology in 1998, recognising his contributions to Indigenous education outcomes, and for spreading cultural awareness of his people around Australia and the world. *(courtesy of Queensland University of Technology)*

Kellaway: 'Do you wanna have a go? I'll teach you how to do a donut?'

Gurrumul nods his head and grins.

Kellaway: 'It's automatic, all you've got to do is jump on the brake, here, and here's the accelerator. And all you gotta do is hard lock and put your foot to the thing, and you'll hear the skidding, and you'll feel it.'

The next minute, the blind musician took off on a practice run, tyres squealing, engine grunting with exhaustion.

'He got right into it,' roars Kellaway. 'Laughing his head off. We had a bit of fun doing that. And then we got the call, "Ah yep, we're ready to get picked up, come pick us up." So I said to Geoffrey, "I'll hide down, and you drive up and pick them up." And so, I was going, "Left! Right!" hiding underneath, just moving the steering wheel a bit. And he's sort of leaned out the window and gone, "Hey, you fellas want a ride?" And Witiyana's gone "What?!"'

This wasn't the first time somebody had given Gurrumul the controls. Former pilot Michael Wyatt tells of the hair-raising time he was flying Gurrumul and some family in a light aircraft from Elcho Island to Biranybirany for a meeting with the band. 'I let Gurrumul fly the aeroplane,' reveals Wyatt. 'He had a wonderful time. He was going up and down, and turning it left and right. And the people in the back started screaming: "He's blind! You can't let him fly! Stop it, stop it!" I said, "Look! We're at 10,000 feet, for god's sake, we can't hit anything." He had a wonderful time, just chucking that aeroplane all over the sky. But it scared the shit out of the people in the back.'

Before the millennium's switchover, Yothu Yindi had also returned overseas to rock Europe on a headlining tour. It was to be their first international sojourn under the watch of tour manager Geoff McGowan. He was in for a bumpy ride.

It began at Frankfurt Airport, where the band members all offloaded their passports onto McGowan for safekeeping. Then came the request: 'Rrupiya ga'!' The boys wanted some of their per diems translated into Deutschmarks so they could do a bit of shopping in the terminal. 'We actually really needed to get on our bus and head off to our first show, because we had a show that night in Cologne,' recalls McGowan. 'Anyway, I went over to the money changer, and pulled out a couple thousand Australian dollars and got it exchanged in Deutschmarks. And while I was doin' it, a guy came and stood next to me, quite a tall bloke, had a really good Armani suit on, long dark hair pulled back … and he was leanin' over the counter lookin' at what I was doing. And I thought, "What's this guy up to?"'

Thinking nothing further of it, McGowan loaded the cash into his backpack, alongside all of Yothu Yindi's passports. Suddenly, out by the buses, two burly men appeared by his side. 'I got mugged!' says McGowan. 'It was violent, and one guy pointed something at me, while the guy behind me removed my backpack, and threw it into the window of a waiting car.'

The muggers took off. Then, Yothu Yindi's tour manager spotted him: standing nonchalantly on the opposite side of the road, the shady bloke in the Armani suit. 'The penny sort of dropped on me, and I thought, "I've just been set up by that guy!" and I screamed out, "I've been robbed!" and all the band just kind of looked at me and just kept gettin' on the bus.' He chuckles. 'So I went after that guy, I charged after him.'

McGowan gave chase through the terminal, 'causing a ruckus', but the crim managed to evade capture. Yothu Yindi had fallen victim to a crime syndicate working the airport. 'Unfortunately, yeah, so they got fifteen or so Australian passports, the bulk of them with Aboriginal faces on 'em, so I don't know what they were gonna do with those,' he says.

With no passports (and no travel insurance!), Yothu Yindi embarked on a chaotic run around the continent, through Germany, the Netherlands, the UK and beyond. 'We had another incident where the trailer on the bus caught on fire,' says McGowan. 'We had an engine bay fire, we had a trailer fire, we were held up with customs.'

By Stu Kellaway's account, the stress finally showed itself when a famished McGowan attempted to pour tomato sauce onto his breakfast and it turned out to be carrot juice. It was a breaking point. But, in McGowan's words, 'we continued on'.

Over their years as an international touring act, Yothu Yindi were privy to some of the most hilarious, incredible and off-the-wall shows and misadventures that it's hard to comprehend them as nonfiction. But they did happen. They played in Bermuda where Sir Edmund Hillary's Mount Everest ice axe was hocked off at auction. A dancer got arrested after chomping into a giant gingerbread house that was reserved for a chef's Christmas function. The band's manager was chased around a Scandinavian hotel lobby with a can opener.

They gigged for German chancellor Helmut Kohl's birthday. Performed to around 100,000 people on a beach in Rio de Janeiro.

'We could play a Koori childcare centre, we could play to Bermuda's 400 richest people, we could play in Bulawayo,' says Cal Williams. 'Didn't matter what the gig was, we had it covered. We could play the biggest rock stage in the world or the Sydney Opera House … We just thought, wow, there's no gigs that we can't do. We can do 'em all. Incredible gigs.'

To Geoff McGowan, 'They are just a brilliant, magic band. It just does something to you when you're touring with them, you know? When they hit the stage, there's a magic everywhere. Something transforms in the venue all the time. People just love 'em.' For McGowan, the magic of that first European tour had somewhat worn off by its end. 'I came back fairly shattered, to be honest. But I couldn't wait to get back into it again.'

Towards the end of the millennium year, Yothu Yindi were preparing to play at the biggest party Australia has ever hosted. They'd be onstage for the globally televised closing ceremony of the 2000 Olympic Games in Sydney, and the opening ceremony of the Paralympic Games, representing the country to a worldwide audience in the billions.

Getting the Olympics had been huge for Australia – and, like the bicentenary twelve years earlier, it had put the spotlight back onto the stories of Indigenous Australians. In spite of the nation's political mood (with Prime Minister John Howard refusing to apologise to the Stolen Generations for the actions of past governments), it was a time of empowerment for First Nations Aussies and their achievements, particularly on the

Mandawuy Yunupiŋu shakes hands with revolutionary former president of South Africa Nelson Mandela at an event in Sydney University's Great Hall in 2000, alongside trailblazing Aboriginal barrister Pat O'Shane (right). *(courtesy of University of Sydney Archives, image G77_4_0372_1)*

sporting field: and Yothu Yindi were helping to provide the soundtrack.

'During the Olympics, they actually used a lot of the music from *Garma* at various events,' says Andrew Farriss. 'I remember sitting there with my family at one of the swimming heats, and a couple of the songs we'd been working on, "Calling Every Nation" was one of them, they played them at the stadium. It was part of that whole experience.'

On 25 September 2000, Yothu Yindi cheered and cried when sprinter Cathy Freeman, a proud descendant of Queensland's Kuku Yalanji and Burri Gubba peoples, won gold in the 400 metres. They'd been taking part in a recorded concert appearance at Moore Park, in Sydney, but paused to watch the milestone race. 'Everyone was so proud of her in the band that night,' says Geoff McGowan.

Away from the track, another strong Indigenous woman was also readying to hit a career-defining moment. Jodie Cockatoo counts being onstage for the Olympics as an all-time high. 'It all just happened so quick,' she says. 'It was a pure adrenaline rush.'

Backstage, the band were surrounded by the other VIPs: celebs, musos and models, who had likewise been handpicked as ambassadors to shine in the spotlight for Australia. 'There was Elle Macpherson, there was Kylie Minogue, and there was Slim Dusty, who I'd grown up and heard from when I was a baby!' says Cockatoo. 'Meeting them, and representing Australia, Aboriginal Australia, on a global stage with the biggest audience you could ever want ... that was the pinnacle, 2000.'

The security manning the Olympic stadium that night was like a trained militia, prepped and ready for any potential terror plot a psycho could try to pull. But, according to the band's tour manager, eyebrows were barely raised when Yothu Yindi rocked up with a gun licence.

'One of the band members from Nhulunbuy was a ranger, and the only ID he had to get into the Olympics was his gun licence,' recounts McGowan. 'We went to the gate to go in and we had to all show our ID, and all he had was this licence for a firearm, which seemed a bit uncanny: massive security around the Olympics and they're letting this guy into the Olympics with his firearms ID!'

On the floodlit stage that October evening, the words of Yothu Yindi's 'Treaty' rang out:

> This land was never given up
> This land was never bought and sold

With more than two billion tuned in (and John Howard in the stands) the political impact of these lines had never packed more of a punch.

For Witiyana Marika, who had largely stepped away from the band since 1993, the closing ceremony marked his triumphant return to the stage. This ceremonial man, who as a teenage dancer had proudly taught his culture to Melbourne schoolkids, was now sharing it with the entire world. 'I was ready. I was recovered. It was one of the biggest concerts I had ever appeared on the stage,' Witiyana says. 'The whole world was watching and Yothu Yindi was there. The impact of Yolŋu power.'

A pride radiated through those onstage. Yothu Yindi showed the world what was possible. How two waters could meet and become one. But if the Olympics was a pinnacle, the crest of a wave, then the band had to prepare for a coming crash. Turbulent seas lay ahead.

19
Fire on the Hill

In the front yard of a home at Gunyaŋara, sitting in a square of shade by a carefully planted flowerbed, Makuma Yunupiŋu recounts some of his life's memorable moments. Jumping in the studio that first time for *Tribal Voice*. 'Pumping the didge' onstage at the Big Day Out until his throat went hoarse. Connecting with fans in nations he'd never even dreamed of. Hunting with his father, Galarrwuy, as a child. Raising up a family with the woman he loves. 'After I had all the fun, after I felt all the pain … mate, look, after about fifteen years, you know, I thought I'd seen it all, felt it all and accepted it all,' Makuma says.

Now in his forties, he's also prepared to speak about the darker turns his road has taken. 'When the unexpected happens, it will put your life on a pause,' he reflects. 'Nobody expects that.'

Makuma's speaking in measured, non-specific terms about a disturbing incident in 2000. A drunken dispute at his home, during which he lashed out and kicked a relative in the head, resulting in her tragic death. Then a trial and conviction. 'Yunupingu was charged with murder and faced mandatory life imprisonment,' wrote Andrew McMillan for *The Age* in 2002. 'In the end, acquitted of murder and manslaughter ... he was found guilty by a Supreme Court jury of doing a dangerous act causing death.' The kick was brutal, but, the jury decided, not premeditated. NT Chief Justice Brian Martin also found Makuma was 'genuinely sorry' for what he'd done and that, 'absent the effect of alcohol you are a polite and well-behaved person who is capable of making plans with others for worthwhile community advancement'.

The former Yothu Yindi musician was sentenced to a three-year stint inside Darwin's Berrimah jail, which was suspended after fifteen months. After his release, he went into exile in Central Australia. As McMillan puts it, Makuma was 'banished to the desert until his victim's family permit[ted] his return to his coastal homelands'.

'I found myself down there for quite a few years, just to isolate myself through customary demand,' Makuma says now on the matter. 'I went through a lot of detox, rehabilitation, a lot of dramatic family changes. Spiritual changes.'

He now appears at peace with it, with a friendly demeanour and a grandkid hopping around his feet. But back then, the episode shocked the Gove Peninsula to its heart. And during the decade ahead, it wouldn't be the only tragic incident to rock the ranks of Yothu Yindi.

But the band wasn't to be overcome. In 2003, they headed out on one of their most exciting tours yet, supporting

Fire on the Hill

Woodstock-era legend Carlos Santana. Through Australia's capitals they wowed huge crowds and reignited the flame of their earlier gigs. Those in the band couldn't quite believe it. On tour with Santana!

'That was huge,' says Jodie Cockatoo. 'My father, in his bands, they used to play that all the time: "Black Magic Woman" ... My dad loved that song. I grew up listening to that song. Next minute, there's Carlos Santana and I'm touring with him! Standin' side of stage watching his gig every night. Woah.'

Each evening during his headline set, Santana would invite members of Yothu Yindi onstage with their yidaki to jam on a medley of Bob Marley tunes, from 'Exodus' to 'Get Up Stand Up'. 'And you know what? He even sang on the mic with me,' says an elated Jodie. 'He came up and sang with me on the mic. Just for a little bit, but far out.'

After the turn of the millennium, Yothu Yindi's personnel had undergone another shake-up. They had a new yidaki player on deck named Danmirrwuy Narripapa 'Nicky' Yunupiŋu, Darwin's Matt 'Marine Boy' Cunliffe on the keys, and the lead guitar was strapped onto a laidback axeman named Robbie James, from the band GANGgajang. Every show during the Santana tour, Nicky would swagger onto the stage and blast his yidaki to an enraptured audience, backed by Santana's world-class ensemble.

'He went onstage and jammed with Carlos Santana, but it was like he didn't give a shit about who he was,' Geoff McGowan laughs of the nightly occurrence. 'He sort of got up there and played his yidaki all the way through a tune, and then he'd just reach forward, pull the mic cable off ... and just sling the yidaki over his shoulder and walk off the stage. I love the way he did that, like, "No big deal. I just played with Carlos Santana, now I'm outta here."'

Robbie James was also on the Santana tour, and remembers a backstage connection between Carlos and the Yothu Yindi band leader — albeit a fairly awkward one. 'Santana would always walk over to our table backstage, and he'd be touting all sorts of philosophies on life,' says Robbie James. 'I sensed a little bit of Santana trying to really learn from [Mandawuy], and connect with Indigenous culture here, but I think [we were] just in band mode backstage. Just having a few laughs and stuff.'

The GANGgajang guitarist had first been conscripted to urgently fill a gap on a 2001 tour of South America. Yothu Yindi's usual strummer hadn't materialised, news of which wasn't transmitted until they were already at the airport, bound for Brazil. The tour was a double-header, Yothu Yindi and 'Sounds of Then (This is Australia)' songsmiths GANGgajang, so it seemed natural to ask for help from the guitarist already onboard. On the plane to Brazil, Robbie James taught himself Yothu Yindi's back catalogue in a 'mad panic' of preparation.

'Got to Brazil, had one quick rehearsal, and then that's that,' says James. 'GANGgajang and Yothu Yindi on the big stages, playing to 5000-seaters, so I had to play in both bands every night, and pretty much winged the Yothu Yindi repertoire for the first couple gigs. But yeah, settled in after a while.'

What began as a stopgap guitar gig transpired into a four-and-a-half-year journey for James, which took him to some of the wildest corners of the world. 'We went to China, we went to the north of Norway – the Riddu Riđđu Festival in the Arctic Circle, North Pole basically – went to Brazil. It was a really busy time, and it was absolutely wonderful,' he says. 'China was such a mismatch of cultures. Walkin' around China with Yothu Yindi and doing gigs was just amazing ... there was a lot of gawking. And it was completely opposite to here: when we played a concert the whole audience was surrounded by police. You're not allowed to show too much emotion. The audience has to pretty much stand there and just not go off at all ... that was very strange.'

At the Riddu Riđđu Festival in 2002, in the far reaches of Norway, Yothu Yindi performed in freezing temperatures alongside some of the world's most extraordinary Indigenous acts, from Mongolian chanzy music to Inuit throat singers. 'Then you had Yothu Yindi from the southern hemisphere, this whole other planet,' says James, chuckling. 'I really felt blessed to have all those experiences.'

As drummer Ben Hakalitz describes it, there was no gig too outlandish for Yothu Yindi. 'This band has played crazy places where no other band has ever gone to,' Hakalitz says. 'We were a rock-and-roll band, then we become a diplomatic band, then we become a band because of somebody's idea on, "Oh, we gotta go play this concert, because we suit this concept and our message is along this line." We'd do shows everywhere, man.'

But away from the stage, not everything was so footloose. Whenever Yothu Yindi returned from tour, it was clear that cracks on the home front were widening. Mandawuy's wife, Yalmay, was stressed by her husband's hard-living lifestyle as a rock-and-roller.

'He was travelling a lot and didn't spend enough time with family, because music was his career. He was married to music.' Yalmay looks back at this tough chapter in their life. 'It was very hard. I had six girls – it was very hard to cope.'

The singer was also drinking heavily. 'The drinking around the community made the life difficult for me too,' says Yalmay. 'Every time he would come home [from tour] he would always go off drinking. And sometimes he would come home, and I know he's home, but he'd go off drinking with family and friends then come home at night time.'

There were raging parties, 'real, full-on loud', and there was always alcohol within arm's reach. 'I was starting to get worried about his drinking,' says Yalmay. 'I tried to stop him, but all he said to me was, "It's my life! It's my life." That's all he said to me. What can I do? What can I say when he said that?'

By 2003, Yalmay says she'd had enough. His behaviour was having an impact on their family. 'I just had enough, so I packed all my things and went out and lived at Yirrkala,' she says. 'I shared a house with one of my teacher colleagues. It was two years we separated. I just couldn't cope with that anymore.'

There were two sides to the story about drinking in Yothu Yindi. On the one hand, it was a spark for bonding between the Yolŋu and balanda families, both on the road and back at Gunyaŋara, where they'd make merry long into the night playing songs, pulling pranks and telling stories by the campfire surrounded by mates, an Esky full of ice-cool VBs at their side. A portrait of unified Australia.

But on the other edge of it, alcohol was having a devastating impact on the band and their communities; some of the effects were immediate and tragic, while others weren't fully apparent until much later on. There were accidents, incidents and, in a heartbreaking climax, there was death. In Makuma Yunupiŋu's case, he blames the disastrous chain of events in 2000 that led to his jail term and exile on one factor: 'It was the grog. The radical blindness of grog,' he says. 'Pushing yourself too far.'

The telltale signs of alcohol abuse had forced their ugly presence into the band even in its earliest years: founding drummer Andrew Belletty still grows emotional talking about it. 'You'd be woken up by the sound of a beer can at seven in the morning in the darkness in the motel room,' Belletty says. 'It was really hard to see that.'

Mangatjay Yunupiŋu, the slender Yolŋu dancer, nowadays regrets the extent of the boozing. He says it was the primary cause of any problems they ever had on the road. 'I didn't like the drinking part of our tour, and most of the time, I had been drinking,' Mangatjay says. 'There was a lot of drinking happening ... it was all this grog; grog this and grog that. Everyone was consumed by grog while consuming it.'

Other Yothu Yindi members talk of how tough it was to avoid alcohol while out on tour and in green rooms around the world – a cool beer was always at hand, and always remained a tempting way to bond with mates and members of other rock groups. 'It's just the nature of the game,' says Stu Kellaway. 'You rock up to the gig from a tour bus in the morning, and there's already beers in the fridge, ready for the rider, and you know, you're having breakfast. You're just surrounded by grog all the time. It's difficult.'

Yalmay eventually accepted Mandawuy's pleas to come back, and the couple reunited in 2005. And while things were on the mend, the same issues continued to come up. 'Things slowly worked out for us,' reflects Yalmay. 'But he still drank a lot. Yow. And I would still tell him, warn him about his health, and he would still say, "This is my life." That's all he said to me, "This is my life." And I would say to him, "You know, I'm married to you. This is my life too."'

Even while performing with Yothu Yindi during this period, Yalmay says her husband would sometimes have a drink or two beforehand to 'make him feel confident onstage. And of course, he gets that from other people too, other people in the position that he was; like Rolling Stones and other singers,' says Yalmay. 'They can do it, he can too.'

By all accounts, Mandawuy could more than hold his own on the sauce – in one instance, bandmates recount an all-nighter he spent boozing at Sydney's Ritz-Carlton bar with Welsh megastar Tom Jones. The pair both resurfaced for TV appearances that same morning. 'Which they proceeded to do with no problems,' says Stu Kellaway. 'It was like two guys with the constitution of rogue elephants, really.'

Fire on the Hill

Just two years after Yalmay and Mandawuy reconciled, they had to deal with a drama that upended their lives once again. Family infighting forced the couple to leave their home at Butjumurru near Gunyaŋara. With their families' houses in Yirrkala fully occupied, Yalmay says they were left with no option but to pack up some personal things and move into a tent on the beach. (Houses in East Arnhem communities, many of them ageing concrete-block homes, are often shared by extended family and friends – overcrowding that contributes to the many hardships faced by the Yolŋu daily, from food insecurity to chronic illness.)

It was terrible timing, as Mandawuy's health was beginning to deteriorate rapidly. Money was also short; in spite of his success, the Yothu Yindi singer had scant savings to his name. 'It was not really good,' recalls Yalmay. 'It didn't suit us in the position that he was in. We didn't have our own house [in Yirrkala] to go back to. We couldn't just go in and move people out.'

After a week or so sleeping rough, they received some distressing news: their home at Butjumurru had been burned in a blaze. While Yalmay says she's never been fully certain about the cause of the fire, NT Police records suggest it was nonsuspicious, the result of a Marngarr Community Council backburn that got out of control. Many of the couple's possessions were destroyed and the house was left uninhabitable. Now they were homeless, and would have to remain in the tent.

'One thing I didn't do during that time, I didn't go to the media,' Yalmay says now. 'Because my mind was so blocked.

I would've gone to the media for housing. I would've taken the media to the beach: "This is where we are, this is where we're living. Under a tent. An Australian of the Year recipient, and look where he is." I would've said that. I just didn't do that. It was later on that I thought about it.' For three months, the pair lived on the beach, out and exposed to the elements. For three months, the singer with a smile to stop traffic drifted further and further into frailty.

In the wake of the Butjumurru fire, the Gumatj Corporation did eventually build a new house for the Yothu Yindi songman, on the crest of a hill in Yirrkala. Once again he and his wife had a home. But by then, Yalmay believes, the singer already knew: something was going seriously wrong with him.

Mandawuy Yunupiŋu receiving the 1992 Australian of the Year award from Prime Minister Paul Keating at Admiralty House in Sydney, 26 January 1993. (Michael Amendolia/Newspix)

Yothu Yindi stage a media promo during a tour in Europe, 1994. From left: Mangatjay Yunupiŋu, Jodie Cockatoo, Bunumbirr Marika, Mandawuy Yunupiŋu, Ben Hakalitz, Natalie Gillespie and Witiyana Marika. *(Franziska Krug/Getty Images)*

Mangatjay Yunupiŋu, Witiyana Marika and Jodie Cockatoo hit the streets of Paris during some downtime from a European tour in 1994. *(courtesy of Yothu Yindi)*

Bassist Stu Kellaway and drummer Ben Hakalitz, who first met and became mates at a concert in Papua New Guinea, pictured together in Paris, 1994. *(courtesy of Yothu Yindi)*

Yiḏaki player Yomunu Yunupiŋu – son of former dancer Malati – with band leader Mandawuy Yunupiŋu, during a concert in Johannesburg, South Africa, in 1996. *(Michael Amendolia/Newspix)*

Yothu Yindi members Malŋay Yunupiŋu and Mandawuy Yunupiŋu with, at right, songman Grant Ngulmiya Nundhirribala, the leader of the Red Flag Dancers from Numbulwar, performing 'Treaty' onstage at the Sydney Olympics closing ceremony on 1 October 2000. *(Martin Philbey, Redferns/Getty Images)*

Jodie Cockatoo, Mandawuy Yunupiŋu and Aussie music legend Billy Thorpe perform Thorpe's hit 'Most People I Know (Think That I'm Crazy)' at the Paralympics opening ceremony in Sydney, 2000. *(Jamie Squire/Getty Images)*

Yiḏaki player Danmirrwuy Narripapa 'Nicky' Yunupiŋu stuns the crowd – and Carlos Santana – during a performance with the Woodstock-era legend in 2003, while Mandawuy looks on. *(David Sproule/Newspix)*

Mandawuy and Yalmay Yunupiŋu together in 2012, during a tough period when the singer was battling end-stage kidney disease. *(Amos Aikman/Newspix)*

Yothu Yindi (with Paul Kelly and Peter Garrett) at a press conference in the Sydney Entertainment Centre after being inducted into the ARIA Hall of Fame in 2012.
Back: Witiyana Marika, Kelly, Garrett, Mangatjay Yunupiŋu, Ben Hakalitz.
Front: Malŋay Yunupiŋu, Mandawuy Yunupiŋu and Jodie Cockatoo. *(Matt Garrick)*

An all-star performance of 'Treaty' at Yothu Yindi's ARIA Hall of Fame induction at the Sydney Entertainment Centre in 2012. From left: Cal Williams (obscured), Geoffrey Gurrumul Yunupiŋu, Paul Kelly, Jessica Mauboy, Ben Hakalitz, Witiyana Marika, Mandawuy Yunupiŋu, Stu Kellaway, Mangatjay Yunupiŋu, Dan Sultan, Malŋay Yunupiŋu (with yidaki, but obscured by Dan Sultan), Jodie Cockatoo and Peter Garrett. *(Matt Garrick)*

Prime Minister Kevin Rudd offers condolences to Yalmay Yunupiŋu at a state memorial service for Mandawuy at Gulkula, the Garma site, in June 2013. *(Matt Garrick)*

Witiyana Marika performs onstage at a tribute concert to Mandawuy at the National Indigenous Music Awards in Darwin, August 2013, alongside the late singer's two-year-old grandson Guruwuk Munuŋgurr. *(Matt Garrick)*

Paul Kelly and Witiyana Marika, surrounded by painted warriors, unveil a plaque dedicated to Mandawuy in his sacred homeland of Biranybirany, in June 2018. *(Matt Garrick)*

Witiyana Marika and singer Yirrŋa Yunupiŋu (with Mandawuy's grandson Guruwuk Munuŋgurr on yiḏaki) performing live with Yothu Yindi at the Yirrkala Yarrapay Festival in June, 2021. *(Michael Franchi)*

Treaty, acrylic on bark, 2018, by Dhambit Munuŋgurr. Despite suffering severe injuries in a car accident in 2007, which have since confined her to a wheelchair, Mandawuy's niece Dhambit Munuŋgurr has gained national recognition as an artist. Showing Yolŋu dancers moving through a group of non-Indigenous people sitting on chairs, *Treaty* references the Yolŋu struggle for recognition and the push for a treaty between black and white Australia. The larger dark figures represent members of Yothu Yindi: from left to right and top to bottom, Dhambit's son and yiḏaki player Gapanbulu Yunupiŋu, her Uncle Mandawuy, Stu Kellaway playing his bass guitar, Witiyana Marika with his bilma, backing singer Jodie Cockatoo, Gurrumul Yunupiŋu on keyboards, and Ben Hakalitz playing the drums. *(courtesy of the artist and the Buku-Larrŋgay Mulka Centre, Yirrkala)*

20
Yolŋu Medicine

It was during a funeral ceremony at Biranybirany that Yalmay realised her husband wasn't telling her the full story about his health. He was off the drink but still woozy and fatigued. 'He was already diagnosed with kidney disease,' Yalmay's now certain. 'He wouldn't tell me, he kept it secret. But I heard it from a nurse.'

Mandawuy had agreed to spend some time in a Sydney rehabilitation facility to help treat his alcohol dependency. While there, doctors had discovered an equally pressing issue. 'As part of the assessment we do a routine blood screen,' psychiatrist Dr Oliver O'Connell told ABC's *Australian Story* in 2009. 'And that ... screen indicated to us that his kidneys had failed.'

While the jury remains out on whether habitual drinking is a direct cause of kidney failure, Mandawuy's doctors say that in his case there was certainly a link between the two. 'We think his chronic kidney disease is due to his diabetes and high blood pressure, which would've been there for some years before being identified,' said Dr Paul Lawton, then the NT's renal services director, on *Australian Story*. 'Alcohol doesn't cause kidney disease. Alcohol dependence, however, makes it very hard to have your other health concerns managed.'

The singer had conceded he was drinking 'between one and four cartons' of beer each day. 'I was just doin' it because I was a rock-and-roll star,' Mandawuy told *Australian Story*. 'That was basically what comes with the job, you know? The drinking came with the singing and stuff like that. But at that time I was young and stupid and didn't quite know [it] would lead up to a kidney failure, in my case.'

The news wasn't pretty. Neither was the name: end-stage kidney disease. It was the beginning of a gruelling journey for Mandawuy and his family, one that saw the singer forced to leave his country in Arnhem Land and live in the concrete backstreets of Darwin for renal dialysis treatment. The constrictive regime of dialysis meant he was hooked up to a machine that operated on behalf of his kidneys at the Nightcliff renal centre three times a week. Due to his advanced illness, his chances of being green-lit for a transplant were low.

'It was really difficult for us to leave, because we didn't have enough money,' says Yalmay. 'Only money that I had was my [teacher's salary] because I was on leave with pay. Lucky. The money that he earned from the band [was gone]. We were moving a lot in Darwin, trying to get a good house for him to live in. At one point, he wanted to get his superannuation money out, to use that money to support him while living in Darwin.'

The family had given dialysis a crack back in Yirrkala – but the singer hadn't properly complied with his treatment. In September 2008, he ended up in a bad way, and was airlifted to Darwin on the brink of a heart attack. They would have to stay in the capital. For the next four or so years, the singer and his wife would endure not just the cultural barriers and bureaucracy of the NT's healthcare system, but also the pain of being separated from their daughters and their land, and the indignity of being forced to live in lousy, cheap housing.

'Rirratjiŋu [Aboriginal Corporation] helped us with accommodation,' says Yalmay. 'Yothu Yindi band, AJ, helped us with the money that he earned from the band. It was just very difficult for our kids to come into town and stay with us. It was good having them around, but then again, it was just difficult, very hard, because the house was too small, too crowded. I was obviously looking after a sick man and that was my main concern.'

In a brick dogbox on Nightcliff Road, the Yunupiŋus sweated through the heat of Darwin's build-ups with inadequate aircon and a lack of working facilities.

Mandawuy's niece Rarrtjiwuy Melanie Herdman was living nearby in Rapid Creek during the period when her uncle was tied to the dialysis machine, around 2008. She'd take him out to his favourite café, the Fannie Bay Cool Spot, where he'd sit silently over cappuccinos. 'You don't need to talk to know that you're appreciated by someone,' Herdman says. 'And I enjoyed that. I wasn't told, but I knew that he appreciated me being there.'

Alongside his physical condition, Mandawuy's emotional state had also taken a dive. 'Again, it's that non-verbal stuff,' says Herdman. 'You can look at someone and know that he doesn't want to be here, he wants to be back home. But because of this treatment that he had to have, three times a week, he wasn't able to.'

In Yalmay's words: 'his soul was crying for home'.

According to family and friends, his circumstances saw him slide into a deep depression. 'You're [a] waning star, no longer as famous and sought after as you used to be, you can suffer a bit of deprivation from that,' Alan James told *Australian Story*. 'But I also think that a lot of it was the amount of premature deaths that he's had to deal with in relation to immediate relatives and friends over the years. That's enough to make anyone depressed.'

This devastating and near-daily parade of death in the Yolŋu community had hit Yothu Yindi for six. In the space of a year, between 2007 and 2008, the group lost three past and present yiḏaki players to suicide, sending ripples of grief through the band and their families. The first was the death of their original yiḏaki maestro Milkayŋu Munuŋgurr in July 2007. He'd ended his life at home in Gunyaŋara after a struggle with alcoholism and depression. Bandmate Witiyana Marika, who was inseparable from Milkay in their teenage years and through some of their earliest performances as Yothu Yindi, says the loss 'just killed my spirit. It hit me. I cried and cried one week for him. He was my beloved young brother.'

Witiyana explains the impact Milkay had had 'right across Arnhem Land. He was a master. All the young people, Yirritja and Dhuwa, they were a fan of him, you know? Every time he would go to Elcho, they would follow him. Every time he'd enter Milingimbi, people would sit around and listen to him. He could draw the people ... Then jumping in Yothu Yindi, oh mate, he'd just blow them away.'

Later that year, another talented yiḏaki player, Yomunu Yunupiŋu, who played on albums including *One Blood* and was the son of former dancer Malati, also fell to suicide. 'He was one of the younger generation to join Yothu Yindi,' says Witiyana. 'He was very skilled, very talented, and he was gone too quick.'

Little more than six months afterwards, the band's current didge player, Danmirrwuy Narripapa 'Nicky' Yunupiŋu, would also be gone. He was involved in a shocking incident that left a young woman hospitalised. It had come just hours after the Gumatj man had danced at a ceremony in front of then prime minister Kevin Rudd.

'Within hours of the event in north-east Arnhem Land ... Nicky Yunupiŋu was dead, a 23-year-old woman was in hospital with multiple stab wounds and an entire Aboriginal community was stricken with grief,' wrote Darwin reporter Lindsay Murdoch for the *Sydney Morning Herald*. 'Police are investigating a tragic chain of events before the death of the 26-year-old didgeridoo-playing member of Yothu Yindi, Australia's best known indigenous band, who danced shoulder to shoulder with his famous uncle [Galarrwuy] in front of the Prime Minister and cabinet on an oval in the tiny community of Yirrkala.'

Once again, the peninsula's communities had been torn apart by a grog-fuelled incident. While the victim luckily survived the stabbing, the musician, apparently believing he'd killed her, took his own life. How, why and what exactly happened became the subject of a coronial inquest. But, whatever the findings, by this stage a few things were already certain. Another young man was dead, a woman had been badly injured, and multiple families had been sent into a spiral of mourning. It was a full-blown community crisis.

By the end of the decade, Mandawuy Yunupiŋu's depression was worsening. Friends say his compliance with the renal treatment remained poor, and his mood towards visitors was often surly and dark. For a handful of years, he hardly even strummed a guitar. 'He was getting so depressed,' says his old friend Kathy McMahon. 'Like, I went and got the guitar [for him] and he nearly smashed it. Got someone to bring it in, and said, "Oh look, [you can] do some music." And he basically just said, "Get out."'

Even if he hadn't wanted music to lean on, Mandawuy had been kept occupied with his role successfully helping steer the Yothu Yindi Foundation. But in 2010, that all changed. A vote for chairmanship of the foundation was clinched by his brother Galarrwuy.

'We had a board meeting where we voted for a chairman, and he wanted to stand for chair again, my husband,' says Yalmay. 'And we had a TV link-in, a teleconference. Galarrwuy and others who supported him sat on the other side, and we were on this side in Darwin. [Mandawuy] had a small group of people that supported him, but then in the end, he [Galarrwuy] won the vote. My husband got up and was so upset, because he wanted to take the chair again, and walked outside. Because he knows that this is his foundation. Then he walked out very upset.'

Those close to Mandawuy say the vote came as a complete shock to them. It also had lasting ramifications for the singer's relationship with his older sibling, his clan's leader. The brothers rarely, if ever, spoke again.

Mandawuy was essentially ousted from the organisation he'd set up with Alan James two decades earlier. James says a 'transition of power' took place, and he and Mandawuy resigned. The Garma Festival, which they'd painstakingly helmed since its inception, had fallen through their hands like sand.

'What I'm proud of is, prior to Mandawuy and I resigning from the foundation that we created and basically built over twenty years ... we did a comprehensive business plan and succession plan, such that when we did leave, it was left in a manner that was sustainable and has proven to be sustainable, in that it still continues today,' James says now. 'I think that in itself is a measure of success.'

Losing his handle on the foundation was a final straw for Mandawuy, says Kathy McMahon. 'He was so devastated by the loss of the foundation,' she says. 'It was bloody horrible. He went down from there.'

Just a decade earlier, the Yothu Yindi singer had been standing in the Great Hall of Sydney University, talking and smiling with South Africa's president, Nelson Mandela, and Australia's prime minister, John Howard. By 2010 he was living basically anonymously in the NT capital.

Mandawuy told *Australian Story* he 'sometimes [felt] like it's not worth it in Darwin. This machine, the motorcars, the aeroplanes and all the things that I hear here. Not the clapsticks and the shouting of the grandsons.' Like so many of his Aboriginal countrymen, he'd fallen prey to incurable kidney disease, and was trapped like a mouse in the Territory health system's endless spinning wheel of appointments and treatment, far away from home and loved ones.

But a chance did wander into his life to rekindle a musical partnership, to hold his guitar proudly once again. He and INXS co-founder Andrew Farriss reunited and co-wrote a song about his struggles with kidney disease and treatment, about bush medicine and its healing power. A song that Farriss says is about 'ancient methods' of healing that he watched the elders use on Mandawuy out at Gulkula to try to rid him of his internal afflictions.

'Some of the elder women ... had set up what almost looked like graves dug in the ground,' says Farriss. 'They would put pandanus leaves and palm leaves down in the dirt, and then they would heat it up with rocks and things, then they'd kind of lay you in there, to try and kill whatever bugs or things [were] in you that were hurting you. They were trying these sort of ancient healing methods, and so, Mandawuy and I worked on a song together called "Healing Stone", because of the stones that they'd put in the earth.'

INXS co-founder Andrew Farriss with regular collaborator Mandawuy Yunupiŋu at the Garma festival site, circa 2007. The pair co-wrote numerous songs including 'Healing Stone', which was released in 2012. *(Jamie Hanson/Newspix)*

Writing in the Sand

Lay me down in a bed of leaves
Cover me with paperbark
Let me feel the heat
From the healing stones
Sweet aroma, pandanus seed

Give me medicine
Strong medicine
Healing medicine
Yolŋu medicine

The collaboration marked the first fresh Yothu Yindi song in a decade. In 2012, the band released a 'best of' compilation with the new track as its title. In the album's liner notes, they speak of the song's importance: 'it's as culturally urgent, profoundly personal and ultimately universal as any song in the world-renowned Arnhem Land band's twenty-seven year history'. 'Healing Stone' was the final tune on the new album: it was also the last new song that Mandawuy Yunupiŋu would release in his lifetime.

21

The Drummer

With Mandawuy crook from kidney disease, Yothu Yindi were on something of an indefinite hiatus. But as one star began to wane, another was burning brightly in the East Arnhem sky. The singer's wäwa from Elcho Island, who'd joined Yothu Yindi as their drummer at just eighteen years old, was beginning to forge a solo career. Geoffrey Gurrumul Yunupiŋu would soon cross borders of language and trends to stun music fans the world over with his mesmeric, high-floating tenor and his upside-down right-handed guitar. 'Unbelievable ... one of the most unusual, emotional and musical voices that I've ever heard,' star US producer Quincy Jones would one day famously describe him.

Even when he was a teenager drumming for Yothu Yindi, those who were in his vicinity say there was something extraordinary about Gurrumul's musical abilities. During rehearsals for the band's *Tribal Voice* album in Darwin, Allen Murphy recalls seeing him in action. 'I was kind of running the studio at the time, and the guys were rehearsing up there, and they had this young blind kid on drums whose name was Gurrumul,' says Murphy. 'And he was playing didge and drums at the same time, while they were playing these songs. And I was going, "What the hell is this?" And he was playing really well!'

From his earliest years growing up on Elcho, Gurrumul had been making beats and sounds from found objects – at times so ceaselessly it would drive his neighbours up the wall. 'He used to bang on anything,' says Sue Reaburn, a former teacher and store-worker trainer who lived across the road from Gurrumul in Galiwin'ku community in the early 1980s. 'He would turn saucepans upside-down, and you know those Sunshine milk containers, lid on, lid off, on the side, he used to just drum. And every so often you'd hear someone screaming, "Shuuuut uppp, please!" Because he'd do it all day and all night.'

Reaburn says one day she discovered a gift suitable for her young neighbour, the drummer, the blind boy who in those days was still simply called 'Miltjiri'. 'I got him a little harmonica thing from school, you know, one of those ones that you blow and it's got a keyboard on it,' she says. 'Just so that he wouldn't drum so much. So he played that a lot … his ability to drum and just pick up music was extraordinary.'

Not long after he'd begun playing with Yothu Yindi, it became evident that Gurrumul wouldn't stay satisfied relegated to the role of timekeeper. 'About a year after he joined, he said he didn't want to go on tour anymore,' says Alan James. 'And I was like, "What? Why not?" and he said, "Well, I don't

The Drummer

like drumming. I like keyboard." And I was like, "What? You can play the keyboard?" and then there was this discovery over time, of course, that he could play everything. So, within another tour or so he was onstage with a guitar, a keyboard and a vocal mic.'

In the studio, Gurrumul was wildly inventive, meticulous, and would sometimes spend hours tinkering to perfect a single sound. 'He had this thing that he used to do with a Coke can,' says *Tribal Voice* producer Mark Moffatt. 'You know how a Coke can tab makes a noise when you flick it? He'd play this thing and cover the hole up with his finger, and he'd play this rhythm by flicking, like a *kalimba* African thumb piano, and make it kind of tremolo by moving his finger up and down on the opening of the Coke can. It was pretty incredible. I've tried it a few times, and the thing breaks off, or my thumbs aren't agile enough.'

Decades since he watched Gurrumul at work on *Tribal Voice* in the early 1990s, Moffatt says he now realises he was witnessing something special. 'This kid had one sense missing which had blown all the others up, big time, particularly his sense of hearing,' believes Moffatt. 'Just stuff like what he could hear, and what he could sing, and how he sang. I never thought about him having a solo career at that point, but when it happened I thought, "Well that was bound to happen." He was just so loaded with talent. But being sightless really did expand his other senses, particularly his musical ability and his ability to hear something and replicate it. Pretty amazing.'

With Gurrumul off the skins, by 1991 Yothu Yindi had eventually settled on session muso Huey Benjamin as their drummer. Benjamin recalls rocking up for an afternoon rehearsal with the band in Yirrkala: what he dubs his 'baptism of peace and patience in the red dirt' after the group failed to show up until hours after their scheduled meeting time.

Eventually, when most of the players had assembled, he was briefed by his new bandmates. 'Stuey and Cal had sort of said, "Hey, wait till you see, we've got this kid, our secret weapon, he's like the Stevie Wonder of Elcho Island. He's really amazing."' says Benjamin. 'You get a bit used to hearing that someone's pretty incredible and they can play like a motherfucker, and you're just like, "Yeah, that's great, great." But I wanted to see it with my own beady little eyes. And anyway, [Gurrumul] arrived the next day, one of his little brothers brought him into the room. He was playing keyboards and guitars. And immediately – immediately! – especially when he was playing guitar, things had a different sort of dimension ... it kinda felt like, "This is the missing link! This is really the gel that's gonna hold it all together."'

Touring with Yothu Yindi also presented Benjamin a chance to hang with Gurrumul and properly get to know this man he describes as 'one of the funniest motherfuckers you've ever met. He was the most wicked impersonator, especially of all the guys in the band,' Benjamin laughs. 'He was absolutely hilarious. Cheeky as anything. You know, when he was in a good mood and wasn't too homesick, he was just a joy to be around. I'm going to break into a hideous cliché, but they really did break the mould when they made that guy.'

In the mid-1990s Gurrumul withdrew from touring with Yothu Yindi, though he would remain a presence in their music right through to their final album, *Garma*. By the late 1990s, he was stationed back on Elcho with a new band on the go. This group, Saltwater Band, comprised Yolŋu musicians he'd known since childhood.

An abundance of natural talent, coupled with Gurrumul's experience touring and recording with Yothu Yindi, meant Saltwater Band learned quickly. They grew tight, playing a fusion of sweet saltwater ska, roots, reggae and traditional grooves, and made a name for themselves gigging throughout the Territory.

'We had a competition at a Galiwin'ku festival, and we won a prize to make an album,' says the outfit's co-founder and co-frontman Manuel Dhurrkay. 'And that first album, it just took us. From that we went everywhere … and Geoffrey, he just stuck with the Saltwater Band. He didn't return to play and join with Yothu Yindi again. And Geoffrey lift the Saltwater Band up, like that …' Dhurrkay motions with his hand: up, up into the air. 'Yow. And then me and Geoffrey together writing songs, and helping each other with vocal harmony, and getting Geoffrey's cousin brothers for more choruses. And you know, it was like, "How did we end up here?"'

Another Saltwater Band original, a family member of Gurrumul's named Johnno Yunupiŋu, says he owes his life to the man. '[For a] long time, I was a petrol sniffer,' says Johnno. 'And [Gurrumul] told me, "Ay, Johnno, come here. I want to talk to you." He said to me, "Stop sniffing petrol. Stop sniffing. That's bad for you. Come and join me. I can teach you how to sing."' The former Yothu Yindi band member took his younger relative under his wing. He helped Johnno hone his vocals. They put in hours practising harmonies, singing high, singing low. 'And here we are,' says Johnno. 'Right now, I'm a singer [thanks to Gurrumul].'

In 1996, an NT University (now called Charles Darwin University) music lecturer named Michael Hohnen had travelled out to Elcho Island accompanied by Yothu Yindi's original guitarist, Cal Williams. It was here during a band workshop that Hohnen first clapped eyes on Gurrumul. This introduction would eventually lead to the most illustrious chapter of both men's musical careers, taking them on an unprecedented international journey together, to set foot on the world's great stages.

'Gurrumul knew Cal really well, because they'd toured together and worked together for years, and so there was basically no need for sussing each other out,' says Hohnen from the headquarters of his Darwin-based independent record label, Skinnyfish Music. 'It was just straight into music making.'

The collected musos at this workshop became the earliest, unnamed incarnation of Saltwater Band. And the track they recorded there would mark the first collaboration between Hohnen and Gurrumul, long before they became musical partners – Hohnen with his double bass and broad smile and Gurrumul with his dark jacket and silent stage presence – even if they weren't aware of this meeting's significance at the time.

Hohnen worked on Saltwater Band's debut, *Gapu Damurruŋ*, then set up Skinnyfish with Galiwin'ku town clerk Mark Grose in 1999 to release it and other Elcho Island music.

By Saltwater Band's third and final album, *Malk*, Hohnen could picture a future for Gurrumul outside of the group.

The Drummer

They were recording at Melbourne's Sing Sing studios, when a chance emerged for the musician to shine alone. 'There were times where the rest of the band would go off and [Gurrumul] would just stay there by himself in the studio,' says Hohnen. 'And so, there's a couple of solo tracks on that record [and] during that time I talked to him about going solo. And when he eventually said yes, we flew [back] to Melbourne and did it.'

Gurrumul's self-titled solo debut was recorded in four or five days in Audrey Studios in 2007. Here, the musician was laid bare – no Yothu Yindi or Saltwater Band around him, just a guitarist and his voice. That voice. A voice that seemed to hark from another realm. 'The vision was just to make this absolutely beautiful record that we really stripped back and basically just let you hear him sing,' says Hohnen. 'And that's what ended up happening.'

Skinnyfish had other projects on the boil, and for a while, Gurrumul's first solo outing sat on the shelf. But Hohnen knew that something rare lay waiting. They finally did reopen it and added the finishing touches to what he describes as a 'very special, natural project'. The album *Gurrumul* was released in 2008.

The public reaction – as Hohnen puts it – turned into a 'phenomenon'. 'It unfolded quite quickly,' he says. 'There was a real groundswell. Then we did the ARIA Awards [in 2008] and when that ARIA award happened, that was really the moment.' *Gurrumul* won the award for best independent release. After backstage prompting from promoter Michael Chugg, the reluctant public speaker even offered a few words of acceptance in Yolŋu Matha: 'Yow Galiwin'ku ŋunhi nhuma ga nhäma family, ga dhuwana ŋarra märraŋal award dhuwal Sydney, yow thank you.' It was met by rousing applause from the music industry crowd.

'Sydney kind of runs the music industry in Australia, and to wake up in Sydney the next morning after the ARIAs, everyone was going, "This is going to be pretty big,"' says Hohnen.

Within just a couple of years, Gurrumul had hit some of the highest pinnacles in the Australian arts world, not least being the subject of an Archibald Prize–winning portrait in 2009. In the ensuing decade he would nab a crate of National Indigenous Music Awards, APRA Music Awards and ARIAs (including, tragically, posthumously as Best Male Artist in 2018).

He was also in high demand from the best songwriters in the Antipodes. Crowded House's Neil Finn counts himself lucky for having had an opportunity to perform with Gurrumul 'on a bitterly cold night in Western Australia. He didn't come out of his tent – they had a tent with a heater in it for him, because he was really, really feeling the cold,' says Finn. 'He almost couldn't make it onto the stage, because he was very cold sensitive. But he did and we sang together, it was really memorable.'

Gurrumul joined Finn from behind the piano to accompany him on a Crowded House classic. '"Better Be Home Soon" was the song that he wanted to do, and it was a really sweet rendition,' says Finn. 'It was a beautiful night. Cold, but beautiful.'

Paul Kelly also shared moments with Gurrumul – the musician he'd first met as Yothu Yindi's teenage drummer

Geoffrey Gurrumul Yunupiŋu's solo career started to take off after the 2008 release of his self-titled debut album, *Gurrumul*. He's pictured here playing in Adelaide's Botanic Park at WOMADelaide, 2012. *(Matt Garrick)*

sitting out by the sea at Biranybirany. In 2015, the pair collaborated on a version of 'Amazing Grace' for Gurrumul's *The Gospel Album*. Sung in his native Yolŋu Matha and interwoven with Kelly singing the traditional lyrics in English, the hymn could melt the hearts of hardened criminals. But the recording also came with its difficulties. For one thing, it was done remotely – Gurrumul had recorded his sections at a studio in Perth and Kelly was then tasked with completing his vocals separately, thousands of kilometres away.

'That was one of the hardest recordings I'd say I've ever done,' Kelly reveals. 'It's a song that doesn't really suit my vocals, or my vocal range. You think "Amazing Grace" is a simple song. In some ways it is, but it's a song made for great singers. Which I don't consider myself that kind of singer. I think my voice is good for the songs I write, and some other songs, but that's a tough one. And also, up against [Gurrumul]! It's sort of like stepping into the ring. You think, "Alright – can I last three rounds? Can I even hold my own here?"'

Gurrumul's rise was meteoric. And like meteors, it was visible to the broader public for just a short fragment of time. But in the ten years of Gurrumul's solo career, the man born blind and without a birth certificate on a remote tropical island played for President Barack Obama and Queen Elizabeth II, and sang with Sting, Briggs and Delta Goodrem. He met many of his own musical heroes, from Vince Gill in Nashville to Stevie Wonder in the UK.

'That was amazing,' Hohnen says of meeting the 'Superstition' singer. 'We went to his dressing room ... he had his big keyboard there and they sort of hung out. But, the thing about Gurrumul was, he would never initiate conversation. So, no matter who it was – if it was Obama, if it was Stevie Wonder, Cliff Richard – you'd get in a room and it was up to them to make the conversation. It was completely [awkward].'

Even if small talk wasn't his thing, there was something transcendent in his voice and music. Something that comforted humans in their hardest moments. 'When his first album came out, the people that responded to it the most, the ones who publicly spoke to us, were either those that had just lost someone or were dying themselves or people who just had babies,' Skinnyfish co-founder Mark Grose told journalists after Gurrumul's death in 2017. He spoke of how entire maternity wards had been soothed by his songs.

'Princess Margaret Hospital in Perth would play his album for the whole nursery,' said Grose. 'It certainly calms children. I can't explain it, I don't think anyone can. For whatever reason his music does have an impact. It's something that touches everyone. It's honest music. It's heartfelt. It's straight from a culture that has a deep beauty and has something in it that us whitefellas don't understand.'

Even if the bulk of the Australian population didn't fully grasp where this music was coming from, thousands felt that beauty, and sought out his songs. His posthumous final album, the stirring *Djarimirri (Child of the Rainbow)*, flew to number one on the ARIA albums charts. It was the first record sung entirely in an Indigenous Australian language to debut at the top of the pops. As Mandawuy had done before him, Gurrumul Yunupiŋu had taken the Yolŋu voice to the nation's highest platforms. And his was a voice that soared. A voice that still cuts raw through the hearts of those who loved him dearly.

'Sometimes I cry, when I feel alone, I think about Geoffrey,' says his wäwa Johnno Yunupiŋu. 'Every time I put his music [on] I start crying … The songs are powerful. Geoffrey's songs. Every time I'm on the stage, every time I sing, I'm crying my heart. And I can feel it. That he's sitting next to me. Right side. Every time, I feel it. Sitting next to me on the right side.'

Whether on a milk crate playing to children in the outback or to a packed Carnegie Hall, there was a note in his voice that never wavered. A note of love for family and for home.

22

The New Guard

Music pulsed up the Darwin Amphitheatre hill, carried in drifts of dry season breeze past the gates, mahoganies and figs of the botanic gardens and out towards Mindil Beach. It was a special night. A chance for recognition. An amped and spotlit opportunity for a baton to be passed between musical generations; between family, mentors, students and countrymen. The National Indigenous Music Awards, August 2012, were humming.

The old man looked out from behind foggy eyes. His hair was thinning, greyed. His voice came through soft and slightly stunted. Was this the same person?

Then, a transformation. Revelation. The curling of a smile cracked into his dial and his teeth beamed white against in the night sky. Suddenly he was there – the portrait from the newspaper clippings. The famous, world-shifting rockstar. The educator. The Australian of the Year shaking hands with Mandela, with Muhammad Ali. The charismatic singer with a ceremonial orange headdress tied around his scalp, charming fans worldwide. The frontman of Yothu Yindi stood leaning into a recorder in the busy backstage area behind the fenceline at the NIMAs, talking with a journalist. Artists and fixers bustled to and fro, making sure the night progressed free of typical hitches. The singer had been asked a question about another band – not his own pioneering force – but one following in his footsteps named East Journey. It's his family. They're of his land, his sound, and largely owe their livelihood to his colossal legacy.

'It's really great to see them following Yothu Yindi's footsteps. Rrawun [Maymuru], the lead singer, he's my niece's son, my grandson, and it's good to see them spark a new era,' Mandawuy said into the dictaphone. He was talking about the same relative to whom he used to strum JJ Cale's 'Magnolia' when Rrawun was but a nappy-clad toddler, when he himself was still just a roughshod young guitarist for Yirrkala band the Diamond Dogs. Before life got involved in proceedings. Before everything.

On this night in 2012, Mandawuy would present East Journey with the GR Burarrwanga Memorial Award, effectively handing over the reins to these younger sentinels. As they posed for photos together backstage, the old guard and the new, there was a remarkable feeling of history repeating itself. Young Yolŋu men streaked in gapan and wrapped in nägas, ready to take the stage and thrill the audience with a blend of the traditional and contemporary.

Yidaki and electric guitars. Body paint and black jeans.

Mandawuy Yunupiŋu (third from left) pictured with rising stars East Journey, from north-east Arnhem Land, who were being recognised at the National Indigenous Music Awards in Darwin, in August 2012. *(Elise Derwin/Newspix)*

The influence of their predecessors was unmistakable – and their idol was there beside them, gently pushing them forward. Onstage, as the trophy was transferred to East Journey, each member embraced the Yothu Yindi founder. There was love and pride, and there were glimmers of sadness. Almost, it seems now, a glint of understanding as to what was approaching. It would be Mandawuy's final NIMAs up on that Darwin Amphitheatre hill. The soft breeze blowing the last notes of the night's music out to the Timor Sea. Gatha Munuŋgurr, the drummer for East Journey, thinks back to that award ceremony, that night of song and sweetness, nearly ten years ago. 'I remember being ready to rock and roll – there was a big crowd happening, we could hear, "East Journey, East Journey!" or "Yothu Yindi, Yothu Yindi!"' says Gatha. 'It was emotional, and happiness, and [Mandawuy] was there to keep us strong, to perform with confidence. How to show to people your music with confidence. It's all about that music you're putting up there, what's really happening in your community.'

For more than a decade, Gatha has also donned the uniform as a Dhimurru ranger, working on country to protect his land and sea. He's now in the midst of a career shift, becoming a schoolteacher out on East Arnhem homelands. In the Dhimurru boardroom in Nhulunbuy, he reflects on one of Yothu Yindi's greatest legacies to East Arnhem Land: the gift of inspiration and mentorship to the bands and musicians who followed their trail. Lessons learned and tricks for survival in a tough world.

'Dr Yunupiŋu was always encouraging, always, to every band,' Gatha says. 'I think it's influenced the whole Arnhem

Land, because Yothu Yindi been to everywhere in the world … putting the contemporary with the culture, and always talkin' about the recognition and the Constitution, about what's right. Always putting all the Yolŋu people on the forefront.' Gatha was among a generation of Arnhem Land kids who fired up their own musical skills from childhood after learning from Yothu Yindi and other Top End bands of the era like Blekbala Mujik and Wirrinyga Band.

As Mandawuy's sickness consumed his life, rendering him a forced recluse in Darwin on dialysis, fellow band members including Stu Kellaway, Ben Hakalitz and Buruka Tau stuck to the path and continued supporting, producing, playing whatever they could with whoever needed it, to help musical hatchlings try to bust through and into the mainstream.

A musician named Brendan Marika was one of those. Now in his forties, Marika thinks back to when he was a teenager being roped into a film shoot happening down on the beach in Yirrkala. The crew was making the video for 'Treaty'. Watch it now and you'll see him – the lanky kid clutching a boom box high above his head. 'That man, the one with the camera, saw I was the tallest boy there,' Marika says. 'He said, "You're the tallest one here, so you take the tape player, and everyone will follow you." I got that tape full blast and playing along with "Treaty", everyone just following me.' He laughs, relishing the memory.

But even more so, Marika – a founder of East Arnhem group Garraŋali Band – relishes what Yothu Yindi proved to him was possible: a future in the music industry. A crack at becoming a recording artist and touring muso. That realisation was life-altering. 'Back in those days you thought it was impossible. And then you sort of asked yourself, "If they can do it, why can't we?" So they sort of gave us that encouragement so to speak, you know? And also empowerment to us Yolŋu, and showed it was very important for us to go out there and share our culture. Music is a very powerful message, a universal language.'

Garraŋali Band hails from the remote homeland of Baniyala (Yilpara), where resources can be scarce and the road can sometimes become boggy or even unpassable for days at a time. But they've still managed to release two albums, and continue to be one of the most popular acts across the wide region. It's in no small part due to Yothu Yindi's mentorship.

Stu Kellaway co-produced their 2010 album with Matt Cunliffe, which also featured input from other past and present Yothu Yindi members. 'It was very special,' says Brendan Marika. 'Having idols that we once had when we were young and seeing them perform, it was really encouraging to see them come and be with us as a family member. Because at the end of the day, we're all family. And that's very important to us; to come together and share music, share ideas and learn from them. What they've been through. And to experience that feeling about music … you feel proud.'

Before the curtains drew on 2012, there would be a reunion. A grand re-entry to the Australian music industry's most glittering stage. The red carpet in downtown Sydney. Twenty years since they first rode high at the ARIA Awards, Yothu Yindi were to be inducted into the ARIA Hall of Fame. They would play the song that had made them a sensation.

The New Guard

Mandawuy Yunupiŋu's thrice-weekly course of renal dialysis was an obstacle, but obstacles can be overcome. He would be there, front and centre. 'When we got there he had to go to hospital for his treatment,' says Yalmay. 'Before he was to go onstage they had a dialysis ready for him, in Sydney. It was very good. Everything was organised from Darwin for him, in case anything bad happened there.'

A televised performance of 'Treaty' was to take place, featuring an all-star backing band including the song's co-writers Paul Kelly and Peter Garrett, and supporters of the Territory stalwarts like Jessica Mauboy, Dan Sultan and Andrew Farriss. 'I didn't actually realise there'd be so many people onstage when I was first asked to do it,' says Farriss from country NSW. 'But it turned out to be something that everybody really wanted to be a part of, which I understand. I was just happy to be there and be a part of it, it was a really good thing ... to pay my respects to that awesome man and the band.'

Some familiar faces from Yothu Yindi's history lined the Sydney Entertainment Centre stage for the occasion: Jodie Cockatoo, Cal Williams, Gurrumul, Ben Hakalitz, Stu Kellaway, Mangatjay Yunupiŋu, Witiyana Marika, and Kevin Malŋay Yunupiŋu on the didge. And although his illness was evident and he was clearly frail, Mandawuy held his place as the band leader, the honey sun in the centre of this Yothu Yindi solar system of friends and family.

'It was a mix of feelings, because by that time he looked sick,' says Cockatoo now. 'But you know, his smile [was beaming]. And he had that strength and that honour to do it for his people, his Yolŋu mob: and for himself, too ... and that performance, he gave it his all.'

Jodie Cockatoo and Jessica Mauboy kicked it off, singing out the opening demand of 'Treaty': *clap your hands and dance!* ... and the crowd, which included megastar US muso Taylor Swift, dutifully followed orders. Behind the band as they rocked out, a painted Gumatj crocodile shone on a giant screen. Right there, Mandawuy's life mission to shine a spotlight onto his Yolŋu people, their culture and world view was proven a success. After the performance, Kelly and Garrett gave an emotional account of the life and career of Yothu Yindi, speaking of how they changed Australia's pop music landscape forever by bringing Aboriginal knowledge to the forefront. They then presented the band members with their golden Hall of Fame trophies.

Cockatoo says she 'still can't believe' she has a gold ARIA among her possessions at home. A lifetime in the music business celebrated by the industry and televised to hundreds of thousands of Australians on their couches: she'd come a long way since her days as a shy kid growing up in Cairns. They all had. 'It was another pinch-me moment,' she says. 'It was overwhelming.'

Mandawuy returned to the stage in a wheelchair, then rose to his feet to deliver a powerful acceptance speech, calling for formal recognition of Indigenous Australians in the nation's most important written law. 'As musicians, recognition from our peers is important to us,' said Mandawuy. 'As Aboriginal Australians, recognition from our Constitution is even more important.' In response, the audience gave a standing ovation

Yothu Yindi's frontman Mandawuy calls for greater recognition of Indigenous Australians, during the band's 2012 induction into the ARIA Hall of Fame. From left: Paul Kelly, Stu Kellaway, Witiyana Marika, Mangatjay Yunupiŋu (obscured), Mandawuy Yunupiŋu, Malŋay Yunupiŋu (obscured), Jodie Cockatoo, Gurrumul Yunupiŋu, Ben Hakalitz (obscured), Cal Williams, Peter Garrett. *(Matt Garrick)*

to these pioneers and preservers of East Arnhem Land culture. In a press conference following the band's induction, Mandawuy said he hoped they would continue to write and record music: 'Hopefully we'll get more moments like this happening in the future.'

Sadly, there would be no more moments like this, at least not with the classic line-up. For their band leader, this show would be his last. His kidney disease was progressing fairly fast and, according to his friends, there were whispers from staff at the Nightcliff renal unit in Darwin that his race was nearly run.

Yalmay began pulling out all the stops to get her husband home to Yirrkala from the NT capital. Mandawuy needed a renal nurse and dialysis facilities available to him on country — an option his family had long been told would not be possible. But Yalmay was relentless. In her firing line was one of East Arnhem Land's Indigenous health services, Miwatj Health. She knew they had the ability to help pull it off. She was on the case of one senior staff member at Miwatj in particular, a bespectacled policy officer named Harvey Creswell. 'I'm sitting there quietly in the Gove office and I got a call from Yalmay in Darwin,' Creswell says. 'And she explained to me that Mandawuy was stuck in Darwin on dialysis and was having a terribly hard time. So could we, as a health service, do anything? My first reaction was, well, almost certainly no.'

There weren't enough resources available to fund a dedicated remote community renal nurse for Yirrkala at the time. But the Rirratjiŋu teacher wasn't accepting this as an answer. 'Yalmay kept ringing me,' Creswell says. 'Every couple of weeks I'd get a phone call from Yalmay saying, "What are you doing?" So that forced me to think about it, and I thought, "Well, I really should do something."'

The search for a solution began in earnest. Miwatj staff travelled down to Central Australia to a place called Purple House in Alice Springs, a revolutionary kidney health organisation funded by Pintupi traditional owners from the proceeds of an auction they'd held for their valuable desert artworks. They'd taken matters out of the government's hands, and were paying for renal dialysis facilities themselves, so they could be made available in their remote home communities. 'They were completely inspiring,' says Creswell. 'The Purple House was a non-government organisation set up by the Pintupi to deliver dialysis back in Pintupi communities like Kintore, because they were in the same position [as Mandawuy in Darwin]. They'd had to come into Alice Springs and live there in a miserable place to get dialysis.'

Kidney disease rates remain at crisis point in the NT. Despite concerted efforts, there are simply not enough resources available to cater for the growing list of patients. Reports show that 'the NT has the highest incidence and prevalence of kidney disease in Australia'.

Back in Nhulunbuy, Creswell says Purple House had proven to Miwatj that there was a way to provide full treatment in Yirrkala. But they still didn't have the money to make it happen. 'I was still thinkin', what am I gonna do? How can we get the money? And in the meantime, Yalmay's still ringin' me every couple of weeks. Anyway, to cut a long story short, one sunny morning the accountant came out and said, "Harvey, we've got this Commonwealth Government grant for chronic disease, for $300,000, what should we do with it?"'

It was a Eureka moment. Creswell didn't have to think twice about where the money should go. 'It was just luck. Just luck that there was this money unspent there for chronic disease,' he says. 'That was the big breakthrough.' Miwatj recruited a dedicated renal nurse for Yirrkala named Rowena Stokell. They bought extra technology and transport. The Yothu Yindi singer was coming home.

By late March 2013, Mandawuy Yunupiŋu was returned to his community and into the loving arms of his six daughters, Yikaṉatjpi, Gayili, Guḻumbu, Bulmirri, Gandhurrminy and Dhapaṉbal. Their dad was finally back. 'It had been really tough ... we were all happy to have him back home,' says Dhapaṉbal. 'He was really happy to stay home, all the grandkids were happy, us girls.'

Back on country, surrounded by his kin and speaking his mother *matha* (tongue), there was a change in Mandawuy's mood. The dark demeanour he'd had while stuck in Darwin was lifting.

Under Nurse Stokell's care, he began to comply better with his renal dialysis treatment. 'When I saw him interacting with Yalmay, or when they brought the grandchild in, you know, he was just so happy,' says Stokell, now working in Broome, still in Indigenous renal health. 'I felt very proud for the fact that he could spend that time he had [left] at home ... I'm sure he was, inside, feeling a lot more at peace, absolutely.'

Although ailing, he continued his support for young

musicians coming through the ranks, including his daughter Dhapanbal. He continued discussing ways to improve education outcomes in the bush. Trading stories, songs and secrets. Knowledge. He was now a senior lawman or, as one old lady described him, a *djarrami* – a seer, a visionary – who had spent years focused on following the vision of his elders. He had now reached the twilight of his own story.

Surrounded once more by the hibiscus and casuarina trees of his home, the songman would sit on the sands of Ganarrimirri with his wife and family, eating fresh oysters from the fire and watching the djäpana as the water slowly darkened out on the horizon.

23
Goodbye, Crocodile Man

Out at Raŋi, the beach camp where as a boy Mandawuy ran free along the sand with his Gumatj and Rirratjiŋu families, a moment of reflection is taking place. It's towards the day's tail end, and Witiyana Marika is bent in thinking pose on a busted plastic school chair, looking out to sea. He's just metres from the mouth of the creek called Yirrkala, from which the community derives its name. A place where the fresh water flows out to meet the salt of the bay. As a toddler, Witiyana nearly drowned in that same stream.

'I was just playing around, and my grandmother, she was concentrating on cutting tucker, *ŋatha*, and the stream was flowing fast,' he says as he peers out to the waves. 'And then the current took me. I yelled, and my brothers all ran, and they heard my mum and my grandmother crying. The water was taking me around into the mouth of the river. It was taking

Goodbye, Crocodile Man

me about half a mile. I was just floating and my tummy was full of water. I was three and a half years old. I nearly died there, right there.'

Caught in a ripping current, he was being swept out to the sea. As luck had it, one of Witiyana's kinship brothers, Bangil Munuŋgurr, spotted the child sinking down into the fast-flowing murky water. The man pulled off his shirt, dived into the creek and swam out. He threw his arm around the young boy and hauled him back to the shoreline.

The toddler had ingested plenty of water, but he spluttered and coughed. He was breathing. 'Why was I saved on that day?' Witiyana asks as the sun sets out in the distance.

Not far from this same spot, on 2 June 2013, Mandawuy Yunupiŋu lost his long battle with kidney disease inside his Yirrkala home. It was a complication of the illness. He'd suffered a heart attack, which his family believes was a result of having too much fluid in his system.

'He used to drink a lot of tea, and he was asked to only drink a little tea, not tea that is full,' Yalmay says. 'It was fluid we were really worried about … but he had to drink a lot of tea. He loves drinking tea. It was like it drowned him, that fluid.'

The shock of his death was immediate. It tore through the community like a category-five cyclone.

Witiyana was staying in a house nearby. In the evening, urgent shouts came suddenly through his window. 'I had just had dinner and then started watching television. And then I heard, "Ah, napippi, pippi, uncle, uncle, uncle!" All the girls, Yalmay calls, "Witiyana, Witiyana!", crying crying, "Come, come, hurry up, hurry up! Something's happened."'

He rushed to the scene. 'I ran, and I ran fast. And they said, "There!" and he was lying on the floor. And I just ran and picked him up and held him against me, on my chest. When I got his wrist, I saw he was gone. Ah, I was crying. I cried, I cried.'

Like a towering eucalypt tumbling in the bush, the Yothu Yindi singer, the man of balance, had been felled. He crashed a stark hole in the canopy, then lay quiet. Silent as the soil.

Witiyana says he began hollering out into the air above. 'Ah, my mummy! My mother! Great crocodile! Oh, my mother, the great crocodile, the firestarter! The fire man! Your flame has flown: *luku-warrwarryun*.' Witiyana replays the distressing moment. 'The great fire, flame, gone to join and to connect with the other clans as it is in the songline and creation. That's what I sang. "Ah, my uncle you have gone, you have gone now ... and with the spark of me, the spark of your child, me, we will together fly. My mother, I am your spark, you are my flame, mother!" I cried for him. And Yalmay cried and the children cried and everybody, we all cried there.'

A vast cloak of grief fell over East Arnhem Land.

The news travelled fast to the different clans and corners of the region. The singer, the educator who spoke of unity, the lawman who raised the Yolŋu voice to the highest platforms on the global stage was gone. Family and loved ones gathered at the house where he lay. The media was soon alerted to this tragic news: the boundary-breaking Yothu Yindi singer had passed away at his home. He was fifty-six years old.

Journalists and editors of the press were served a warning – no photos of his face were to be used and the singer's first name was not to be referred to during an undefined period of mourning. This plea from the family was respected by outlets and the news ran out: 'East Arnhem Land has lost an educator, a musician, a brother and a friend,' reported local newspaper the *Arafura Times*. 'Mr M Yunupingu changed the landscape of Australian music and made the rest of the nation aware of Yolngu people and this part of the world.'

Across the eastern seaboard, the nation's leaders reacted. The singer's political friend, Midnight Oil frontman turned Labor MP Peter Garrett, was serving in the House of Representatives. He used its podium to vent the grief of the Yolŋu, of Australia, of himself. 'Today is a day for sorrow but also a day for pride: for the pride all Australians feel in his creativity and character and culture,' Garrett told the Australian parliament. 'The pride we feel in the achievements of his life is a foretaste of what we will feel when the First Australians take their place in the first document of all Australians: not just respect, but self-respect. But that is to contemplate on a future day. For now he is gone and like so many Aboriginal people he is gone too young. He was right: too often words *are* cheap. His death shows us how high a price we all still pay for Indigenous disadvantage.'

Lawmakers from across the political divide followed suit in paying tribute to this crocodile man, this man of fire. This man whose flame burned vividly but was extinguished far too soon.

A state memorial service was announced by the NT government, to be held later that month at Gulkula, the escarpment site where the singer had once dreamed of building

Gumatj leaders and warriors, headed by clan chieftain Galarrwuy Yunupiŋu (centre), opened the state memorial service to Mandawuy Yunupiŋu with a stirring buŋgul at the Garma site, on 30 June 2013. *(Matt Garrick)*

a bush university. It was to be televised nationally. Along with his family, clan groups, bandmates and companions from his many stations in life, dignitaries from across the country showed up, including the surprise last-minute addition of Labor prime minister Kevin Rudd. Rudd's attendance at Gulkula was a shock not least because it came just three days after he'd rolled Julia Gillard in a bloody political spill to reclaim the top job. So last-minute was Rudd's appearance that the service's organisers had hand-drawn a 'reserved' label on a seat for him. At one point during the memorial, a senior Gumatj elder thanked everybody for coming, naming different clan groups and local dignitaries but forgetting to thank Rudd; the man then came back onstage thirty seconds later and offered, 'And thanks to the prime minister for coming!' to a rousing laugh.

In an open-air hall filled with family and friends, speakers remembered Mandawuy as 'one of the nation's great teachers', a 'man of balance' and someone 'who gave the opportunity for the Yolŋu voice to be heard'. The love was great for this man who built bridges towards reconciliation, helped change the face of NT education and blessed the world with memorable music. There were also those in the room who spoke of him as a loving husband, father and family man.

Yalmay Yunupiŋu took to the stage wearing the orange headband of her husband – his sacred Burrkuwurrku, made from the feathers of lorikeets threaded with string. 'He took this headband to the world promoting Yolŋu music, language and culture, in his attempt to bring down white Australian racism,' she told the crowd. 'His headband was a symbol of strength and power, identifying who he was.' In the moving speech, Yalmay looked back at her marriage to Dr Yunupiŋu. 'We had an amazing journey together; growing up, working together in education, teaching in Both Ways curriculum development.'

She said at the beginning of their life together, she'd never expected he would become a globally renowned leader, and she spoke of the impact Yothu Yindi's music had on the planet. 'Yothu Yindi grew up to be a much bigger band, and before too long, they were world famous. On stage there was always didgeridoo players, blowing to the north, south, east and west; spreading his messages of Yolŋu strength, culture and survival.'

Others came onto the stage one by one to pay their respects, including a special performance by Gurrumul Yunupiŋu and his local band, the Y Boys. Peter Garrett MCed the service, as well as joining in to sing with family in a rendition of the hymn 'Just a Closer Walk With Thee'. In spite of their differences towards the end of Mandawuy's life, his elder brother Galarrwuy was a commanding presence throughout the service, and led the Gumatj warriors in a stirring buŋgul.

Mandawuy's relative and spiritual Gumatj elder Djuŋadjuŋa Yunupiŋu said it had been a long journey for his clan and his people: 'Not only Yolŋu and the Territory, but throughout Australia.' Djuŋadjuŋa relayed something once told to him by his famous family member. 'He said to me: catch the rainbow, our mother's clan, before it fades away. Catch the beauty, before it fades away. Let us hold each other's hands and march together, and raise one flag, so we can all call Australia our home.'

Paul Kelly, in a grey suit pinned with a ribbon of yellow, presented a eulogy at the service, which spoke of his friend and fellow songwriter's impact on Australia. By Alan James's account, the musician had been tweaking and perfecting his speech all morning, until just before it was due to be delivered. When the moment came, though, Kelly didn't even glance at his words. 'That music went around the world, in this country and in others,' he said. 'Young people were inspired to pick up their instruments and play. You could see and hear Yothu Yindi's influence everywhere. You could see and hear it directly, in those directly influenced by the band. But their influence was much wider and more subtle than that. Their example gave pride and encouragement to Indigenous bands all over the country. And to all bands and singers and artists, they showed us a way.

'All great art contains contradictions, and struggles to reconcile opposites,' Kelly told the crowd. 'This was Yothu Yindi's daily work, their daily bread. Balance. And we are all richer for it. Balance is the heart of life, it's the heart of art. Balance is the heart of the dance. I thank you, man of balance. I thank you, brother. Long may you dance.'

Like the rains of Biranybirany where Kelly and Mandawuy wrote the first lines of 'Treaty' together, tears were fogging the eyes of those present at Gulkula. The saltwater flowed down their cheeks.

Back in Yirrkala, another tearful celebration would soon get underway. A traditional funeral saw a meeting of yothu yindi clans at the community's ceremony grounds to farewell Mandawuy under Yolŋu lore. Coloured clan flags were

Talented musicians and former Yothu Yindi members Rrawun Maymuru and Gapanbulu Yunupiŋu, with Jodie Cockatoo (right), performing at the National Indigenous Music Awards in August 2013 as part of an all-star tribute to Mandawuy. *(Matt Garrick)*

hung and a semi-permanent structure was built to house the deceased. The funeral featured what attendees describe as some of the 'most powerful' buŋgul they'd ever seen. The weeks of ceremony wound on, and by late August, the clans were preparing to hold a traditional burial to properly return this crocodile man to his ancestral home. However, a tense dispute over where the singer should be interred threatened to cast a pall over proceedings. Disagreements are not uncommon before the burial in Yolŋu funerals, but in this particular case, considering the national profiles of both the Yothu Yindi singer and his family members, the stakes were somewhat higher.

For the sake of unity, the dispute was eventually resolved. Gumatj warriors danced into the Yirrkala ceremony grounds, and the singer's body was transported thirty kilometres back to Gunyaŋara, where he was buried by the sea. Down by the home of his totemic bäru – the saltwater crocodile – the singer rested, burdened by disease no more.

Towards the end of the dry season in 2013, a powerful performance took place at the National Indigenous Music Awards in Darwin. It was the first Yothu Yindi show without its lead singer. There was a spirit in the air at that concert, something profound. A moment of catharsis for Mandawuy's mourning bandmates, and, importantly, for his fans. Witiyana brought Mandawuy's grandson Guruwuk Munuŋgurr onto the stage and the two-year-old danced alongside his relatives. Singers Rrawun Maymuru and Gapanbulu Yunupiŋu did justice to their lost elder on lead vocals. Band members from across the eras were joined under the spotlights by friends and family such as musicians Archie Roach and Shellie Morris and actor David Gulpilil.

In reflecting on the night, Witiyana says, '[Mandawuy's] spirit was in the heart of the people. He was right there present, in his band members, and his nephews and grandchild. It was hard for me. I got emotion, and I cracked out in "Timeless Land" when we sang that. Just broken tears, as I sang along: 'This is a timeless land, this is our land' ... I just cried on the stage as I was singin'. And all the people there, it moved 'em.'

Long after the mourning period, odd little moments can sometimes come firmly into focus. In the weeks leading up to her husband's death, Yalmay Yunupiŋu had noticed a breed of black bird gathering around her home in unusually large numbers. Dozens of crows had taken over a flowering hibiscus tree in the front yard. 'We didn't have crows, that tree didn't fill with crows,' she says. 'And when we came back from Darwin, you know those hibiscus flowers, out in the front there? Those trees were filled with crows, day in, day out. Day in, day out. Crows, every day, crows. And after he's gone, the crows stopped coming. That's one thing that I always think back to. What was that crow telling me? What does it mean? They don't sit here anymore. It was very difficult for us, even him. After he would come back from having dialysis, I would say, "Let's sit outside and have lunch outside." He would simply say no because of the crows. Just sit inside and eat inside. That was the strangest thing that I've come across. What is it? I still ask myself this question. It's very strange.'

In the years since her husband's passing, Yalmay has continued to honour his life in many ways, not least by her

Yothu Yindi musicians Stu Kellaway and Mangatjay Yunupiŋu perform in the Darwin Amphitheatre at the National Indigenous Music Awards in August 2013, as part of a special tribute show to late lead singer Mandawuy. *(Matt Garrick)*

steadfast commitment to bettering education outcomes for Yolŋu.

She's also spent many hours puzzling over signs and symbols that she tries to comprehend. Like the crows. Or a tiny moment of tenderness between husband and wife that happened just hours before he passed away. 'The funniest thing, the night before he died, we were sitting there, there were these friends from Melbourne who'd come and visited us … we had a lot of laughs, we were talking about things in the past. And after they left – I would always say to him, "Do you want me to shave your beard?" and he would say no to me all the time. And it was very strange that night, he got up and went to me and lay down, and said, "Shave me. Shave my beard." And that's the only time he's asked me to shave him. Yow. And again, that's very strange too. A lot of times I sit down and pick up all these puzzles. Why? Why? What happened? What really happened? What does it all mean? And that's why I think that he never really meant to go.'

Little more than four years after the death of the Yothu Yindi singer, Gurrumul Yunupiŋu would also be gone. By 2016, kidney failure had grounded Gurrumul from touring, as it had Mandawuy, and without nurse-assisted renal dialysis on Elcho Island, the musician had become increasingly trapped in Darwin.

Gurrumul had been admitted to hospital seven times in one year after he'd repeatedly skipped dialysis because, as Michael Hohnen told ABC Darwin reporter Jane Bardon in 2017, 'he hated it. He had an enormous support team of family and doctors and an extended social group [in Darwin] and out bush. But some people don't like dialysis, and when he didn't want to do dialysis, he used to hide.' In July 2017, the Elcho Island musician had again left the strict routine of renal treatment, choosing instead refuge with family in the city's northern suburbs.

An itinerant camp in the trees down a dirt track on Casuarina Beach marked the road's end for this saltwater man. After a hospital social worker raised the alarm about his prolonged absence from dialysis appointments, Larrakia Nation ranger Vaughan Williams (a brother of Cal and Todd) tracked him down at the long-grass camp. Gurrumul didn't want to leave the camp, but asked Williams to come back the next day. 'He said, "Come back tomorrow, wäwa. Renal day is Thursday,"' Williams recounts.

In one last urgent push to try to save the singer, Williams returned with three others in the morning. Gurrumul was in a bad way. In a last mercy dash, they delivered him back to hospital care. But it was too late. Kidney disease, on top of existing ailments he'd harboured since childhood, took their fatal toll on the prodigy. On 25 July 2017, he passed away at forty-six years old.

Another tree thundered to the forest floor. The world mourned the devastating loss of another national treasure. 'While publicly reticent, behind the scenes he was known as incredibly funny, compassionate and ambitious,' read the tribute in the next day's *NT News*. 'Despite his blindness, Dr G Yunupingu had a musical vision and forged a singular path that thousands will continue to marvel at for decades to come.'

Both Yunupiŋu musicians, Mandawuy and Gurrumul, carried something special, a certain genius, something perhaps so rare that it's hard to put a finger on exactly what it was. A relative of both men, Djuŋadjuŋa Yunupiŋu, describes them as follows: 'For me, they were two disciples who went out into the world, and preached our culture, our customs, our law, and identified that we Yolŋu, in this part of the continent, still have culture, beliefs, a story to be told to children. Balanda ga Yolŋu.' Yolŋu disciples sent to light a flame in the hearts of those who cared to listen.

While the campfire dimmed after their departures, those who still sit around it now try to sing the songs ever louder, until the dawn cracks above their heads in luminescence – like the great Gumatj gurtha blazing across the sky.

24
A Flame Reignited

It's 12 January 2018: almost thirty years to the day since the young men from Yothu Yindi, blackfellas and whitefellas together, marched through the streets of Sydney protesting the bicentenary in 1988. Now the band is back up onstage.

At the Enmore Theatre in the musical heart of Sydney's inner west, it's a sell-out show. The place is packed with people of different generations, different races, here to see this remarkable act from Arnhem Land return to the stage, twenty-five years since their biggest hit.

They've got a new singer – a nephew of the original frontman named Yirrŋa Yunupiŋu. Standing beside him is Yirrmal Marika, the son of Witiyana, and on the other side of the stage, Dhapan̠bal Yunupiŋu, Mandawuy's musician daughter. They're blasting through the encore, the song that runs through their blood. It's 'Treaty'. And the crowd is going off.

After a few years in the record industry wilderness, there'd been a reconnection of sorts. Gavin Campbell, the former Melbourne nightclub owner and DJ from Filthy Lucre, the genre-bending trio that remixed Yothu Yindi's 'Treaty' to wild acclaim in the 1990s, wanted to tap back into that feeling. It was approaching the twenty-fifth anniversary of the release of 'Treaty' and Campbell had some fresh ideas for a new series of remixes, so he got in touch with Alan James and Stu Kellaway to see if there was anything that could be done.

'I'd been DJing the whole time since the early 1990s, and I'm meeting young DJs, and they'd say to me for years, "Oh, I play 'Treaty'! I played it at such and such," and for a while I didn't believe them. I thought, "Oh, it's too old now,"' says Campbell. 'But lo and behold, it just kept coming at me. And I realised that "Treaty" was really popular still, if not more popular now, because the festival circuit in Australia was so massive. And it's a no-brainer; you play "Treaty" outdoors in Australia and everyone's gonna go off.'

After tracking down the master tapes and (this time!) getting the sign-off from the band, Campbell sent them to a bunch of different DJs who each interpreted the song in their own way. There was a techno mix, a deep house version, a hip-hop reworking.

Yothu Yindi were unsigned by this point – in Campbell's words they were 'defunct'. But with this new project on the go, Yothu Yindi re-signed to Mushroom Records, which via an arm of the company called Bloodlines released a new album of remixes, featuring hip musicians of the new generation like Wicked Beat Sound System and Yolanda Be Cool.

A Flame Reignited

Some of the remixes started to gain traction on the festival circuit, and the request came through to Campbell: 'Gavin, do you think we can do a live "Treaty" moment?'

'And I said, "Okay, leave that with me,"' he says.

The DJ approached Yothu Yindi. They were up for it. They'd rebrand as Yothu Yindi and the Treaty Project and perform remixed versions of their classic tracks. They'd freshen up their line-up with young blood like Yirrŋa and Yirrmal, who would perform alongside surviving original members like Witiyana and Kellaway.

'The band were excited,' says Gavin Campbell of the revival. 'We put together a new concept for Yothu Yindi, which was an electronic thing.'

This new group played one 2017 festival show in rural Victoria, but then the calls kept coming through: Yothu Yindi were back in demand. It turned into a two-year journey for the Treaty Project, which took the band to the Enmore, Melbourne's Hamer Hall, the Byron Bay Bluesfest and the closing ceremony of the Commonwealth Games on the Gold Coast.

'I could still pinch myself,' says Campbell. 'I still can't believe all that really happened. It was extraordinary. I'll confess, there was a couple times at rehearsals and once onstage where I was in tears, because I couldn't believe what I was experiencing, and the audience.'

For the next-generation members of Yothu Yindi, it was a special feeling being up onstage and singing out the music that's been part of their lives since they were babies. For Dhapaṉbal Yunupiŋu, this was coupled with the emotion of missing her father, but she could do it knowing he'd be proud as she carried his life's mission into a new era. 'It was *manymak*, fun on the road with the Treaty Project, working with them, singing all Dad's songs, and joining with all the other band members,' says Dhapanbal. 'It was really amazing to be able to sing Dad's songs onstage and sing with the actual Yothu Yindi band.'

At one of the Treaty Project's most triumphant shows, a return to the grand Hamer Hall in the centre of Melbourne, Dhapanbal joined with singers Emma Donovan and Deline Briscoe to perform one of Mandawuy's earliest songwriting efforts from the mid-1980s; the tune he'd written after a funeral in Yirrkala called 'Yolngu Woman'. 'It was amazing, a really good song choice – strong women singing that really powerful song,' Dhapanbal reflects on the moment. 'It's a song about being a strong woman in the community, a strong cultural woman, standing strong.'

Yothu Yindi and the Treaty Project breathed new fire into the old songs, with a cast of young Yolŋu talent in support. One of those was Witiyana's musician son Yirrmal. In recent years, Yirrmal, who sings in a hypnotic, wavering tenor, has found his own career windfalls. The beat-dripping track 'Marryuna' he recorded with hip-hopper Baker Boy, a fellow Arnhem Lander, was number 17 in 2017's Triple J Hottest 100, and the pair's 2021 track 'Ride' has been tearing up the youth radio station's 'most played' charts. Yirrmal has also joined forces with songwriters like Jordie Lane, Shane Howard, Archie Roach and Neil Murray, and has the ear of a younger generation. But he's never forgotten his roots.

Yothu Yindi and the Treaty Project rock Melbourne's Hamer Hall in 2019. Front of stage from left: Witiyana Marika, Yirrŋa Yunupiŋu and Dhapaṉbal Yunupiŋu, and special guest singers Emma Donovan and Deline Briscoe. *(Matt Garrick)*

'I always acknowledge that man that sang to me and gave the baton to my generation,' Yirrmal says of Yothu Yindi's founding singer. 'And [Gurrumul] too. An amazing musician, such an incredible talent and left such an amazing legacy. Someone had to pick it up, and build it.'

Yirrmal says the message of Yothu Yindi's 'Treaty' still gives him 'hope' each time he sings it: 'Not hope as fate but hope as a blessing and a warning. It makes me stronger as a Yolŋu,' he says. 'I will sing my heart out for this country so everyone can hear and say, "Wow. This is the strongest culture in Australia and still not recognised. But they are still singing it proudly and so resiliently."'

At Treaty Project shows, wherever they played, audience members would be invited onto the stage – often Indigenous kids, mums, dads – to dance and celebrate alongside the band. DJ Gavin Campbell remembers some of these as 'oh my god' moments, moments he counts as 'the most significant work I've ever done'.

He says seeing the impact of 'Treaty' on modern crowds was a revelation: how in spite of the song's political reality – that there's still no treaty – the audience always reacted with joy. 'When you see the joy in mob when they're dancing to it, when it's being performed live for them, you think to yourself, "They're not angry!"' the DJ looks back on those shows. 'There is anger and disappointment in there, but they're not bringing that to the stage ... they're bringing all this joy and laughter and dancing.'

Watching Yothu Yindi's new singer, Yirrŋa Yunupiŋu, in action these days, you would be forgiven for thinking you were standing at the Darwin Amphitheatre twenty years ago. Yirrŋa's voice has the same power, and in his eyes shine a hope and knowledge of good things to come. Yirrŋa knows he has giant shoes to fill. But he walks in his uncle's footsteps with respect, with legacy in mind, and with an ability to bring those songs to today's generation.

'[Mandawuy] was a great man, and a humble man, a knowledge man, and he's a leader – sharing a message,' says Yirrŋa, sitting outside the Nhulunbuy High School rehearsal room. 'He's gone now, but we're here to build a bridge for our generation, for our future, for the kids, just to do the same things as he was doing, and he's been through.'

Yirrŋa is also helping to fulfil part of Mandawuy's dream – that Yothu Yindi would continue across generations long after he was gone. In many ways, Yothu Yindi is more than a band. It's a cultural ambassadorship, teaching others about the Yolŋu voice, about working side by side: Indigenous and non-Indigenous. A global nation coming together. It isn't something that can just form and break apart like a normal rock group. As with the strict Yolŋu cultural system it's named after, with no clear start and no ending, the hope is the songs will continue to carry on and be played indefinitely over generations.

'It will keep going, yow,' says Witiyana. 'Generation after generation after generation. If the band and the people and the singers and the leaders will put their mind on one thing; to carry out this legend of Yothu Yindi.'

Yirrŋa also fronts a band called King Stingray – a self-proclaimed 'Yolŋu surf rock' group that's been going gangbusters across Australia thanks to their catchy output like 'Get Me Out', 'Lookin' Out' and 'Hey Wanhaka'. This band also counts another Yothu Yindi offspring as a member: Roy Kellaway, the son of the original bassist, Stu, and his wife, Andrea, a stalwart of East Arnhem Land's health and education sectors.

'My dad's been a big role model for me, and for all of us really,' Roy says. 'He's the vibe-master, and there's so much to be said about the way in which he conducts himself as the humble facilitator of good times. We're just trying to keep playing music and having fun, and I've seen my dad do that for so many years – he just loves playing music. In the music industry there's all these different people involved, and sometimes you can forget that you're just doing it to play music with your mates.'

By the beach in Yirrkala, Roy and Stu Kellaway sit reflecting on this crazy, multi-generational ride. Roy, a sweet-natured, long-haired guitarist and qualified podiatrist, watched and heard Yothu Yindi from his earliest days on Earth. He cites himself as one of the band's 'biggest fans'. He's also now been one of their members, having played with the Treaty Project and at Yothu Yindi shows in recent years. 'It was so exciting – obviously everyone loves Yothu Yindi, and you're just like, "Woah, this is amazing!" But to imagine what it would've been like being the band [back in the day],' says Roy. 'Getting that momentum as a band of your mates, the excitement that that would come with; doing things for the first time, going, "What the hell, look at all these people here for us!"'

Stu Kellaway offers his input: 'That's what we were feeling!' There they were: a group of young men and women

A Flame Reignited

from remote Australia in their twenties and thirties, black and white, blazing through 'Treaty' to a crowd of fired-up kids in the city. A sweaty, exultant postcard from the far reaches of the north, sent down bearing a message of peace and unity.

'Treaty' arguably opened doors in more ways than any other Australian song before it. To urban Aboriginal kids on the east coast, it showed a strength, an unbroken connection to history, to the land and to lore. Mandawuy's niece Rarrtjiwuy Melanie Herdman says it was only after she'd lived in Sydney in 2019 that she realised the profound effect her uncle's music had on Indigenous Australians outside of Arnhem Land. 'The influence that not just the song "Treaty" but Yothu Yindi as a band had on Sydney and the inner city and Redfern and those communities that I got the opportunity to live in ... I can't describe how crazy they were about the band, even now. Without knowing who I was, I would meet people and they'd be playing "Treaty" and they'd be playing "Djäpana", and they'd be playing all these songs on their phone, in the car, in schools, because I guess it provided them with a sense of direction and vision and hope, and continues to.'

Growing up, Herdman says she'd 'taken for granted' the access she'd had to her family members in Yothu Yindi and what they taught her firsthand. 'We as Yolŋu people haven't been exposed so much to, I guess, what [Indigenous people] down south have been, in terms of colonisation and losing their language and culture and having to fight constantly for their rights ... and I think I know now why Yothu Yindi are so important, and why their music is so important to all these other people around Australia.'

Inspired by her uncle's journey and life lessons, Herdman is enrolled at uni and on the path to a law degree so she can continue working towards Mandawuy's Both Ways vision for Australia. 'I reflect on the work that he did, and I continue,' she says. 'Now that I'm back in uni, that's my passion: to continue to take his legacy of Both Ways, and drive it further than just education. Because while his platform was education and his music, I think that if the Yolŋu, and the Northern Territory and the rest of Australia and the world think about it, this Both Ways approach should be applied to every part of society.'

In Yirrkala today, if you go for a short stroll around the community, from Buku-Larrŋgay Mulka art centre's wood workshop to the boat ramp, chances are you'll still hear 'Treaty' booming out of windows or on a cracked iPhone down by the rocks at sunset. Somehow this song, cobbled together brick by brick from Biranybirany to Darwin, Melbourne and Sydney, still crackles with intensity decades on. Maybe it's the political inaction on proper Indigenous recognition (there have been seven prime ministers since Hawke's promise). Maybe it's the pride in past heroes and in Yolŋu Rom. Maybe it's Cal Williams's funky guitar licks and Milkay's yidaki hovering over the groove. Maybe it's all of it.

Another Yothu Yindi band member, the dancer Mangatjay Yunupiŋu, also reflects. Now in his sixties, he says if he had his time over, he'd do it all again in a heartbeat. 'If I had a chance to form another band, try to get out and run – because that's what it is, trying to get out and be someone – I'd still give it a try,' says Mangatjay.

He doesn't have to look too far for the chance. Yothu Yindi still exists, still gigs as a rock combo, splicing traditional buŋgul and manikay with hot electric guitars. Stu Kellaway's still there, adding coal to the engine, keeping the fire burning for the long haul. Witiyana's still there – the legend who dropped the jaws of thousands in packed Sydney beer barns when he was just in his twenties. And Mangatjay, too, he got back onto the stage just this year, in 2021, aged sixty, when Yothu Yindi performed to a thrilled crowd at the Sidney Myer Music Bowl in Melbourne.

'I keep sayin', "Nah, nah, I'm not doing this anymore,"' Mangatjay says. 'But that's bullshit.' Sitting on a rug in a Darwin park, eating fried dim sims on a sunny, early dry season morning, the dancer chortles away. Deep in his heart, he knows that if the call comes through asking him to perform, he won't be able to turn it down. He'll be there. After all, it's family.

'He shed his blood, sweat and tears without discrimination': Yalmay Yunupiŋu gives a moving speech to her late husband at a ceremony held at Biranybirany homeland in June 2018. *(Matt Garrick)*

Epilogue

Back in Biranybirany, the sweet, sad ceremony – Mandawuy's memorial and plaque unveiling in June 2018 – is moving along. Five years since the Gumatj songman departed and the guests are cross-legged on their mats, watching the speakers as they approach the handmade podium, one by one, each with a different drop of wisdom to impart. Many familiar faces dot the crowd. Witiyana in his fire-emblazoned näga stands watching. Yalmay, a streak of white clay across her forehead, has spoken a steely ode to her other half, describing him as 'a mover and a shaker, shedding his blood, sweat and tears without discrimination'. The educators Leon White, Trevor Stockley, Greg Wearne and John Henry, they're all there, together in their grief. Some of the original Diamond Dogs are there. The elders are there. And perhaps most importantly, the children are there. The kids of Yirrkala School and the homelands, the kids for whom Mandawuy Yunupiŋu devoted years of his life to improving theirs. The next speaker approaches the podium with its yellow fabric, the words 'YOTHU YINDI' and 'TREATY' woven into it.

The musician in the blue polo shirt steps up to the microphone. Paul Kelly. He shares what impressions he's been left from his friend, Mandawuy, Dr M, and what they spoke of as they sat together in the sand writing the first lines of 'Treaty' all those setting suns ago. 'While we were here, Dr M, my friend with the big smile, he showed me his country and shared his philosophy with me – a philosophy based on balance,' Kelly offers, returning to the theme of his eulogy at Mandawuy's original memorial service. 'Balance was a word I heard a lot over those few days. Balance between Yolŋu and balanda, balance between fresh water and salt water, balance between Dhuwa and Yirritja, balance between protecting culture and sharing culture. We're still on the long path to proper recognition of Aboriginal sovereignty. And more than ever we need balance in that struggle.'

The wind whips sand around the feet of the gathered guests. Together they sit, far away from the cities of the south with their bars and buses, cafés and billboards, handbags, department stores and queues. Together this small huddle of people digest the sad reality that Kelly has raised: that the Australian Government has so far failed to properly reconcile with its first residents.

Not too far from this spot, once a year in the dry season, a procession of Akubra-donning politicians steps off the plane at Gove Airport and navigates the twenty kilometres on red dirt to plant their boots on the sacred soil at Gulkula, for the Garma Festival. There, they shake hands, they pose with

Epilogue

Gumatj leaders for a photo opportunity, they furrow their brows and make myriad pledges to the watching media. But year after year, as their convoy of taxpayer-funded Toyotas departs in a whirling cloud of dust, all that's left is the wind blowing off the escarpment. Nothing changes. There is no treaty. Business remains unresolved. Yunupiŋu's dream of a brighter day is still a distant light on the horizon.

>   Now two rivers run their course
>   Separated for so long
>   I'm dreaming of a brighter day
>   When the waters will be one

Glossary of Yolŋu Words

Balanda – non-Indigenous person
Bäpurru – clan nation
Bäru – crocodile
Bathi – (sacred ceremonial) dillybag
Bäyŋu – none, nothing
Bilma – clapsticks
Buku – face/forehead
Buŋgawa – boss/leader
Buŋgul – ceremony/dance
Dhäwu – story
Djäma – work
Djäpana – sunset
Djarrami – mirror/a visionary
Djorra – book
Ga – and
Ga' – give it (to me)

Gapan – ceremonial clay
Gapu – water
Gara – spear
Gu' – come here
Gurrutu – kinship
Gurtha – (ancestral) fire
Guya – fish
Latju – good/beautiful
Lipalipa – canoe
Ma' – ok
Madayin' – sacred/secret
Makarrata – peace making ceremony
Mala – group
Mälk – skin name
Manikay – song/songline
Manymak – good
Märi – maternal grandmother
Miltjiri – blind person
Miny'tji – colours/painting/ancestral designs
Mukul bäpa – paternal aunt
Mulka – culturally safe and legitimate
Näga – material worn around waist
Ŋanitji – alcohol
Ŋapaki – non-Indigenous person
Ŋapipi – maternal uncle
Ŋatha – food
Ralpa – respect for one's elder
Raypirri – A matter of being sensible, discipline
Rom – law, culture, Constitution

Glossary of Yolŋu Words

Rrupiya – money
Wäŋa – home
Wäwa – brother
Yaka – no, not
Yäku – name
Yapa – sister
Yiḏaki – didgeridoo
Yirralka – homeland
Yolŋu – Aboriginal person of East Arnhem Land
Yolŋu Matha – Yolŋu Aboriginal languages
Yow – yes
Yuwalk – true

Some Key Concepts

Dhuwa and Yirritja Everyone and everything in the Yolŋu world is divided into one of two categories: Dhuwa or Yirritja. Animals from the sea and sky, plants, people – they all fit into one of these two halves of the whole. For example, the white cockatoo (*Lorrpu*) is Yirritja and the red-tail black cockatoo (*Ṉatili*) is Dhuwa. They are the two pillars of all life, together making the whole Yolŋu universe, as handed down by the creators.

Galtha The reconciliation of different perspectives, or the process for agreeing on a compromise, in order to find a way forward. As the late Dr Raymattja Marika described it in 1991, galtha is a 'term used for gathering together ideas as a starting point for sorting out important issues and problems, ceremonies, and individuals' roles … in these ceremonies. Galtha literally means "the starting point".' The concept is used across East Arnhem Land in fields such as wildlife management and education.

Garma A term to describe coming into a ceremony to join and share wisdom, culture and understanding in a public arena where everyone is treated respectfully.

Yolŋu Rom Rom means 'law' – but Yolŋu Rom is all-encompassing. It is Yolŋu society – law, discipline, the Constitution, the cultural and everyday rules that Yolŋu abide by. It is a foundation block that will remain forever.

Yothu yindi Yothu yindi is part of the Yolŋu kinship system, gurruṯu. It's a system that allows Dhuwa and Yirritja beings to co-exist respectfully. It's a system of balance. Yothu yindi dictates marriage, ceremonial obligations and land ownership between individuals and between entire clans. It is a cycle with no beginning and no end, and has existed forever and will carry on infinitely. Yothu and yindi refers to a 'mother and child' relationship; the mother must always be there to care for her young one, and vice versa.

*

This glossary and key concepts were written and compiled in collaboration with Ellen Gapany Gaykamaŋu, a senior Gupapuyŋu woman who holds the wisdom and knowledge of her country, Djiliwirri, and is a senior teacher, linguist and qualified interpreter at Aboriginal Interpreter Service, and language and cultural consultant at Charles Darwin University (CDU). For a greater understanding of Yolŋu language, life and culture, CDU is home to an award-winning, internationally respected Yolŋu Studies Centre, which offers lessons and courses from beginner level, and is available to anyone around Australia. Learn more or enrol in a course at learnline.cdu.edu.au/yolngustudies/study.html.

Acknowledgements

Thank you to Nicola Pitt, Zach Hope, Lucy Desoto and Stu Thornton (see, I remembered!) for your help and encouragement in this project's early days. To Egle, John and Louis Garrick, Sarah Bentley, Brendan Moore and Alex Bowen, for the support and steady drip of homecooked meals, and to Nick Reid, Michael Hazell and Aleks Arsenic for the comic relief.

Thanks to Gove FM's Robbie Stewart for always coming to the rescue, and to Gumatj Corporation's Klaus Helms and Allan Rungan for many things – not least sorting me out with a desk. To the crew at Buku-Larrŋgay Mulka art centre and The Mulka Project, particularly Will, Joseph, Bec, Ishmael, Arian and Dave – your knowledge, friendship and support are always endlessly appreciated.

And thank you to the Yolŋu Studies Centre at CDU, Nori, Gapany and Mutha, for your patient help with the glossary and concepts, and, Nori, for your amazing work with the transcriptions. To the team at NT Archives, particularly Brian and Katherine and, at the NT Library, Patrick and Cathy, thanks a lot for your enthusiastic assistance. To those who helped me with editorial checks in one way or another – Rarrtjiwuy Mel Herdman, Charlie Ward, Lindsay Murdoch, Ted Egan, Michael Hohnen, Ian 'Jumbuck' Redfearn (and others I've probably omitted!) – thanks for casting your expert eyes over it: priceless.

To my colleagues at ABC Darwin, especially my bosses John McElhinney and Sara Everingham, a huge thank you for believing in and supporting this project. To the ABC Books editorial team, Jude, Scott, Nikki and Nicola, thank you for your thoughtful and thorough edits and advice, your expertise and insights, and thanks to the whole HarperCollins team for backing this book and bringing a dream into reality.

Thank you so much to Kylie Stevenson, for keeping me sane in the line of fire, for constantly pushing and advising me. And to Grace Heifetz, for your calm assurance and care, even when everything's been ready to hit the fan! So much appreciated. To my wife, Ange, who I met in Nhulunbuy, thanks for always being my number one, for your boundless positivity, for being a super mum and an incredible burst of energy and heart. You're the wheel that keeps this whole thing turning. To everyone in Nhulunbuy and Yirrkala who gave me a good tip or grabbed me for a friendly yarn, thanks for making me, Ange and our son, Gus, always feel like we're home.

Thanks also to the legendary Diamond Dogs – Gumatj elders Djawa and Balupalu Yunupiŋu – for your time, humour

Acknowledgements

and love of music, and to the educators, particularly Leon White, Kathy McMahon, Kevin Kluken, Sue Reaburn, Helen Verran and Greg Wearne, for your steadfast advice and assistance. To the Swamp Jockeys and the Williams brothers, Todd, Cal, Benny and Vaughan, thanks for all of your positive contributions.

And to all the members of Yothu Yindi, past and present, who poured their hearts into the microphone for this biography, my sincerest thanks. It's been an honour hearing all of your heartfelt perspectives. Likewise, to the many others who shared their stories for this book, from Yirrkala, Gunyaŋara and Nhulunbuy to Darwin and across Australia, an enormous thank you. To Alan James, a huge thanks for your support and advice on the manuscript, and for sharing your amazing tales. To Stu Kellaway and Witiyana Marika, the living legends – it's been a wild ride writing this bio, and I'm forever grateful that you had the trust in me to pull it off. Thanks so much.

I save the biggest thank you for two incredible people without whom this book wouldn't have happened; Yalmay Yunupiŋu and the late Dr B Marika – a trailblazing force of nature and a friend and inspiration to many, myself included, and it's still hard to believe that you've left us; to paraphrase your niece Mayatili, the land is still heavy from your loss. All those hours you both sacrificed to sit by the sea at Raŋi, going through drafts, sharing ideas and your stories from the past: it was a warm-hearted experience that gives me great optimism for a future we can still achieve, of a Both Ways Australia, living 'under one dream'. Marrkapmirr.

Notes

Author's note
page
xvi   *'Language is power':* Andrew McMillan, 'Yothu Yindi: From the Heart', *The Edge* magazine, 23 May 1989, pp. 30–31.

Prologue
4   *'fire is my clan symbol. Fire is my life force':* Mushroom Pictures, *Tribal Voice*, director Stephen M Johnson, 1994.

1. Diamond Dogs
10   *The brothers' father, Mungurrawuy, was a traditional Gumatj composer:* Mandawuy Yunupiŋu, Yothu Yindi/DoRo Productions, *Yothu Yindi: One Blood*, 1999.

2. Child and Mother
24   *Some Yolŋu thought they were being bombed':* Matt Garrick, 'Roy Marika: On the frontline for freedom', *NT News*, 21 August 2016, p. 20–21.

26   *'from time immemorial':* Yirrkala bark petition, 1963, nma.gov.au/defining-moments/resources/yirrkala-bark-petitions.

26 '*[The petitions were created] to try to help explain*': Mushroom Pictures, *Tribal Voice*, director Stephen Johnson, 1994.

26 Senior clansmen gathered at the top of a sacred hill, 'Spears Along Cliff-Top', *Daily Telegraph*, 19 May 1969.

27 Millirpum v Nabalco: https://aiatsis.gov.au/sites/default/files/catalogue_resources/SF26-7_5.pdf; https://library.museum.wa.gov.au/fullRecord.jsp?recno=5264.

30 '*Yothu yindi is child and mother*': Yothu Yindi/DoRo Productions, *Yothu Yindi: One Blood*, 1999.

30 '*My inner life is that of the Yolngu song cycles*': Galarrwuy Yunupiŋu, 'Tradition, truth and tomorrow', *The Monthly*, July 2008.

36 '*thinking man's drinking man*' and '*there are a couple thousand people at the show*': Andrew McMillan, *Strict Rules: The Blackfella – Whitefella Tour*, Niblock Publishing, Darwin, 2008, foreword and p. 218.

3. The Educator

40 '*The end result is to get people to think like Yolŋu*' and '*I had accepted the reality*': 'Yirrkala says it's time to apply self-determination', *Land Rights News*, September 1988, p. 18.

44 '*We discussed his disappointment*': John Henry, 'Biranybirany Galtha 2018: Both Ways Learning', booklet produced by Yirrkala Community School, 2018, p. 58.

46 '*On a political level, Indigenous and non-Indigenous Australians*': Aaron Corn, *Reflections and Voices: exploring the music of Yothu Yindi with Mandawuy Yunupingu*, Sydney University Press, Sydney, 2009, pp. 34, 61.

48 '*listened to the Yolŋu voice*': Bakamana Yunupiŋu, 'Nambara philosophy of education', Yirrkala Community School, 1986.

48 *The Methodist missionaries had only arrived in Yirrkala in 1935:* Dr B Marika, *Rirratjingu Ethnobotany: Aboriginal plant use from Yirrkala*,

Arnhem Land, Australia, NT Parks and Wildlife Commission, 1995, pp. 7–11.

4. Swamp Stomp

62   '*song about white people and Aboriginal people*': Yothu Yindi – 'Mainstream', *Blah Blah Blah*, ABC TV Australia, screened 1988, youtube.com/watch?v=K3SBcMByEEI.

63   '*the fabulous Flienetts*' and '*raggedy bush bands*': 'Swamp Jockeys last stand' and 'Bakamana Yunupingu & Witiyana Marika team up with the Swamp Jockeys', Swamp Jockeys press biographies, Library and Archives NT, Andrew McMillan Collection, reference MS68.

5. Back in 1988

70   *they were incorrectly billed:* Kevin Cook, Heather Goodall, *Making Change Happen: Black and white activists talk to Kevin Cook about Aboriginal, union and liberation politics*, ANU Press, Canberra, 2013, p. 351.

72   '*the Collingwood diehard*': Bob Gosford, 'A living wake for the "Jesus of Westralia Street"– Darwin Railway Club, 3 December 2010', *Crikey*, 6 December 2010, blogs.crikey.com.au/northern/2010/12/06/a-living-wake-for-the-jesus-of-westralia-street-darwin-railway-club-3-december-2010/.

73   '*They stayed in Sydney for a few weeks*': Andrew McMillan, *An Intruder's Guide to East Arnhem Land*, Niblock Publishing, Darwin, 2008, p. 255.

77   '*What we're trying to do is bringing both worlds together*': *Sing Loud, Play Strong*, produced and directed by Jo O'Sullivan, Central Australian Aboriginal Media Association, 1988, youtube.com/watch?v=NTP65qOMREk.

6. The Good Oils

83 *'the rights of Indigenous people'*: Justin Mitchell, 'Garrett, Midnight Oil return with 2 unknown, ethnic bands', *Rocky Mountain News*, 10 November 1988.

85 *'labelling the fire an "accident"'*: Bruce Weber, 'John Trudell, outspoken advocate for American Indians, is dead at 69', *New York Times*, nytimes.com/2015/12/10/us/john-trudell-outspoken-advocate-for-american-indians-is-dead-at-69.html.

7. The Highway Beckons

92 *'It's Not U2, It's Yothu'*: *TIME*, 7 November 1988, time.com/vault/issue/1988-11-07/page/2/.

92 *'The curtain comes up'*: 'Black rock takes land rights to US', Arts, *Sydney Morning Herald*, 12 November 1988.

95 *'Michael was a staunch supporter'*: Rachael Hocking, 'First Nations musicians remember Michael Gudinski', NITV, 2 March 2021, sbs.com.au/nitv/article/2021/03/02/powerhouse-first-nations-musicians-remember-michael-gudinski.

98 *'Given the burgeoning international interest'* and *creditors' notices*: Library and Archives NT, Andrew McMillan Collection, reference MS68.

100 *'A lot of people sorta tend'*: National Film and Sound Archive, *Into the Mainstream*, directors John Whitteron and Ned Lander, Inma Productions, 1989.

8. The Brother

109 *'In this bicentennial year'* and *'There shall be a treaty'*: ABC News report from Barunga Sports and Cultural Festival, 1988, facebook.com/watch/?v=10156573372809873.

110 *'A better understanding between cultures'*: Helen Davidson and Calla Wahlquist, 'Australian dig finds evidence of

Aboriginal habitation up to 80,000 years ago', *The Guardian*, 19 July 2017, theguardian.com/australia-news/2017/jul/19/dig-finds-evidence-of-aboriginal-habitation-up-to-80000-years-ago.

114 *'from a century of servitude'*, *'The Gurindji were not merely protesting'* *and fight for justice:* Charlie Ward, *A Handful of Sand: The Gurindji struggle, after the Walk-Off,* Monash University Publishing, Melbourne, 2016, pp. xxvi, 34, 183.

116 *'Nhämirri? Dhuŋgarrayyu 1963yu':* Galarrwuy Yunupiŋu, address to the National Press Club, Canberra, 10 November 1977 (Gumatj transcription by Charles Darwin University's Yolŋu Studies Centre), nla.gov.au/nla.obj-194379429/listen.

118 *'Governments and mining companies':* Australian of the Year Awards, 'Galarrwuy Yunupingu AM: Aboriginal Leader and Land Rights Advocate', 1978, australianoftheyear.org.au/recipients/galarrwuy-yunupingu/81/.

118 *'just another whinging, whining':* Former NT Chief Minister Shane Stone, 'Stone Family in Australia – Chapter 12: The "Chief"', stonefamilyinaustralia.com.au/shane_stone/story/chapter-12-the-chief.

119 *'It will be something to remind any government':* Galarrwuy Yunupiŋu's speech at Barunga Sports and Cultural Festival, 1988, Australian Institute of Aboriginal and Torres Strait Islander Studies, aiatsis.gov.au/explore/articles/barunga-statement.

9. Well I Heard It on the Radio

123 *called The Messengers in the US:* Caz Tran, 'Reflecting on the sonic postcards Paul Kelly dispatched on Gossip', Double J, 1 March 2021, abc.net.au/doublej/music-reads/features/paul-kelly-and-the-messengers-gossip/13202754.

10. Into the Mainstream

145 *'is a form of song that is about fun':* Rita Metzenrath, '"Treaty" by Yothu Yindi', Australian Institute of Aboriginal and Torres Strait Islander Studies, aiatsis.gov.au/blog/treaty-yothu-yindi.

152 *'truly Indigenous album':* Mandawuy Yunupiŋu's speech at the 1992 ARIAs, youtube.com/watch?v=6TVRJoLojQo.

154 *'ethnic group':* Mikel Toombs, '2 ethnic groups help in getting Midnight Oil's message across', *San Diego Union*, 5 November 1988.

11. Hollywood Calling

157 *the first Aboriginal band to sign:* Hollywood Records press material, 1992, Library and Archives NT, Andrew McMillan Collection, reference MS68.

158 *'In a week in which musicians':* Richard Harrington, 'Brawling to the beat', *Washington Post*, 21 July 1991, washingtonpost.com/archive/lifestyle/style/1991/07/21/brawling-to-the-beat/f8f6dfba-e4bd-400d-bfc2-aaf97653fc76/.

162 *'Yothu Yindi is an electrifying molten'* and *'Yothu Yindi builds what they do':* Yothu Yindi press material, late 1993, Library and Archives NT, Andrew McMillan Collection, reference MS68.

163 *Bob Weir would venture to East Arnhem Land:* Bob and Wendy Weir, *Baru Bay: Australia*, 1995, seawifs.gsfc.nasa.gov/OCEAN_PLANET/HTML/barubay.html.

12. Australia Tunes In

169 *'building bridges of understanding:'* Australian of the Year Awards, 'M Yunupingu, Aboriginal educator, musician and ambassador', 1992, australianoftheyear.org.au/recipients/m-yunupingu/96.

169 *'I think that this year's going to open a lot of avenues':* National Film and Sound Archive of Australia, 'M Yunupingu Australia of

the Year', Network Ten, 1993, nfsa.gov.au/collection/curated/m-yunupingu-australian-year.

169 *'To be able to get Australian of the Year with my brother'*: Chips Mackinolty, 'Yunupingu: he's our Australian of the Year', *The Age*, 27 January 1993, p. 1.

171 *'Isn't it reasonable to say'*: Paul Keating, 'Australian launch of the International Year for the World's Indigenous People, Redfern', 10 December 1992, pmtranscripts.pmc.gov.au/release/transcript-8765.

174 *Alan Jones described Mandawuy's Australian of the Year win:* 'Jonestown', *Four Corners*, 6 May 2002, ABC TV, abc.net.au/4corners/jonestown/12240362.

174 *'To promote people because of their colour'*: Australian of the Year Awards, 'First Australians', australianoftheyear.org.au/first-australians/.

176 *'I was wearing lean jeans'*: Mandawuy Yunupingu, 'Black and White', *Rolling Stone*, 1992, no. 471, pp. 33–34.

13. Freedom

184–5 *'Ganma has many meanings'*: Bakamana Yunupiŋu, Helen Watson and Stephen Kemmis, 'The Ganma Project in mathematics curriculum', Yirrkala Community School publication, 1986.

185 *As Andrew McMillan would observe:* McMillan, *An Intruder's Guide to East Arnhem Land*, p. 269.

186 *'The Djungguwan ceremonies'*: Yothu Yindi press biographies; Library and Archives NT, Andrew McMillan Collection, reference MS68.

187 *'reflects our own Yolŋu ties to land'*: Corn, *Reflections and Voices*, p. 97.

14. Raypirri

201 *'night bugs that had never seen floodlights'*: Alistair Jones, 'Mandawuy's sober mission', *Good Weekend*, 23 October 1993, pp. 23, 25, 27.

15. A Global Nation

215 *Keith Richards once threw a television:* Avishay Artsy, 'The rock 'n' roll legacy of a Sunset Strip hotel', *KCRW*, 18 May 2015, kcrw.com/culture/articles/the-rock-n-roll-legacy-of-a-sunset-strip-hotel.

218 *'It was a once-in-a-lifetime opportunity'*: 'Storyteller Julie Gungunbuy', *Birds Eye View*, StoryProjects podcast, 2020: birdseyeviewpodcast.net/julie.

16. One Blood

225 *'I was blown away with this bloke!'*: DoRo Productions, *Peter Maffay: Begegnungen*, directors Rudi Dolezal and Hannes Rossacher, 1998.

226 *'We've been to Ireland before'*: Yothu Yindi/DoRo Productions, *Yothu Yindi: One Blood*, 1999, youtube.com/watch?v=1wMNdNbwnHk.

231 *'I have done research on benefits'*: Pauline Hanson, 'Pauline Hanson's 1996 maiden speech to parliament: full transcript', *Sydney Morning Herald*, 15 September 2016, smh.com.au/politics/federal/pauline-hansons-1996-maiden-speech-to-parliament-full-transcript-20160915-grgjv3.html.

231 *'Which living person do you most despise?'*: Rosanna Greenstreet, 'The questionnaire', *The Guardian*, 29 September 2000, theguardian.com/theguardian/2000/sep/30/weekend7.weekend7.

17. Garma

237 *'For several years the Yolngu community leaders'*: The Yothu Yindi Foundation, 'Proposal for the establishment of the Garma Cultural Studies Centre', February 1997, pp. 1, 5, 6, 13, 15, 16.

18. The New Millennium

249   'recognition for Mandawuy's lifelong work': Phillipa Hanrick, 'Mandawuy honoured for his cultural dedication', *Inside QUT* (Queensland University of Technology newspaper), 5–18 May 1998, p. 1.

19. Fire on the Hill

260   'Yunupingu was charged with murder': Andrew McMillan, 'Poison cousin's death tears a clan apart', *The Age*, 29 June 2002, theage.com.au/national/poison-cousins-death-tears-a-clan-apart-20020629-gduch7.html.

260   'Makuma was "genuinely sorry"': The Queen and Gavin Makuma Yunupingu, NT Supreme Court transcript of proceedings, 24 June 2002

20. Yolŋu Medicine

272–6   *Quotes from* Australian Story: 'Message from Mandawuy', ABCTV, Australian Story, 19 October 2009.

273   'Within hours of the event': Lindsay Murdoch, 'Aboriginal celebration spirals into tragedy', *Sydney Morning Herald*, 30 July 2008, smh.com.au/national/aboriginal-celebration-spirals-into-tragedy-20080730-3n0p.html.

21. The Drummer

279   'Unbelievable': Quincy Jones official Facebook page, 14 March 2015, facebook.com/watch/?v=10153132551954631.

xx   'When his first album came out': Tamara Howie, 'Our children blessed by Dr G', *NT News*, 27 July 2017, p. 6.

22. The New Guard

301   'the NT has the highest incidence and prevalence of kidney disease': NT Health Department, 'Northern Territory Renal Services Strategy 2017–2022', p. 15, digitallibrary.health.nt.gov.au/

prodjspui/bitstream/10137/1438/3/DoH_RenalServices_Strategy.pdf.

23. Goodbye, Crocodile Man

307 *'Mr M Yunupingu changed the landscape':* Matt Garrick, 'Loss of a legend', *Arafura Times*, 5 June 2013, p. 1.

307 *'Today is a day for sorrow':* Peter Garrett, 'Goodbye to my dear friend Yunupingu', *The Guardian*, 4 June 2013, theguardian.com/commentisfree/2013/jun/04/Australia-yunupingu-peter-garrett.

309 *speakers remembered Mandawuy:* Matt Garrick, 'Vale Dr Yunupingu: nation bids farewell to a Crocodile Man', *Arafura Times*, 3 July 2013, pp. 1, 3.

316 *Gurrumul had been admitted to hospital:* Jane Bardon, 'Dr G Yunupingu: Indigenous musician found "wasted away", friend says "we owed him better"', ABC Darwin, 26 July 2017, abc.net.au/news/2017-07-26/dr-g-yunupingu-found-at-darwin-camp-indictment-on-society/8745532.

317 *'While publicly reticent':* Matt Garrick, 'Born blind but with a singular musical vision for the planet', *NT News*, 27 July 2017, pp. 6–7.

Some key concepts

339 *'A term used for gathering together ideas':* Dr Raymattja Marika-Munungiritj, 'Some Notes on Principles for Aboriginal Pedagogy', *Batchelor Journal of Aboriginal Education*, December 1991.

Yothu Yindi Discography

Albums and singles

1989

Homeland Movement (Mushroom)
Singles: 'Mainstream', 'Djäpana'

1991

Tribal Voice (Mushroom)
Singles: 'Treaty', 'Tribal Voice', 'Treaty (Radio Mix)'

1992

Tribal Voice, extended version (Mushroom)
Singles: 'Djäpana: Sunset Dreaming', 'Djäpana: Sunset Dreaming (Radio Mix)'

1993

Freedom (Mushroom)

Singles: 'World Turning', 'Timeless Land', 'Dots on the Shells' (featuring Neil Finn), 'Gapu (The Tidal Mix)'

1996

Birrkuṯa – Wild Honey (Mushroom)

Single: 'Superhighway'

1998

One Blood (Mushroom)

Singles: 'Treaty 98', 'Mainstream' (featuring Liam Ó Maonlaí), 'Our Land'

2000

Garma (Mushroom)

Singles: 'Community Life', 'Romance at Garma'

2012

Healing Stone: The Best of Yothu Yindi (Mushroom/Liberation Music)

Single: 'Healing Stone'

2017

Yothu Yindi: The Remixes (Mushroom/Bloodlines)

Yothu Yindi Discography

2018

Single: Yothu Yindi and Gavin Campbell, 'Treaty '18' (featuring Baker Boy) (Razor Recordings)

2019

Single: Yothu Yindi and the Treaty Project, 'Mabo' (Razor Recordings)

Lyrics Permissions

Thanks to the following organisations and artists for permission to reproduce Yothu Yindi lyrics in the text:

Mushroom Music Publishing and Yothu Yindi for licensing
- the use of Yothu Yindi's lyrics:
'Djapana', 'Freedom Song', 'Homeland Movement', 'Mainstream',
- 'My Kind of Life', 'Tribal Voice', 'Yolngu Boy', written by
- M. Yunupingu (Mushroom Music)

'Mabo', written by M. Yunupingu/G. Yunupingu/G. Yunupingu/
- S. Kellaway (Mushroom Music)

'Timeless Land', written by M. Yunupingu/W. Marika/S. Kellaway
- (Mushroom Music)

'Treaty', written by M. Yunupingu, C. Williams, G. Yunupingu,
- M. Mununggurr, S. Kellaway, W. Marika (Mushroom Music)
- and Peter Garrett and Paul Kelly

'Yirrmala', written by M. Yunupingu/G. Yunupingu/S. Kellaway
- (Mushroom Music)

'Dots on the Shells', written by M. Yunupingu (Mushroom Music)
- and N. Finn

'Our Generation', written by M. Yunupingu/S. Kellaway (Mushroom Music) and A. Farriss

'Superhighway', written by M. Yunupingu (Mushroom Music) and A. Farriss.

BMG Rights Management (Australia) Pty Ltd for permission to include the lyrics of songs co-written by Yothu Yindi and Neil Finn ('Dots on the Shells') and Yothu Yindi and Andrew Farriss ('Superhighway', 'Our Generation', 'Good Medicine' and 'Healing Stone').

Sony Music Publishing, Paul Kelly and Peter Garrett for licensing the use of Yothu Yindi's co-writes with P. Kelly and P. Garrett:

'One Blood': Written by Paul Kelly and Mandawuy Yunupingu © Sony Music Publishing (Australia) Pty Limited Licensed by Sony Music Publishing (Australia) Pty Limited International copyright secured. All rights reserved. Used by permission.

'Treaty': Written by M. Yunupingu, Cal Williams, Geoffrey Gurrumul Yunupingu, Milkayggu Mununggurr, Stuart Kellaway and Witiyana Marika (Mushroom Music) and Peter Garrett and Paul Kelly (© Sony Music Publishing (Australia) Pty Limited Licensed by Sony Music Publishing (Australia) Pty Limited). International copyright secured. All rights reserved. Used by permission.

Ted Egan for permission to use the lyrics for 'Gurindji Blues' and 'The Tribal Land'.

Matt Garrick is a writer and ABC News journalist based in Darwin who has written extensively about politics, Indigenous affairs and music. He previously lived and worked in north-east Arnhem Land as the editor of Nhulunbuy's local paper, the *Arafura Times*, as a freelancer, and as Yothu Yindi's media coordinator in 2018. *Writing in the Sand* is his first book.